HOW TO GET YOUR SON BACK

7 Steps to Reconnect and Repair Your Relationship

Kevin Fall, PhD, and Austin T. Fall

Life Doctor Publishing
Kansas City

Dr. Fall and Austin would love to hear from you. Please stay connected!

Email: info@LifeDoctor.com
Facebook: www.facebook.com/RealLifeDoctors
Blog: www.LifeDoctor.com/blog

Editorial work and production management by Eschler Editing
Cover design by Jerry Dorris jerry@authorsupport.com
Interior print design and layout by Marny K. Parkin
eBook design and layout by Marny K. Parkin

Published by Life Doctor Publishing
First Edition: November 2017
Printed in the United States of America
10 9 8 7 6 5 4 3 2 1
ISBN 978-0-9996810-2-2 (Hardcover)
ISBN 978-0-9996810-0-8 (Softcover)

HOW TO GET YOUR SON BACK

To Alex,

Words fail to capture and express my love for you. Your infectious laugh, desire to help others, and second-to-none parenting are *truly* inspiring.

Love,
Dad

To Grandma Carolyn,

Thanks so much for being a steady figure during a turbulent time in my life. Coloring my memories of you are warm feelings of love and comfort. You were a safe place where a young boy with an unlimited supply of insecurities and self-doubt learned confidence—because you saw something special in me.
I will hold your memory near until we meet again.

Love,
Austin

CONTENTS

ACKNOWLEDGMENTS

Austin and I would like to especially thank Marcia Fall—wife, best friend, and stepmom—for her unending love and support.

We'd also like to thank the editorial staff at Eschler Editing (EschlerEditing.com) for their expertise and dedication in helping us make this book a reality.

And Anna DeStefano of www.howyouwrite.net, our editor and dear friend. We cannot begin to express our appreciation for your tireless engagement on this project.

PREFACE

As parents of troubled teens and young adults, it's deceptively easy for us to lose the keys to our children's hearts and brighter futures.

Our teens and young adults are navigating the confusing and often painful journey of maturing into adulthood. They're making mistakes and enduring consequences that can impact their lives for a long time to come. And on a daily basis, we as parents are told we're not welcome. Our help isn't needed. We couldn't possibly understand. When we try to get them to talk, we're only in the way and making things worse.

How do I know this?

Because I've been right where you are, feeling the same isolating hopelessness and making so many of the same missteps with my own son. I was failing as a parent no matter how hard I tried to reach my teen. Yes, I'm a licensed psychologist. But counseling is my second career. It took taking a long, hard look at myself— and beginning to do my own "personal" work—before I realized how much I craved helping other parents who find themselves at a similar crossroads.

My son's behavioral and relationship issues were in rapid decline.

Though I loved my boys, my parenting choices were, at best, ineffective.

At my worst, I was impatient, emotionally all over the place, and, due in large part to the way I was raised, "controlled" my kids using psychological and physical intimidation—and at times outright abuse. Don't get me wrong. I was doing the best I could. I simply didn't know enough about myself or what my son was going through to make better choices. I only wished I'd figured some of that out sooner, before things with Austin became so critical.

Over time, that wish evolved into sparing other parents of learning the hard way that relating to their troubled teen or young adult and becoming part of his journey (instead of another enemy for him to battle) is the most important *and* most effective step a parent can take in helping a child.

I am a father first. And before I received my training and years of clinical practice, I almost lost Austin to his descent into his darkest days.

He was only thirteen, and then fourteen, and then fifteen, and soon twenty and was drinking, hiding more of himself from the world, getting into trouble with the law, and identifying more and more with a small group of destructive peers telling him it was funny and cool—the damage and pain he was causing himself and others. He was gone from me and desperate for the approval of the only friends he had left. There seemed to be no way to pull him back.

As Austin will soon share, back then the last thing he wanted was to reverse his course. Things were fine exactly the way they were. He was going to make it on his own. He no longer needed my or anyone's help.

I'd somehow squandered my healthy relationship with my son,
who was struggling through life feeling defective and unlovable.

He was bright and capable of anything. He could overcome all the mistakes he was making and choose a different path. I was certain of it.

But where had his confidence gone? Where was his belief in his true identity—that wonderful boy I'd known the first twelve years of his life? He seemed hell-bent on growing into the absolute worst version of himself: the troublemaker the world, and too often in those days, the version his own father reflected back to him.

And yet I was determined to never let go.

Austin and I are writing this book, exposing our ugly and painful past, as well as our successes and his now-bright future, to bring a message of hope to other parents of troubled teens and young adults.

Because we know you'll never let go of your son or daughter either.

There's no limit to a parent's love. There's no mistake your teen or young adult could make that would sever that forever bond. And yet there are countless obstacles in your way these days as you battle to connect and maintain a positive, loving influence over your son's or daughter's often too-solitary path into adulthood.

NOTE: This book is written from a father-and-son perspective. The majority of the recommendations we offer will be, for the sake of pronoun simplification, directed toward your work with your "son."

However, the same material applies equally to troubled daughters facing this pivotal moment in their development.

So bear with us going forward, and when we say "son," know that we're talking about your teen or young adult regardless of gender.

The reality is that parents can truly change only one thing in their relationships with their children: themselves.

My training has taught me that, but so has personal experience.

Your most effective impact and the best use of your time and energy lies in handling your own journey as you work to see and understand the deep struggles underlying your son's acting out and destructive behavior. Your best play is to put yourself in the most positive, powerful position you can to maintain a healthy influence over your son's actions and to improve his understanding of the consequences he faces because of his choices. To do that, you must tap into the most powerful human force in your teen's or young adult's world: the attachment relationship. Through your relationship with him, you will be able to guide him to achieve the purpose, confidence, and independence he craves.

As you work our seven-step game plan to getting your son back, you will repair your parent-son relationship.

You will rebuild trust in both directions, admitting your own mistakes, taking responsibility for the effect your parenting choices have had on your son, and asking and offering forgiveness. This will put you on a successful path to earning your maturing son's confidence and to once more being a welcome guide in his life.

Austin and I offer our stories as examples of how badly things can go wrong and as inspiration for you to redouble your efforts to help your teen or young adult attain his unlived potential. Because we believe the stakes are too high not to.

> *You cannot assume that your teen or young adult will "grow out of" his troubles or "find his own way."*

He needs your help regardless of what he may be telling you. And in order to reach him, you as the parent must be the first in your relationship to risk becoming completely vulnerable.

Our sons are well aware of our shortcomings.

They're far more savvy than we were at their age, and they see straight through our pretenses. By and large, they no longer respond to an all-knowing, do-it-because-I-say-so authority figure.

Teens today respect authenticity.

If our relationships with them are to succeed, our openness and honesty about our own problems and failures is an incredible gift we must find the courage to offer. Consistently. Every day. This book calls you to become the very best you can at doing just that. And in return, as you begin to help your son once more, you will tap into the power of your own imperfect humanness.

Beyond my son's and my personal experience, I'll share my experience in the area of interpersonal psychotherapy.

With Austin's input and help, I'll offer steps for analyzing and understanding your personal situation with your son. We'll offer strategies for repairing and rebuilding the connection and communication you've lost and for growing your parent-child relationship in new directions and to new heights you've possibly only dreamed of.

To supplement these high-level solutions, additional resources to further assist you with your unique circumstances are offered in appendix C.

Your son, like mine, is worth all of that and more. He is not a lost cause.

This book is for parents who've tried various strategies, perhaps even counseling, and yet their teen or young adult persists in continuing down a destructive life path.

Austin's and my story will seem extreme to some. And yet the steps and strategies we recommend ultimately worked for us—to the extent that he is now coauthoring this book.

Additionally, in the last eight years, with these same techniques, I have helped a large number of my most at-risk clients: young men with severe mental illness, many of whom were housed in lockdown facilities due to patterns of violence, dangerous behavior, and a wide range of intellectual disabilities. I'm grateful and humbled by the positive impact I've been able to have on the lives of others grappling with our shared core need to form healthy relationships.

Our goal now is to transform and help as many failing parent-teen relationships as we can.

All we ask in return is that you become 100-percent engaged in the process.

I thank you in advance for your trust.

I hope for you the same success with your son or daughter as I ultimately achieved with Austin. While the road you're traveling can be long and not always easy, it is well worth the journey. Buckle up as together we work through the challenge of reconnecting with your teen, repairing your relationship, and transforming your bond with your son into a deep, rich relationship that endures for a lifetime.

Kevin Fall, PhD

INTRODUCTION

I am a psychologist.

My area of expertise is human connection and the obstacles that prevent us from having productive relationships. For years (while I helped my own troubled son deal with his issues), I have studied, conducted research, and facilitated therapy to help individuals overcome the barriers that prevent them from having healthy relationships. That's the "practical" foundation for the seven steps and the Parent Playbook Austin and I will soon share. The rest—the stories and reflections and analysis of all I did wrong as a parent before I learned how to do better—is me talking to you as a dad scared out of his mind, determined not to lose Austin against what at times seemed insurmountable odds.

The most tormenting emotional pain I have ever experienced involved my son.

A combination of worry for him, anxiety, and a desperate longing to solve our problems occupied not only my head but affected me physically in the form of digestive issues and chronic sleeplessness. I was a parent, my son was in trouble, and nothing I did to help or "set him straight" was working.

Since you're reading *How to Get Your Son Back*, chances are that you are having difficulty with your own teen or young adult. Your child's issues likely fall somewhere within the following spectrum:

- Not applying himself in school
- Isolating himself
- Bullying
- Stealing from family members and friends
- Substance abuse
- Drug addiction
- Anxiety
- Depression
- Violence
- Legal problems

If any of this sounds familiar, you've likely experienced some of the same emotions and feelings I've described. Yet I'm here to tell you that as painful as parenting through these challenges may be, it is better than the alternative.

> *Giving up and becoming apathetic is the worst thing parents can do.*

Letting your teen or young adult go, not fighting to get him back, is not an option.

Even as you face your child making one irreversible mistake after another—even when in the direst of straits your teen refuses to accept your help—there is always another chance to connect. There is always hope for bridging the communication gap. And even though you're already working yourself ragged as a parent, it's time to formulate a new game plan and work even harder.

I could not shut down emotionally nor dismiss my parental responsibility regardless of how tempting it seemed at times to walk away. I'm glad you can't either. Your son needs you.

This book is designed for parents.

Our recommended strategies target parents of teens and young adults who range in age from eleven or twelve up to thirty.

Austin's stories and analysis are as valuable as mine, if not more so. In his sections, Austin details his more troubled years. His clarion voice is essential, sharing firsthand insight into the emotions and conflicts and fears teens and young adults often refuse to discuss with their parents. Our strategies are not geared toward children.

Our seven-step game plan is designed to prepare you, the parent, to better deal with similar confusion, anger, dangerous behavior, and sometimes violence in your son.

NOTE: We wanted to share one last reminder that while the title of this book targets "sons," our strategies apply to parents struggling with teens and young adults of both genders.

For certain, there were other players impacting Austin's and my journey together.

We can't possibly cover everything that happened as my connection with my son broke down and as I struggled for years to find my way back to being an active, positive presence in his life. What we do share with you, though, comes from our personal desire to shine light and hope into the often-difficult parent-child relationship.

Our goal with How to Get Your Son Back *is to help parents reaching for something, anything, that will help them get through to their child.*

Our Seven-Step Game Plan

In *How to Get Your Son Back,* we will ask you to work hard to customize this program to your family's unique needs.

You will study, think carefully about, personalize, and implement an array of strategies built around the key stages of your relationship with your teen or young adult.

The game-plan steps are numbered: applying these strategies works best when you implement them in the order in which they're offered.

However, your situation and relationship with your child is unique to your experience.

For that reason, at the opening of each chapter we share a brief "Field of Play" note, highlighting for that step the core challenges you and your teen or young adult face. We also wrap up each chapter with a "Your Next Play" summary to help you once more orient your and your son's progress to the material covered in the chapter and to the work ahead.

Think of your son's challenges as your *opponent* and our seven-step game plan as your *offensive strategy.*

> With How to Get Your Son Back, *you will no longer defensively react to your teen's or young adult's troubled behavior and poor choices.*

Instead, your play will be to improve yourself and your relationship so you can influence your son to make better, healthier choices for himself.

Following our seven-step game plan, you will transform your relationship.

Step One Step Two	**You reconnect and repair your relationship with your son.** You develop a firmer relationship foundation based on trust and credibility.
Step Three Step Four Step Five	**You build on that solid foundation and begin to more successfully influence your son's behavior** by allowing his crisis to motivate change, by setting an example (modeling better choices and behaviors), by initiating and welcoming honest conversation, and by offering lovingly set boundaries and expectations. **Using your deepening relationship as a springboard, you will help your son heal.** Your teen or young adult will more fully engage in the game plan and with the health-care professionals helping him achieve his best.
Step Six Step Seven	**You spread your wings as a more confident parent when you have an authentic relationship with your child.** Leading by example, you inspire your son to join you in creating a more meaningful present and future life together.

Right now, you hold more power as a parent than you can possibly imagine.

We will show you how to capture and maximize that power.

What if I told you that your son really wants your approval and support?

Austin and I will show you how to tap into this longing so you can help your teen or young adult change. Even more meaningful and rewarding, you will learn how to build a deep, meaningful, and productive relationship with your son.

You do not need to be a psychologist to implement these seven steps.

How to Get Your Son Back is a dynamic, practical game plan for any parent wanting to better relate to a troubled teen or young adult.

However, these recommended strategies can only go so far. The effectiveness of the work you undertake depends almost entirely on you, the parent. Your commitment to understand, practice, and execute the skills we discuss means everything. Each parent must build his or her own playbook, uniquely designed to help their son find a better path.

> **NOTE:** Remember as you practice your game plan that we recommend you not explain these concepts and strategies to your son.
>
> Your teen or young adult is unlikely to buy into the journey you're about to undertake. Not just yet.

Your Parent Playbook

As you work through our seven-step game plan, you will build your own Parent Playbook.

Buy yourself a notebook, and be prepared to use it.

Take it with you wherever you go, so it's never out of reach when you have a few moments to review, or think more deeply about, or plan for your next opportunity to work with the questions and recommendations and exercises we offer.

But know up front that our work together won't be seven "quick steps" to making everything better.

Each family dynamic is different.

There are no hard-and-fast rules that, if followed, guarantee overnight success. You and your son have a great deal of work ahead of you.

Austin and I strongly recommend you share your Parent Playbook with the health-care team helping you and your son. Our game-plan recommendations are often most effective when pursued in conjunction with the work already being done with doctors and therapists.

Think of your Parent Playbook as a well-informed, motivational journal.

You will build your playbook yourself, making the notes you want, tracking whatever progress seems significant, and getting to know yourself and your son more positively, compassionately, and *honestly* than ever before.

Use your playbook to inspire you and to hold yourself accountable. Refer to it often as you consistently work on your relationship with your son. Track your progress as you both embark on this path of healing.

I can't tell you exactly what to do as a parent or what to record in your playbook. But I can tell you that consistently writing about your journey, giving voice and form to your innermost fears and doubts and regrets and dreams, will encourage you to explore even more deeply every aspect of your growth. And then eventually to open those very personal spaces to the people you care about most in your life—which is the very essence, in my experience, of giving and receiving compassion, acceptance, and love.

Record in your playbook whatever jumps out at you as you read each game-plan recommendation.

Not all of what Austin and I share will speak to you at first glance. You may read everything sequentially, from Step One through Step Seven (our recommendation), or you may be searching for something specific that will help you right now, in whatever difficult circumstance you're facing with your child.

And then you will circle back to the other steps once you're able. The key is to keep reading and wondering and searching for the answers you need.

Don't worry about keeping neat, organized, linear notes if that's not your thing. Write whatever you feel led to write, however you have to, as you work through your steps. Keep relating them to your son and yourself, learning and growing and healing as you help him do the same. Make time regularly to review your path through the notes you've left in your playbook.

> *Let your subconscious and your journey speak to you about all you've accomplished and the bright future ahead as you keep listening to and fighting for your teen or young adult.*

How We'll Work Together

Austin and I have made our seven-step game plan as approachable, easily understood, and practical as possible

We want you to feel confident as you apply our techniques to your family's unique dynamic.

Our process for rebuilding your parent-child relationship is designed with the goal of you beginning with Step One and progressing forward one step at a time from there. We strongly believe that you will achieve more immediate and consistent results in following this approach. However, we understand that not everyone succeeds using the same learning style.

To better assist both parents reading sequentially and those searching for a specific tool or concept, each game-plan step is presented in an easy-to-follow progression:

The Field of Play	We orient you to each step's key elements:
	• Your "game-plan" challenge
	• Your progress on your journey as a parent
	• Your son's progress on his journey to recovery
	• The current status of your parent-teen relationship
	• Your goal for this step
The Parent-Child Disconnect	**Austin and I share our personal journeys.** You'll find first-person accounts from our past detailing the painful and overwhelming situations Austin dealt with as a troubled teen as well as my (often misguided) parental reactions, including the mistakes I made in trying to cope with and help a son who was spiraling out of control.
	These will be real-time "story pairs," one from Austin and one from me, depicting two points of view of the same series of events. We'll relay what occurred without additional commentary in the hope that, while difficult to remember and convey, our stories will provide an opportunity for other parents to see that they are not alone on the challenging path they're traveling.
	NOTE: Timeframes, Austin's age, and the locations of some events will not necessarily flow linearly. Instead, we've sequenced the stories to best frame and support each step's message and recommendations.
What Happened?	**It's time to get serious about your game plan.** As a therapist, I help you break down the psychological, emotional, and behavioral elements at play in my and in *your* parent-child relationship.
	I'll clarify the dynamics and challenges of each step's field of play. We'll explore what's at stake for a child and parent in a similar situation, as well as the misunderstandings and missteps that at the time blocked Austin and me from successfully working through his problems. I'll share all I can, frankly and in laymen's terms, from my years of professional experience.

What to Do?	**From a parent's *and* a psychologist's perspective, I provide specific strategies for better dealing with a teen or young adult on a similar field of play.** Austin offers a teen's take on what would have worked better for him. He shares the kind of help he really needed from his father and how having it might have changed the painful outcome and consequences he and I unfortunately faced.
What's Most Important?	**Your Parent Playbook is our focus as we reinforce the key parent-child relating elements to keep in mind as** you execute your game plan on the playing field you share with your teen or young adult, and as you prepare to move forward to the next step of your work together.
Your Next Play	**We review your work so far:** • Your current step in the game plan • Your focus as a parent moving forward • Your teen's progress due to your work together • Your improving relationship dynamic due to your work together • Your goal in the next step: looking ahead

Behind the Game Plan

It would be impossible for Austin and me to cover every teen's or young adult's behavioral issues or every struggling family's dynamic.

Rather than going for a one-size-fits-all approach to solving specific problems, we instead focus on the power of the parent-child relationship—and your innate ability to affect your approach to relating with your child.

Regardless of the situation you and your son find yourselves in, you, the parent, can always change how you respond to your teen. And with sustained commitment to the work you need to do, you can and will improve that floundering relationship, so help can finally be offered and received in a loving and impactful way. Without a doubt, I see this as one of the most underused strategies for empowering parents of troubled sons.

To give you an overview of some of the concepts that will follow, for the moment, think of your relationship with your teen in terms of an employer's to his employee.

John Maxwell describes *positional leadership* as the lowest level and most ineffective style of leadership. With this method of influencing behavior, a worker decides to do what he's asked primarily because of his leader's power over him: if the worker doesn't complete the assigned task, he will be fired. In parenting terms, now consider situations in which you've threatened and attempted to coerce and punish your child in a genuine and desperate attempt to finally get him to listen and behave better. That, too, is the application of positional leadership—you're asserting your parental power over your troubled child. And while these tactics may render short-term results, the long-term consequences to your relationship (and your son's willingness to follow your leadership) can be profoundly destructive.

Using *How to Get Your Son Back*, your new game plan can best be summarized by what Maxwell terms the highest level of leadership: *influential leadership*. Consider that boss and his worker again, only this time they're relating in a much different manner. The influential leader is in the game *with* the subordinate, working alongside him. He inspires and respects rather than wielding demands or punitive measures. He doesn't use his position of authority to intimidate or bully subordinates into doing things his way. The worker knows he is valued and listened to and, through the leader's deliberate building of trust, is in turn willing to follow—even when not certain of the method or outcome.

The influential leader motivates not based on position but rather through credibility, experience, communication, and inspiration.

This is the "big-picture" parenting game plan you will learn to master as you read on.

The Fine Print

I can't stress enough that the success of our recommendations depends almost entirely on you, the parent.

You must be willing to engage and take the initiative with your child. You must be consistent in implementing your game plan and Parent Playbook strategies. Doing this vital work is *your* responsibility, as the parent. Yours is not a passive role. You are embarking on a long journey to inspire your teen or young adult to reach his potential.

Becoming an influential parent is a full-contact sport. You must abandon your "sideline coach" mentality, suit up, and be a leader on the playing field.

Our seven-step game plan will "dirty" you up.

You won't always get each step or strategy right the first time, or even the second. But both you and your child *will* get better the longer and harder you practice.

Remember that these recommendations are based on research, theory, and experience. I have used them extensively with my own son and with my patients. They are proven methods that yield inspiring results.

Before you begin, acknowledge that your teen or young adult did not develop his behavior overnight, nor did your relationship with him begin to misfire in only the past week.

Depending on your son's age and maturity, the degree of dysfunction in your relationship and his troubling behavior has likely been escalating for years. Reversing that course will take time. And *How to Get Your Son Back* is an authentic, long-term approach. Surface changes aren't enough. You and your child deserve a deeper, lifetime transformation that will enable you to successfully weather any challenge to come.

> **NOTE:** Therapy may be an essential component of healing your relationship. If either of you is also dealing with mental illness, this book is not intended to address your condition.
>
> A diagnosed or suspected mental illness must be treated in therapy by a qualified professional.
>
> Keep in mind, however, that much of therapy's success occurs beyond the parameters of the therapeutic session. The strategies recommended within this book can supplement and complement your or your son's therapy—if, and only if, your therapist agrees that they would be helpful.
>
> I highly recommend you share your Parent Playbook with your therapist and request to use our seven-step game plan along with your prescribed rehabilitation plan.

And finally, one last disclaimer . . .

There are no guarantees when it comes to human behavior.

The strategies we recommend in *How to Get Your Son Back*, the same as therapy itself, do not always work. There are mental illnesses that make it difficult to build reciprocal relationships (two-way relating built on communication that depends on give-and-take, trust, and honesty).

However, *How to Get Your Son Back* offers tools that can help any parent improve their connection with their child and better influence the behavior of a troubled teen or young adult. Our seven-step game plan is a fresh opportunity to commit fully to doing everything humanly possible to love and help your son.

In the end, that's all any of us can do.

That, and having faith that the results you've longed for will follow.

STEP ONE: STOP FIGHTING!
You Are Not the Opponent

Your Game-Plan Challenge	**Reestablish a foundation of understanding, empathy, and support with your teen or young adult.**
You, the parent, are	frustrated by your teen's or young adult's escalating pattern of destructive behavior and poor choices.
Your teen or young adult is	not communicating and is battling you, himself, and his world at every turn.
Your relationship dynamic is	disconnected; everything you say is either ignored or seems to make your relationship and his behavior worse.
Your Goal for This Step	**Shift first your perspective, so you can reconnect with your teen or young adult and begin to work together.**

THE FIELD OF PLAY

Your son is facing the battle of his life.

He is struggling. Whether he admits it or not, he feels out of control. Enemies loom everywhere he looks. His worst opponent is himself, and he likely knows it. Don't be another negative, ridiculing "Will you ever get anything right?!" voice beating him up for the mistakes he's making. Instead, relearn how to be with him, to fight *with* him, through every challenge and struggle he faces.

Failures are far too common for our troubled teens; opportunities to succeed seem practically nonexistent.

You, as the parent, must shift this perspective in your child—by first addressing it in yourself. You must help him see and take advantage of his next chance to handle his life better. Your job is to reflect the opportunities still available for him to find happiness, beginning with the very next choice he makes. And then the next.

You must become part of his struggle rather than being one more in a long line of people and circumstances opposing him.

Think of your relationship with your son in terms of our sports metaphor. In this step, you will begin to build your Parent Playbook.

Rather than a coach, consider yourself more in terms of a team captain. And consider this very important question: How will you lead your team to victory if your energy is focused on judging and reprimanding your teammate for past mistakes and fumbled opportunities rather than calling and running the next play?

> *At his age and level of maturity, your son is not yet equipped to solve his issues on his own.*

He needs your leadership to help him understand his circumstances and options. He will grow to better care for himself and to employ more effective tools and coping techniques by first watching you demonstrate more compassionate, empathetic methods of relating.

To accomplish this, you must see his world from his perspective as well as from the viewpoint of a loving, engaged parent.

It is absolutely essential to communicate this awareness and support and patience. He must internalize your intent to help him with how *he* sees himself needing help. You can't achieve this connection until you learn to curb and stop projecting your disappointment and frustration on his current circumstances.

To get in the game with your son, you must begin to struggle *with* him—not *because* of him or in reaction to something he's done. You are on the playing field sharing his journey, eyes forward, engaged in the next potential success rather than jeering from the sidelines, forever circling back to the last disappointment. You will never stop believing in your team's ability to succeed. You will fight beside your son, leading and supporting, your palm gently planted between his shoulder blades, your confidence steadying him as you walk forward together.

You will first make needed changes within yourself.

And as we discussed in the introduction, you will learn to shift your own view of what's happening, which will in turn improve your ability to relate to and then help your son recognize and confront his problems. Over time, you will both grow from this reestablished place of connection and understanding.

Your son will ultimately learn to accept your perspective and influence as that of a leader *sharing* his problem-solving and coping issues rather than as the opposition calling him out and punishing him for his mistakes.

> *Your Step-One game plan is to reestablish a foundation of understanding, empathy, and support.*

Following and practicing the recommendations in this step, you will learn to proactively relate to your troubled teen from a position of positive influence.

THE PARENT-CHILD DISCONNECTION

As Austin became a teenager and his struggles and problems escalated, my frustration with his issues grew into a never-ending, dysfunctional pattern I couldn't control.

I repeatedly explained the importance of education and how failing or dropping out of high school would literally cost him hundreds of thousands of dollars in forgone salary over his lifetime. I tried to convince him he would always have to answer to an authority figure, even when he was older and on his own: "If you think your teacher has power over you now, wait until your boss controls your paycheck." It didn't matter what I said or how dire I made the consequences seem. Austin refused to modify his behavior.

As my frustration grew, so did my concern for his future.

I lectured him, but the *next* lecture was never more effective than the previous hundred or so. Out of options, though, I kept preaching. If I found just the right things to say in the just the right way, I thought, something would finally click and I'd save my son from himself. Of course, that didn't happen. At least not the way I'd thought it would.

But as you'll see in our stories, I kept lecturing.

Austin: A Teen in Crisis

While not as traumatic as some, my story is more intense than that of many of the teens I've heard from.

It is a story of the hurt I endured and the hurt I caused others on my spiral into making life choices that seemed destined to land me either in prison or the morgue.

No two stories are alike. Mine won't be the same as your son's. But I'm betting parts of what I'll share will sound and feel and seem uncomfortably familiar, maybe reassuringly so, helping you accept that you're not alone in your relationship issues with your child.

All parents of troubled teens have one vital thing in common if their goal is to reconnect and once more influence their child's behavior.

It is absolutely essential to understand his *experience of what's happening in his life.*

You must be able to adjust your view of your teen's world. You must be willing when necessary to allow your son's experience and thoughts and reactions to become your primary focus, rather than your own. Without this perspective, how will you understand enough of what he's going through to be able to make an authentic connection? How will you know how to help him?

An obvious wrinkle in this plan, as many of you already know, is that your troubled teen is not going to hang out with you and invite you into his world or come right out and tell you what he's thinking. *Never* going to happen. I wish I'd been able to with my dad. I wish even more that he'd found some way to reach me sooner regardless of how hard I fought to hide away all I thought was ugly and broken about myself.

I share my difficult stories throughout this book to show you this "secret" side, your child's side, of what you and your family are going through.

My goal is to inspire you to never, ever give up on caring for and encouraging your son to fight his way back to feeling positive and hopeful about his chances to live a successful life.

Troublemaking from a Young Age

Many of my earliest childhood memories have become vague, but what I do recall is significant.

At a very early age, my life began heading down the wrong path.

I remember living in Wichita, Kansas, where I was born. I get the times and locations confused now, because we moved to

Dallas, Texas, when I was still very young. Dallas is where my parents' marriage and our family and my life began to unravel, one thread at a time. It's where the worst of what you're about to read of me began.

What I Saw

When we were all still living together, my parents fought frequently.

Their conflict and negative energy and way of relating became mine. The thing that stands out most as I look back is how much it hurt that very young me to hear them fight—especially when they were arguing about something I'd done—and how I wanted so badly to be somewhere else.

I am guessing I was about two or three years old when I took the Clorox bleach from the back of the toilet and dumped it all over my little brother, Alex, and the room where he was sleeping. Dad and Mom started screaming at me; dad tossed me on the couch, and I remember him screaming at my mother for leaving the bleach where I could get ahold of it. I just laid there with my face buried in the back of the couch and my eyes closed, crying uncontrollably, while the raging continued around me. There was no way to block it out.

I never knew when my parents would start fighting again. Every child wants a peaceful, stable home to grow up in, where the people raising him love each other. That wasn't in the cards for me. Not a lot seemed safe. And I was so young. I guess the only control I had was to start blaming myself for all of it. There had to be a reason, right? And I was the one who kept screwing things up.

Before I knew it, I was the oldest of two brothers in a broken home headed by a newly divorced, single mom who was now responsible for holding everything together. I was the man of the house.

At least I wanted to be.

Things I Did

One day my mom had just mowed the yard and was taking a nap.

She worked so hard, and I wanted to help around the house. I saw the weeds growing up around everything, especially along our fence. I could trim them for her. The idea made me excited and proud. *Mom is going to be surprised*, I remember thinking. *It'll make her so happy when she sees what I've done.*

I found the weed trimmer in the garage and discovered that the string it used to cut grass and weeds was a tangled mess. I had no idea what I was doing, but that didn't stop me. I could fix that. I could get it operating again. I was going to help my mom.

I sat on the kitchen floor and fought for over an hour trying to untangle yards of slippery string. Yes, in the kitchen. Of course, I made a huge mess: grass clippings and fuel were everywhere, and I wound up tangling the stuff even worse than before I'd started. Not to mention I had no idea how to insert the line back into the trimmer once I was finished. *If* I ever finished.

Stories like this remind me of just how young I was when I first began feeling as if I were a mess. I was totally out of my depth, trying and failing to help my mom and little brother. In moments like this—when I genuinely wanted to do my best for the people I cared about—those tangles got inside me and held tight; they grew roots deep enough to echo throughout my lifetime. I was worthless, you see, when I had to accept and admit that I'd failed. I'd wanted to be the man of the family. What kind of a "man" couldn't even fix a weed trimmer?

My mother was not happy about the giant mess I made. Of course, as an adult looking back, I can't say I blame her. But her disappointment and frustration and the anger that came my way were absolutely crushing. I grabbed the trimmer and tossed it back into the garage and started to sob.

I was seven at the time. Not much more than a baby, but I was the man of the family—and real men didn't cry. I remember hating myself for not controlling those tears, even though I made it back to my room without anyone else noticing. I crammed my face into my pillow and blamed myself for everything (the way I was certain everyone else did) and mentally kicked myself around for hours.

I felt like a nothing.

Who Was I?

My little brother, Alex, was nine, and I was ten.

We had been inside the cool climate of our air-conditioned home for most of the day, sheltered from the scorching, humid Maryland summer. We were bored and sick of feeling cooped up, so we resorted to "picking at each other" (that's what my father called our arguments back then). My little brother and I couldn't agree on which sport to play when we finally did go outside. Finally, we heard my dad's voice from downstairs. "You guys ready? I'm done listening to you pick at each other. We're going to go throw the football at the park." So that settled that.

I put on my shoes while Alex dashed down the stairs.

"Shotgun!" I yelled. "I called it!"

Dad heard and said, "He called it. On the way back," he told Alex, "you can sit in the front."

As we rode to the park, Alex and I continued to silently irritate each other. We were both mad by the time we arrived. It was game on.

Dad headed into a field beside the playground. He dropped his wallet and keys to mark the halfway point on our makeshift football field. That was our first-down marker. We each had four downs to make it to at least the halfway point, and then another four plays to score a touchdown. The game we played back then was passing only; Dad was our all-the-time quarterback.

Alex and I traded touchdowns until the sun sank behind the tree line, making it difficult to see the ball. Dad said, "All right, you each get one more possession. It's about time to head back."

Knowing it was the last possession, my little brother and I played our hearts out. On the first down of Alex's drive, he ran a long slant route, catching the ball well past midfield to set up first and goal. The next play, I hung back about five yards beyond the line of scrimmage, knowing I had to protect the end zone.

Dad yelled, "Hut!" snapping the ball to himself.

Alex tried another slant in the opposite direction, but Dad threw a bad pass that was too far behind him. Alex did his best to adjust and catch the ball, but I was in far better position and easily intercepted. I celebrated by subsequently spiking it into the ground, making Alex cry. As brothers, we were overly competitive and couldn't stand the thought of losing to each other. Crying was a common feature of our games, but Dad wasn't having any of it this time.

"You guys are a bunch of babies!" he erupted. "I bring you out here and play football with you for hours, and this is what I get—a bawling mess. I should have brought a towel so you guys could soak up the tears! Get your butts to the car now. You both lose."

Dad picked up the ball and threw it at me as hard as he could but missed.

Now I was about to break down.

My father was angry with me, and that cut deep. Plus, I'd lost my chance to beat my brother by scoring the final touchdown. While Dad went to fetch the ball he'd heaved at me, Alex and I walked to the car together, making chilling eye contact without saying a word.

Our fight was over. So was the fun we'd had. For a while there, we'd felt so close to our father and each other—even as we competed to prove who was best. It had been an amazing afternoon. Now we'd ruined everything.

Dad was more than angry. He thought we were losers.

Our father was ashamed of us.

⌐

I wanted to get to know my grandpa more.

He did a lot of the cool things I had heard about at school, like hunting and fishing. Also, in our small Kansas town, everyone knew and liked Grandpa. He had lived there his entire life, working for the same company since right after high school graduation. He had tons of friends and couldn't go anywhere without striking up a conversation. I was proud that everyone knew he was my grandpa.

One of the neat things I noticed about him was his spitting all the time. I didn't know why, but whenever he spit, it was brown.

One day, when I was ten or eleven, I asked, "Grandpa, what do you have in your mouth?"

"That's Grandpa's chewin' tobacco. Boy, you'd better stay away from it; it ain't good for you. Grandpa shouldn't be doin' it either."

Of course, I wanted to start chewing after that. But there was no way to get my hands on any tobacco of my own. So I just started spitting. It was as close as I could get to being just like my grandfather.

I often asked him to tell me stories about his childhood. He told me about getting into lots of fights.

"You see these false teeth?" He flipped his dentures around in his mouth. "The reason Grandpa ain't got no teeth left is from fighting all the time. Well, that and trying to pole-vault over a clothesline." He got a good laugh out of me with that one. "Hell, your grandpa got into a fight damned near every day. Times were a lot different back then. Nowadays they'd hang you for doing half the stuff I did."

He told me about the time he'd ramped his car off the Santa Fe Railway's loading dock, prompted by a dare, which caused the axles to snap and all four tires to bend outward. "Hell, I had to drag that son of a bitch to the junkyard with a tractor!"

The way he'd fought a lot when he was my age and all the rowdy stuff he'd done back then made him sound so cool. Everyone still thought he was. He was a great man, and he made me feel good when he took me places. Being with him made me feel important.

I wanted to be just like him when I grew up.

⌇

I felt blessed to have both my grandpa and my father in my life.

Each of them loved me a lot. They would have done anything for me; I always knew that. Their love for me was never in question, and neither was mine for them. I worshipped the ground they walked on (especially my father) and found myself trying to be like both. My father became my "professional" ideal; my grandfather was the best of what it meant to be "country" and "down-home."

In a way, having them as role models created a kind of hybrid pattern for me to follow—good and bad. But it was also confusing. Who was I? A raw redneck or a polished, white-collar professional?

Switching back and forth depending on who held greater influence in my life at any given time left me feeling confused. When you're that young, identity is everything. Not knowing who you are (or wondering who you should be) really dings up your self-confidence.

When I was around kids my own age, I didn't know how to act. I wanted to be like the adults in my life. I felt weird and anxious around other boys, like I didn't belong. I'd never let anyone know it, but when I was with other kids, I had, like, zero self-confidence. I guess that's why I started picking friends the way a lazy person picks apples—from the lowest hanging branches.

If the kids I hung out with felt as awkward as I did, they were less likely to reject me—which would have been the worst thing I could imagine happening. Everyone liked my dad and grandpa. So I needed everyone to like me; however, I had to make that happen.

I realized when I was around twelve or thirteen that I felt most comfortable around the troublemakers and outcasts who were just as insecure and confused as I was. It strikes me as ironic now how much I turned to those same guys for guidance and advice. We were truly the blind leading the blind.

I'd handpicked the "safe" people I surrounded myself with, knowing they wouldn't challenge who or what I was while I was still trying to figure that out for myself. Until, slowly at first, and eventually so rapidly I'm not really certain when it all locked into place, I became one of those outliers who frequently got into trouble at school and fought and started cursing at a young age.

Even more destructive and more of a concern to my successful father, I wound up not caring about grades or my future.

Because, really, "What's the point?" all the confused kids around me kept demanding.

⤳

Maintaining that tough-guy identity became an emotional wormhole.

My senses were continuously on high alert, my mind constantly thinking of ways people might verbally or physically attack me. I wasn't innocent when it came to that kind of bullying.

Anytime there was an opportunity to make fun of someone, especially in public, I would. Like I said, the thought of being publicly humiliated was my biggest fear. I was terrified of someone "putting me in my place" or exposing me for the phony I knew I was.

One night when I was seventeen, a friend of mine and I were riding around in his old blue Chevy flatbed truck. He received a text from his cousin, who invited us to a party. We went. There wasn't anything else to do.

We arrived at a bonfire-style party out in a field, with trucks lining each side of the path down to the fire pit. As usual, I was drunk out of my mind. This was an older crowd, and I felt threatened just being around them, but, of course, I wasn't going to let anyone know that. These guys were older and more experienced. The sober me would have known I was out of my league. But I was hammered, so I ran my mouth off.

I walked by a crowd of guys and recognized one of them. He was the older brother of a girl I found super annoying. I remember saying something bad about his sister and then walking the other direction, not giving a moment's thought to the hornets' nest I'd just poked. Suddenly big brother tackled me from behind and began choking me.

As a frequent fighter, I was familiar with being hit in the face and how that felt, but I had never been choked. His arm tightened around my throat. Although I was drunk, I remember time slowing down—I know now that this was due to the adrenalin pumping through my body. There was nothing I could do but lie there, getting my drunk ass choked out.

I was reaching the point of passing out, and as the possibility of death crossed my mind, I thought about God. It was a surreal moment. Everything was a blur—the sound of the older guy's friends cheering and rooting him on faded into the background as I lay there completely vulnerable, no longer fighting back, about to black out. And all the while I was calmly, silently praying, asking God for His forgiveness.

For some reason, big brother let me out of the headlock before I was completely gone. I pulled right up, and, of course, forgot to turn my mouth off autopilot. It was running like a Cummins diesel. The next thing I knew, I had three much older, much bigger guys wanting to kick my ass. Somehow it finally registered that I was outmanned, at which point I shut up, did some listening, and got myself out of there in relatively one piece.

It took me a long time to mentally recover from the public humiliation, not from the fear. The thought that I might have died or deserved the choking never really registered. Instead, every time I went out, I was hypersensitive and aware of my surroundings. It felt as if people were always talking bad about me behind my back. I could still hear that guy's friends jeering at me and egging him on. My body was in constant fight-or-flight mode while my thoughts swirled with who else viewed me as a nothing who deserved to have the life choked out of him. I was a wreck; weak and damaged.

My persona as a fighter had taken some serious hits, and my small-town, redneck reputation was literally all I had back then.

What Would I Become?

Their conversation grabbed my attention and wouldn't let go.

Several of my classmates had huddled together talking about their recent fishing expeditions. They took turns swapping stories about how much they had caught and the size of their biggest catches.

It was if they were speaking a different language, as I did not understand any of it. They laughed at each other's stories and bragged about who was best and who knew the choicest fishing spots. Once again, I felt like an outsider, missing out on a bond other guys shared—guys who already seemed more like men than I'd ever be.

Lucky for me, my grandfather was an avid and experienced outdoorsman. It was as if he were born in a duck blind. Nearly all my grandfather's hobbies involved either a shotgun, a bow, or a fishing pole. I called him, and he agreed to take a friend and me fishing. I was thrilled, though not so much about the fishing part. *Now* I would fit in with the other guys. I would have my own stories. I would be the kid with the cool grandfather who took people to the best places to catch the biggest fish.

My friend and I awoke before dawn and sat out on the porch, anxiously awaiting my grandfather's arrival. As I saw the lights of his old red truck heading down our road, I yelled, "Here he comes. Let's go!"

Grandpa stopped the truck and reached across the cab to open the door for us. He playfully said, "Get your little asses in here. Grandpa's taking you two out for breakfast, then we're going to head out and do a little fishing."

I was so proud.

We were eating breakfast at McDonald's when Grandpa asked, "How's your breakfast, kids?"

"Good!" we told him.

When I asked him the same thing, he responded, "Well, it'll make a turd, or push one out." My friend and I burst out laughing, which prompted grandpa to jokingly say, "What in the hell are you two laughing at? I'll kick a turd out of you boys a foot long!" We all laughed, and I'd never felt more like I belonged.

He took us to a large farm pond. We spent the entire afternoon fishing. My friend and I caught lots of fish and had a great time. I remember the look on my friend's face when he was reeling in a large fish. He was so excited, and I'd been the one to make that happen.

Thanks to my grandpa, I was finally an insider.

╌

My "rougher" friends got into frequent fights.

I continued being drawn to that kind of "masculine" behavior. I'd started bullying kids back in elementary school, and old habits die hard. I started trouble because I thought that was the mark of being a man. Overall, my personality was firmly entrenched on the "badass" side of the spectrum.

In my mind, fighting and cursing were what being a man was all about. I wholeheartedly embraced the lifestyle. I remember actually standing in front of a mirror once and practicing "the glare": squinting my eyes and raising my upper lip as if I were Clint Eastwood in *The Good, the Bad, and the Ugly.*

Being an adult like Eastwood and my grandpa was something I so badly wanted. In my mind, I would have even more credibility and respect once I was a man like them. I would finally, forever belong.

∽

When I was younger, being one of the bigger kids in my class became a big part of who I was.

Classmates rarely challenged me, so I started bullying them at recess, kicking them in the shins with my cowboy boots whenever I could get away with it. I didn't think about what I was doing or how I was making others feel. The important thing was the small niche of "bad-news" friends I was making. Being like them, only better, soon became what I wanted most.

One of my best friends would often use the phrase "I don't know." He said it so often it was weird, but before long I was saying it all the time too. It was the ultimate statement of cluelessness and stupidity, but it felt right.

Early on, I learned to do whatever and say whatever and become whatever I thought I had to in order to feel "right."

∽

My grades deteriorated the further I progressed in school.

Being in class was difficult. For one thing, I couldn't pay attention for a sustained period of time. "Smart" wasn't my problem. I simply couldn't focus. As my grades slipped, I honestly tried to listen to my teachers and take notes. But it all started feeling impossible.

I was too ashamed to ask for help; real men didn't ask for help. So, like my outlier friends, I quit trying. My dad's lectures about the importance of education were humiliating and painful. It couldn't have been any clearer how ashamed he was of me. But it was just noise, I told myself. I didn't care. I could handle it.

I mentally checked out of school. But the last thing I wanted was to appear stupid. I compensated by becoming the class clown, which had the added allure of playing into my tough-guy persona.

English was a class I thought was stupid and pointless. "Because I already speak it," I'd rag to anyone. To my teenage mind, singing songs differentiating the various parts of sentence structure (prepositions, pronouns, conjunctions, etc.) was asinine. Worse yet, I thought the teacher was a jerk. Back then they all seemed to be. But this one guy—the more I could do to piss him off, the better. Forget the consequences; I simply didn't care.

One day before English class, my friend Jack and I decided to run by the vending machines to get some snacks and soda, knowing we would be late. About ten minutes after class started, we made our way into the room, both of us wearing cowboy boots and dirty jeans from the welding we'd done in shop. I walked in first; Jack trailed behind. My arms were full, with three cans of soda and two snack cakes.

We sat down, and the teacher asked, "Austin, why are you guys late?"

I responded, "Well, we were running behind because we had to pick up after people who'd left a big mess over at the vocational shop."

Just as I spouted what was so obviously a lie, right on cue, Jack cracked open a can of pop as loudly as he could, breaking the tense silence. He began gulping it down as if it were the first time he'd tasted soda. His short legs were crossed as he propped his black cowboy boots on the unoccupied desk in front of him movie-theatre style. His cavalier attitude annoyed the teacher. I laughed, sort of trying to keep it to myself but not really.

"Okay, I just want to get this right," the teacher said. "You two were late because you had to pick things up, but yet you still had time to stop and get food and drinks?"

Jack replied, "Yup. It's called priorities."

The class erupted in laughter. The teacher told him to take his sodas and enjoy them in the school office, to which Jack responded, "Fine with me." He scooped the unopened cans of soda and snacks using the bottom of his dirty white T-shirt as a pouch, then walked out of class without a care in the world.

I lowered my head, still laughing, thinking the attention was still on my friend. Worried about losing my snacks, I crammed an entire cupcake in my mouth. When I looked up, I discovered the teacher's attention locked on me. "What did I do?" I asked, my mouth stuffed full and open, my half-eaten food on display as everyone around me waited for a response.

Of course, they were all laughing too. Which prompted me to keep up it and lean even harder into my disgusting behavior.

"Austin, take your desk and move out in the hallway," the teacher said. "I would send you to the office, too, but I don't want you near Jack, so just sit out in the hall."

Tears of laughter were flowing down my classmates' cheeks. Not knowing what to do with the remaining cupcake in the open package, I crammed it into my already full mouth like a compactor ramming refuse into an overflowing garbage truck.

I sat in the hall, removed from the spotlight and instantly bored. No way was I going to read the assigned material, so I kept drinking and eating, not a care in the world. The classroom was located near the stairwell at the end of the hall, so numerous people walked by. That hallway had become my second home, so it didn't bother me.

From the floor below, I heard Breanne's voice and footsteps coming up the stairs in my direction. Breanne was a good friend of mine who was easy to make laugh. Making her laugh always made everything, anything, seem right. As she walked up the stairs and around the corner, the sight of me sitting out in the hallway started her giggling.

"Austin, what did you do?" She was heading to a class down the hall.

I used my legs to propel me and my desk backward, and I said a line I'd heard in a movie somewhere, "Walk with me."

We had the equivalent of a "walking meeting," only with me scooting my desk backward to keep pace. The sound of those four metal legs screeching on the old linoleum floor made her laugh hysterically. So I kept scooting, acting as if I were serious about having a dialogue. Breanne laughed so hard that she couldn't even talk.

Something stopped me from behind. It was the wall. I had scooted my desk to the opposite end of the hallway. Breanne walked into her class. I positioned myself where I could see her. I started making faces, nodding in agreement with whatever lesson was being taught in her class.

Her teacher finally saw me and slammed the door, leaving me alone and isolated in the mess I'd made, still pretending it was fine with me that this was what my life had become.

Kevin: Parenting 911

Most parents want their children to achieve more in life than they as parents have.

We want them to avoid the painful mistakes we endured and to use our wisdom and hard-earned experience as stepping-stones from which to launch themselves onto a better path. I wanted Austin to have the good things I had achieved, like financial freedom. As I saw it, he had it all—he was talented, smart, good-looking, and had a personality that wouldn't quit.

So I was in the clear, right?

No worries about how things would turn out for him . . . or me.

The Dreams I Had

From beneath a surreal swirl of strange activity, the doctor announced, "It's a boy."

My reaction was "Yeeessss!" All my prebirth plans would now become reality.

During her pregnancy, my wife and I hadn't wanted to know the sex of our first child. But I'd had a feeling it was going to be a boy. Now, I thought to myself, *Oh, the fun this little guy and I are going to have!*

That first night in the hospital, Austin laid on my chest for hours. I could not believe it. I was finally a dad, and this was my son. I looked at each detail: his hands, his feet, his face. He looked exactly like his grandpa Jim. Austin was perfect. I couldn't stop kissing his head. I was instantly in love. There is no feeling like the birth of a child. As a parent, I know you get that.

The very next day, I executed the plan I'd been formulating for months. I went to a store and bought Austin a football jersey. Everyone between that store and the hospital got to see my son's new jersey whether they wanted to not.

Some strangers would smile and nod; others would kindly comment, "Aw, a little football player."

I thought, *No, you don't get it. He is going to be a major college linebacker and business executive. For real*! I had visualized it all. Austin would grow up to be the starting linebacker for the Oklahoma Sooners. When he wasn't leading his team in tackles, he would be a distinguished scholar. He would eventually attend law school, but that might have to wait for a year or two, what, with him being drafted into the pros and all. He was going to have such a sweet life, and I would proudly watch it all unfold.

About eighteen months after Austin was born, I was blessed with my second son, Alex. For the next two years, the boys and I often played on the floor and out in the yard. We made up silly games: don't get smashed by the couch cushions, cars, stunts on the couch, fights on the floor with Daddy. Anything to entertain and exhaust two of the sweetest, funniest, most active boys you'll ever meet.

Laughter was an important part of our silly play. I had learned from the best. My father had played the same way with my two brothers and me. As a kid, my front yard was a football field. And when that wasn't our thing, my brothers and I played more made-up games than I can possibly recount.

I was determined to re-create the same idyllic experience for Austin and Alex.

Time for a Reality Check

Unfortunately, not all dreams are given a chance to flourish.

The boys got older, and I began to enjoy them even more. Sure, there were occasional dustups and timeouts, but the three of us had so much fun together. They were at the ages where we could have conversations, go for walks in the park, and play for hours. I was beginning to learn to be present with them. Whenever we were together, I would focus on them rather than on my work or the other matters wanting to rent space in my head. Sounds perfect, right?

Unfortunately, my marriage began to deteriorate. How could that growing conflict not have distracted me from the boys? Ultimately, when Austin and Alex were around age five and three, their mother and I separated and then divorced. We were living in the Dallas area at the time. I stayed there for business after she and the boys moved to Kansas.

I missed Austin and Alex dearly, so I would visit on as many weekends as possible, driving the sixteen-hour round-trip from Dallas to Kansas. My parents lived near the boys and served as their primary day-care providers while their mother worked. Their house became my home base when I was in town. Following an eight-hour drive on Friday after work, I'd land at my parents' at around three in the morning. The boys would already be there.

I remember quietly walking into their room as soon as I arrived. It was so good to see them. They looked like angels.

I'd kiss them good night. Exhausted, I'd hurry to bed, knowing the door to my room would soon blast open with two boys shouting, "Dad!"

Continuous play would ensue for the next thirty-six hours, followed by an agonizing eight-hour return drive to Dallas, my heart overflowing with grief after a gut-wrenching, tearful good-bye.

Was It Him or Me?

What early on seemed to be trivial issues for Austin—inattention and not completing his homework—developed into major problems over time.

By the fourth grade, he was acting out in class and fighting on the playground, a pattern that escalated throughout junior high and high school, resulting in multiple suspensions. The teachers and I agreed that intelligence was not Austin's issue. He simply refused to apply himself. Countless conversations with Austin, his teachers, and the school's administrative staff led to zero improvement. I felt helpless to remedy the situation. As his parent, I felt deep guilt and regret, certain the mess his mother and I had made of our marriage was contributing to his behavioral issues.

Things He Did

As Austin became a teen, our time together and the length of our phone conversations gradually diminished.

He liked to hunt, and he worked whenever he could, so there was little time in his life for me. I would make visits, but they were less frequent, and usually I would see much more of Alex. When he was available, Austin always took my calls and talked to me, and he'd end each call with an "I love you, Dad." Our love for each other was still solid. His waning confidence, troubled behavior, and nonexistent life direction, however, were ongoing issues. My concern for him—the path he was on, his friends, his poor performance in school, and his growing legal troubles—continued to mount.

I worried about his future, about how the mistakes he was making could be life altering and how the hardships he was creating for himself were stacking up. What had happened to my dreams: my two sons attending a major college, playing football, dating lots of pretty girls, balancing fun with making the grades that would lead them to successful, rewarding careers like mine? For Austin, those dreams were in serious jeopardy.

As a parent reading this, you are likely familiar with that ache in your stomach and the persistent worry and fear that go with having a troubled teen or young adult. When the phone rings and the number calling is somehow associated with your son, you instantly feel sick and angry.

We think, or, worse yet, we say, "Why can't you get it right? It's not that hard!"

Who Were We?

Before long it seemed as if the only news I received from or about Austin was negative. Home, school, church, and the police—it was mostly all bad.

The continual drip of trouble was difficult for everyone. I know Austin hated to call and tell me what had happened next. When he would call, he typically got right to the point and took responsibility for his actions. His sense of self, the way he felt about himself, took a constant beating.

You could see the effect of this almost nonstop negative feedback from the adults in his life in how he carried himself. He was willing to take ownership for his behavior, but that didn't keep him from heaping more and more trouble onto his plate. The load was getting heavier and heavier.

His eyes were becoming hardened, his humor more dark and cynical.

He was drifting away from me.

What Would We Become?

To quote my mother, I talked to Austin until I was "blue in the face."

While he would tolerate my lectures, it was apparent he was not listening and really had no interest in what I was saying. It was incredibly painful.

When Austin achieved success, it was as if he didn't know how to handle it. During his eighth-grade year, he went out for track and wound up throwing shot put and discus. He certainly had the size and strength to compete, but the last thing I'd expected was for him to be as talented as he was.

He would typically get second in the shot put, but in the discus he was in a class all his own. Early in the season, he broke the school record by twenty-five feet. He won most meets by that much and more. He'd had no formal coaching. He was purely a natural.

I remember going to Austin's last eighth-grade meet.

The high school coach, a division-one college athlete himself, was drooling over the prospect of having Austin as a freshman. Others would cheer, "Good throw, Austin!" and in response, avoiding eye contact with anyone, my son would respond in self-disgust, "I freaking suck today."

He hated being in the spotlight, and his responses to others took on an ugly edge. If you hadn't known him earlier in life, you would have instantly disliked the young man he was becoming. He came across as angry and always wishing he were somewhere else. The next year, Austin informed me he was not going to go out for high school track. I couldn't believe it. I didn't understand his "I just want to work and make money" excuse.

I know all parents are prone to overestimate their child's ability. But given Austin's size and strength as he entered high school, grabbing that college scholarship I'd always hoped for him would not have been out of the realm of possibility. Why would he give this up? Why not at least try? So many kids would have loved to have his talent, but it was as if he were determined to flush his potential down the toilet.

And I was powerless to stop him.

WHAT HAPPENED?

How well do you know your son?

What really motivates him?

You can see in the stories you've just read that as son and father, Austin and I were experiencing, at least on the surface, the same out-of-control journey. But we were far from working together as a team.

From the Psychologist

Many of the parents I have worked with have used varying strategies in an attempt to alter their teen's or young adult's behavior.

I have seen parents try to control, smother, baby, helicopter, coerce, guilt, and even shame their sons into change. I was no different. But while these tactics may have worked while our children were younger, and while we may have experienced short-term success with our more positional leadership approach, these methods can have significant negative, long-term costs.

> *When a child is in an accelerating behavioral spiral, the most painful aspect of a* positional *parenting approach can be the shame and humiliation your teen or young adult feels as a result of your parenting.*

Positional parenting often conveys that you think your son is not capable. You may be repeatedly projecting reminders that he or she is failing, not good enough, and won't ever be able to do things right, all of which can feed the disconnection between you.

Today I work with parents of equally troubled teens or young adults.

These are intelligent, well-meaning adults whose bright-minded children are making bad decisions. Their relationship with their sons has often deteriorated to the point where attempts at conversation quickly explode into anger, with disrespectful name-calling and brutal insults. I have heard moms and dads say, "I just hate being around him."

Of course, not all sons and parents fight openly. Sometimes the relational rift is silent and passive. I have heard parents express concern about their sons lying and sneaking around. Others talk about their children "running over them" and blatantly disrespecting them.

> *When we and our kids are at our lowest, it's common for parents to have no idea what to do to earn back the respect and trust we fear we've lost forever.*

We no longer have influence over the choices and behaviors our son seems to be intentionally inflicting on himself and everyone around him. We grapple for any lifeline that may help us break through—often to our and our son's detriment. I certainly made mistakes early on that haunt me to this day.

Attempts by the parent to control a troubled child's behavior using a domineering "power approach" conditions him to believe he is not capable of making the right decisions on his own. Alternatively, if you helicopter parent your son (rescue and protect him from consequences), you're risking his never learning to take responsibility for his actions—a key developmental skill for emerging adults. I have seen parents baby and coddle their son to the point that he feels emasculated, leading him to resent the very person moving heaven and earth to care for him. This overly cautious, "well-intentioned" sheltering also fosters an unhealthy dependency—conditioning your teen or young adult to feel ill-equipped to handle challenges and adversity on his own.

And, finally, using coercion, guilt, and shame as parenting tools destroys the very trust we're working so hard to protect.

> *These critical mistakes we make as parents of increasingly troubled boys can create deeply rooted resentments in our teens and young adults—resentments we may spend years attempting to overcome.*

Austin Checks In

Looking back, I think the watershed moment for me was my parents' divorce.

I "failed" to take over the responsibilities my dad abdicated when he left. I heaped guilt and shame on myself, because surely that's how everyone else saw me. After all, all of the out-of-control, scary things happening around me and my little brother were my fault.

Trying to fill that leadership chasm in my and my sibling's lives wasn't a position assigned or delegated to me. I wanted it. I felt an internal, urgent obligation as the oldest son. But what did I know about taking care of myself, let alone anyone else?

At far too young an age, I was determined to become the man of the house. But how was I supposed to learn those vital developmental skills? My father was no longer around on a regular basis to talk to me or model how to mature into what I wanted so badly to become. And when he was around—or rather, when I was around him at his new place—things had changed between us. For reasons I didn't understand, everything felt off.

As time passed, I became more and more frustrated and felt as if I was a worthless case—an inadequate trifle of a "man." No matter where I turned, I couldn't make things better. So, naturally, the problem had to be me, right?

Nothing scared me more than pissing my father off.

When dad was angry, each and every time I messed up, fear and rejection came calling, waves and waves of it. What would he do? When he lost his cool he would yell, intimidate, threaten, shake, and spank, sometimes even with a belt.

I so badly wanted his approval. Every time I disappointed him or let him down, it felt like I was losing him. And there was never any reassurance that I wasn't. My dad didn't know how to do that sort of thing then. And I didn't know how to tell him what I needed.

> *Over and over, my heart broke for how badly I was screwing things up between us.*

You see, in my mind, it was all my fault. I was worthless because I couldn't make it better. My dad was my idol; my heartstrings were tied to his fingers. No one back then could have damaged and eventually severed those ties as skillfully as my father. And the only weapon he needed was his words.

I was a failure.

That's how I interpreted the trouble I got into—and how I figured everyone else did. At a very young age, even before all the rest, I struggled with confidence. That's just who I was. My father didn't seem to notice, so making me feel better about myself wasn't on his radar. Soon, when anything bad happened in my life, I internalized it. I must have been the cause. For years to come, that assumption colored my world.

And don't get me wrong. I don't tell these stories to play victim or assign blame. I'm not an armchair quarterback saying that if I'd been the father, I'd have done better. Parents in the thick of what I put mine through do everything they can, everything they know how, until they learn and know better. My dad did, at least.

> *I'm wanting you to see the origin of the destructive, negative self-view that devastated my early life.*

If you do, and if you're hearing and seeing something eerily familiar, maybe it will help you and your son understand and talk and work better together on helping him avoid the mistakes I made. That's what I'm hoping for.

Kids feeling worthless. Children knowing for a fact that they're letting their parents down. Teens feeling the crushing defeat of never being able to make things right again. When a teen or young adult watches the secure foundation of his family and the unconditional love he craves disappearing, where is there to go but pull further away and disappear even deeper into emotional and behavioral darkness?

WHAT TO DO?

Kevin: How I Became a Parent-Leader.

A Ray of Hope

One day Austin's high school principal called me.

My son was in trouble again. Knowing I was wasting my time and a vacation day, I reluctantly took off work and drove the three-plus hours for the meeting. It would be painful to sit through another "Austin did this, and Austin did that" conversation, but I would try to encourage Austin to take school more seriously with another one of my "super successful" dad lectures. After all, they had worked so well up to that point.

Perhaps the principal sensed I needed some encouragement. After the short meeting with Austin, the man asked to speak to me privately, then said, "The thing about Austin—if I go to him and ask him if he did something, he will look me in the eye and admit it. Most kids his age won't do that. Heck, a lot of parents won't do that. They will look away and lie, but not Austin. I appreciate that about him."

I thanked the principal. His words were medicine to my tired soul. Deep in my heart, I knew Austin was a good kid. I knew he had character. For the moment, I was proud of him. Austin was worth the fight. Though my lecture that day had little to no effect on his behavior, I had some hope. I could work with character.

So can you.

Time to Dig In

It is time for a new parenting strategy—one through which you will discover your greatest strength and gain influence with your son. This strategy is designed to empower both of you. You will reconnect and deepen your relationship. By using this approach, you will help your son become a better communicator and partner, skills that will later help him in his career and in other aspects of his adult life.

> *To achieve influence with your son, you must enrich and deepen your relationship with him.*

You need to better understand your son, his priorities, and his desires. Otherwise, who is he? How can you know him if you don't understand what motivates and drives him? Of course, there are millions of relationships out there, including parent-son relationships, that exist solely on a superficial plain of communicating about sports, news, and the weather.

But once again, I'll ask you the hard question I faced in the mirror as Austin and I stood at the same emotional, developmental precipice as you now do.

How intimately do you know your son and what really motivates him?

A New Perspective

One day I was thinking of ways I could help Austin.

Suddenly I was prompted to look at him from a new perspective, one I had never before considered. It made me feel extremely uncomfortable.

What if Austin were dead? *I wondered.*

I'd *never* wish that for my son. But I found the exercise enlightening—and scary as hell. My first recommendation: take that same question out for a spin in your own parent-child relationship. See if the answer doesn't dramatically shift your perspective of your teen's or young adult's behavior and troubling choices.

I found myself suddenly staring the down the reality that if Austin *were* dead, I would be in more pain than I could possibly imagine. So many things would be left unsaid between us. I would never have another chance to hug him or to tell him how much I loved him and how sorry I was for failing him as a parent. I would have missed my chance to show him how forever my love for him would always be, or how much I wanted to know him better, even if I didn't understand how to reach through his hurting to make that happen.

Uncomfortable motivation?

Yes.

But a highly effective exercise to reengage your fight for your son's well-being and to revitalize your determination to *never* find yourself in that scenario no parent ever wants to face.

Core Behavioral Motivators

Perspective is key for your son too.

Similar to Austin's experience, when I was younger, my negative view of myself dramatically impacted the relationships in my life. I've worked hard to change the way I perceive myself, and in the process I've improved my ability to successfully relate to others. Changing my self-image had a dramatic impact on my life, which later became the genesis of my decision to become a psychologist.

During my studies, I scoured a treasure trove of scientific articles detailing common barriers to forming connections with others—a skill essential to developing and sustaining healthy relationships.

You'd think bonding with someone you love as much as your child would be a given; our caring for each other naturally deepens throughout those newborn, toddler, preschool, and, for some of us, elementary years.

> *Unfortunately, many families must confront life changes, obstacles, and conflicts that prevent the organic progression of this innate parent-child bond.*

We often don't realize how disconnected our paths have become until problems arise that require partnering and working together to solve. And then, somehow, the harder we try to "fix" those problems, the worse we seem to make things.

For years, I have researched and studied the problems individuals have in developing and sustaining healthy relationships. Conducting research and working with therapy clients, including many parents and their sons, it's become clear to me that there are three *core behavioral motivators* that drive the actions of most human beings regardless of age, history, gender, race, sexual orientation, etc. I'm confident these are also the key motivators that you, as a parent of a troubled teen, must recognize when observing your teen's actions and reactions, in order to better understand him and improve your effectiveness at influencing his choices and behavior.

> *In this section, in remembering your overall "step" objective to stop fighting with your child and to no longer be an opponent, you'll gain insight into the behavioral motivators that follow.*

As you learn about each one of these motivators, try to focus on how they influence *your* son's reactions to his world. Relearn the basics of who and what he is, and *why* he makes the choices he makes. Because he does have a goal for each action and reaction—even if his motivation is subconscious and he has no idea why he's continuing to "mess up."

Constant trouble is the last thing most of us want for our lives. It's likely that your child, at least early on, has been working day in and day out to not make the same mistakes (or worse) over and over again. He'd change things if he could, but he can't. And in order to help him, you must begin to see him and his actions differently.

With this new framework as your guide, your son's life and his actions will no longer seem so foreign or inexplicable. Your confusion will dissipate, allowing you to better communicate your acceptance of and patience for your child.

> *This "bridge of understanding" between his experience and yours will diffuse much of the tension and bewilderment you currently bring to your relating with him.*

You will be better equipped to become the nonanxious presence he needs you to be so you can help him lift himself out of the emotional spiral he's lost himself in.

Once I began walking this path with Austin, my reaction to his behavior became more measured and positive, and less reactive and frustrated. My deeper understanding changed our connection for the better. It was a start, at least—one I'm honored to have been able to help some of my most challenging clients achieve.

Behavioral Motivator One: We All Want to Belong

Human beings are biologically, neurologically, and emotionally wired to live in a community.

Throughout early human history, individuals who lived in groups were more likely to survive than those who lived alone. Isolated individuals were more vulnerable to attack and less likely to independently provide for all their needs. Those who lived in groups had numbers on their side. They could better defend themselves and were able to pool their talents and skills to meet the requirements of life. It is a commonly held theory by social scientists that humans are hardwired to live in communities.

> *Loneliness is a painful trigger for individuals who live in isolation to join a clan, the goal being to ensure their chance of survival.*

The purpose of community and relating has evolved over time.

These days, being with others is rarely necessary for actual survival. But meaningful relationships are now believed to be one of the most important aspects of life. In his book *Triumphs of Experience*, George Vaillant summarizes a seventy-five-year-long Harvard study of the secrets to a fulfilling life. Its findings demonstrate that in modern life, feeling love and a connectedness with others is key to happiness and fulfillment.

Our teens and young adults seek inclusion among groups that define who and how successful they are.

As school and friends become a larger part of their lives, teens attribute a greater value (and more of their self-worth) to gaining the acceptance of their desired peer group. The cost of acquiring this inclusion is adopting group norms, which could include a wide range of beliefs and behaviors that clash with those taught at home, creating internal and external conflict. Sooner or later, the instinct to belong tips the scales, and the importance of belonging to the group takes priority over relating to and identifying with parents.

Austin's story is rich with this need for belonging.

Recall that he was not so much interested in fishing with his grandfather. His *primary* desire was to be included in and admired by a group of school friends. Fishing became a group-acceptance delivery device. He also talked about spending summers with me and his yearning to gain my acceptance. Even his bullying of other children could be explained, to some extent, as motivated by a desire to have his friends view him as an authority figure.

Not all choices rooted in the need for acceptance are destructive. Austin's relationship with his grandfather, for example, grew to become a healthy, valued connection. Austin admired and emulated his grandfather—a well-known, well-respected man in his small town. But also note Austin's choice to imitate his grandfather, adopting his mannerisms in order to gain masculine appeal and broader social acceptance.

If left unchecked, our subconscious need to belong will continue to feed and drive behavior at every available opportunity.

Behavioral Motivator Two:
We All Want to Avoid Rejection

Once a person gains acceptance into a group, the behavioral priority shifts to protecting their inclusion in that group, that is, avoiding rejection.

The evolutionary history of tribes reveals that as long as an individual abided by the rules of the group and did not jeopardize the safety of the clan, he was typically allowed to remain and enjoy the benefits of belonging. However, if a member violated the rules, for example by stealing food from others; engaging in practices contrary to the group's culture; or endangering the health and well-being of the group, such as contracting an infectious disease, group membership would be in jeopardy.

Group excommunication (in addition to threatening one's safety and survival) meant humiliation: the most painful of evolutionary emotions. Humiliation meant reduction of social status. Shunned from a group, your status was reduced from insider to outsider. Humiliation was akin to stigma, the bearer shamed and exposed and marked as unworthy of belonging. Defense strategies were needed to protect the ex-tribe member from experiencing the resulting pain. The defense strategies—a subconscious coping mechanism for protecting oneself against painful emotion—would then cause the outsider additional problems with forming future interpersonal relationships.

Shame, like connectedness, has evolved over time.

Humans first feel this powerful emotion around age two. At other times, it presents as the result of trauma. Most often it invades our lives more slowly, subtlety, and without detection.

> *Shame is the self-belief that one is broken, defective, or dirty at the core in a way that cannot be fixed.*

If left unchecked, shame develops into a trait known as shame-proneness, whereby if a negative life event occurs, our instinct is to internally blame ourselves.

This destructive self-view is extremely common for young men experiencing behavioral problems. Don't be fooled—shame-prone young men often present themselves as unreservedly confident. But even though your troubled son may appear not to want or need your help, he likely feels deeply insecure.

In Austin's story so far, he's shared that his greatest fear, beginning at a very early age, was being exposed for how he viewed himself—worthless.

Reflect on his blaming himself for the fight between his mom and me when he spilled the bleach. When he couldn't start the trimmer, he internalized his failure to meet his ideal of a man into feelings of inadequacy and "being nothing." And yet, notice the inconsistency between this inner view of himself and his outward behavior at the time as a tough and self-sufficient young man. In an attempt to avoid the likelihood of further humiliation, Austin honed in on creating and feeding his tough-guy identity. His shame and fear of being exposed was so great he developed the defense mechanisms we discussed earlier.

Human reaction to shame is individual and unique and depends on our circumstances, history, and personality. Some of us defend against our "worthlessness" being exposed by withdrawing and avoiding. Others attack, putting themselves and others down. Employing these defensive means, humiliation may be successfully avoided. But this destructive behavioral pattern hinders the ability to establish and maintain healthy relationships and consequently results in even more unwanted ostracizing and ridicule being focused on a person already experiencing deep pain and blaming himself for not being able to stop the emotional spiral he's experiencing.

Behavioral Motivator Three: If We Can't Belong and Avoid Rejection, Something Has to Give

Austin has shared that he lived in constant fear of humiliation and rejection.

His actions, however, regardless of how damaging to the vital relationships in his life, were driven by a subconscious urge to feel valued by others.

All humans share this core need to belong.

Balancing between his fear of humiliation and his need to belong required my son to manage his self-presentation: a method by which we perceive and adjust our approach to others based on their impression of us.

Remember his difficulty paying attention in class? He will share more later, but for now it's important to understand that at the time, Austin was dealing with undiagnosed ADHD. He was unable to focus on or retain the material presented through no fault of his own. And yet his circumstance required him to negotiate behaviorally between his need not to be seen as "stupid" and the compulsion to protect his social status of being a "tough guy" among his peer group. This internal conflict resulted in his new persona as a rebellious class clown who did not care about school.

> *Being a class clown wasn't about being stupid; it was a way of*
> *securing a more positive impression of him. So that's the path*
> *Austin chose.*

It's interesting yet disheartening to think of the amount of energy Austin spent preventing humiliation while at the same time making his life and his chances of feeling adequate and wanted exponentially more difficult. Consider, as I have, what he might have accomplished if all that powerful, creative energy had been focused on something more positive than surviving and not being "banished" from his peer group.

Our technology and social-media driven society forces troubled teens to face this loneliness/shame cycle in real time, twenty-four hours a day, seven days a week, 365 days a year. Public shaming and cyber-bullying threats abound.

> *In today's reality, for those with poor self-esteem or a shame-*
> *based life view, the likelihood of humiliation and being ostra-*
> *cized is a nonstop threat. For the shame-prone, self-focus*
> *becomes a social-survival necessity.*

Our children are constantly on their devices, which create a conduit for the escalation of childhood anxieties.

If our troubled teens are not online, they are missing out. If they're not posting, tweeting, streaming, etc., they risk disapproval and overt taunting. They must remain relevant at the risk of incurring public humiliation and ridicule.

Battling this constant threat of isolation and humiliation, our teens and young adults tend to become even more self-focused, basing their behavior and appearance on the feedback of others as if their very survival depended on it. Many of the parents I've worked with are gravely concerned that their sons have become immovably self-centered and narcissistic.

A Note from Austin: What I Really Wanted

For the past nine years, my father and I have talked about writing this book for all the reasons we've already shared.

He's the doctor and parent, and this is a game plan for parents. So a lot of what you'll read is focused on things you need to do and understand about yourself.

> *But for these first few steps in our game plan especially, I think you can't know enough about what it's really like behind the scenes in your son's world and in his mind.*

Talking about theories and goals is great, but nothing hits home like being back in that moment with me, during the worst days of my life and seeing how I treated myself and others.

I still have a note I wrote to myself when I was twenty-one, just before beginning my first semester of college. This was around the time when I began understanding how I'd seen myself as a young child and how the thoughts I'd had about myself were not actual truths. Instead, I began to realize they were lies I'd grown to accept as fact. It took me until my twenties to question more deeply those core beliefs that had for so long impacted my choices and actions.

This was me. Inside me. This was me damaging me, and I couldn't make it stop.

Some of this—a lot of it, maybe—is your teen too.

> *Find a way today to understand why your teen or young adult is feeling the horrible things that are driving him to act in ways he knows will hurt him.*
>
> *Accept how badly he's hurting and why he will do anything to make that pain stop.*

January 2, 2009

The many lies of my life started back when I was a little boy. To be honest, I am not too sure I can remember the exact time they started. It always felt as if they were a part of me.

Examples of the lies:

1. *I am not enough.*
2. *I am just snot-nosed kid. What do I know?*
3. *I am ugly.*
4. *I do not deserve anything good or worthwhile.*
5. *If people know the real me, they won't like me.*
6. *If people know my story, they will reject me.*
7. *If I act vulnerable, people will see it as weakness or as a flaw in my character.*
8. *Why try? I am sure to fail anyway.*
9. *I never can get it right.*
10. *Being me is completely stupid.*
11. *I should have never been born.*
12. *Something is definitely wrong with me.*
13. *I am not nearly as good as others.*

This list goes on and on, but I am sure you get the point.

WHAT'S MOST IMPORTANT?

Understanding what motivates your son is only the beginning.

Knowing that he wants to belong and avoid rejection and is negotiating a precarious path between these core behavioral motivators is critical "head" knowledge. By clearing this first hurdle, you are positioning yourself to tackle deeper challenges.

In this step, your ultimate goal is to reconnect with your teen or young adult.

Keep striving for that. Keep honing your skills at recognizing the emotional triggers at play as you more closely observe your son's struggle, as you find your way to joining him there, and as you perhaps begin to see your own struggles through the same lens of understanding and acceptance.

All human beings grapple with the same core needs. Allow yourself to see your son's struggles at play within yourself and your relationships, and you'll open a gateway to more closely connecting to what he's experiencing.

Understanding Is Mere Information. Relating Is Transformative.

As you come to recognize your son's grappling with the conflicting motivational triggers driving his destructive behavior, and as you grow to better relate to his challenges, a transformation occurs—within you.

You will more clearly recognize the challenges you have faced in your own life, as well as those you're currently battling. The need to belong and feelings of inadequacy are core motivators you share with your son. They are pervasive in adult society as well as simply part of being human.

> *We all share the tendency to filter our reality through the perspective of what others think of us, and then allow that skewed view to control much of our decision-making.*

The only difference between you and your child is your experience in handling these behavioral challenges. With age, we acquire knowledge that helps us navigate our choices and actions with less regard to what others think or our place in an unforgiving social hierarchy that often seems to thrive on exclusion and rejection. Our teens, however, aren't there yet. They need our help. But they'll only accept it if they see *us* accepting that we're as flawed as they are in the same core, fundamental ways.

When you understand the shared challenges you and your son face, you develop deeper empathy for his situation.

You begin to relate to him from a place of "We're in this together." You know the challenges he faces because you've been there yourself, and you don't want him to have to travel that path alone. You know his pain and confusion. You're sorry for how much his fear is costing him because you've made similar missteps and endured similar consequences. You've grown to recognize the cost of destructive, angry words and of the judgment that has widened the disconnection between you—at times causing him to react with rage.

Never again, you say to yourself.

It is time to break this vicious cycle.

Judgment and anger will melt away, replaced with compassion.

A deeper emotional connection will help *you* discover that you and your son have been on the same side all along.

> *You'll find your anger replaced with compassion. Your son will no longer seem so obstinate. Instead, when you observe him, you'll identify with a hurting child who'll do anything to be accepted by you.*

You'll discover a kindred spirit, a wounded soul doing his best to white-knuckle it through circumstances far too complex for someone his age to be facing alone. And yet "alone" has become the only way he feels safe. You've been there. You know *exactly* where he's coming from.

When I began to address my own parenting behavior and the motivations behind it, I finally saw Austin's actions through a different lens. Our interactions gradually transformed in a way I could not have predicted. The relationship barriers and potholes separating us became opportunities for me to reach out and around our differences so I could once again connect with him. We were finally on same playing field, on our way to becoming a team once more.

Dive into understanding the behavioral motivators I've described—both in yourself and in your teen.

Change *your* way of seeing things, and your son will detect this shift in your perspective. As your parenting approach softens and becomes more compassionate, there will be more room for him to accept your presence and for you in turn to respond even more positively.

> **NOTE:** This is only the first step in your overall game plan. You're not looking for a miraculous resolution to your and your son's issues. Instead, you are relearning how to relate to him.

You're striving for a new, more effective approach to engaging your son's emotions.

You're taking that first, vital step toward responding to his situation by extending respect and kindness rather than disappointment and discipline. You're committing to release the judgment, suspicion, and accusations that have heightened his defenses and caused him to retreat from you and the world at large.

You're reaching out to pull him closer by more honestly understanding where he's coming from.

Your Parent Playbook

We've talked a lot about shame-prone individuals seeing themselves as unworthy or defective and the cycle of humiliation and rejection that can result, and how this can be the root of a destructive behavioral pattern that can lead any of us to become a threat to our own well-being.

By now I'm guessing you are looking for something a little more specific in helping your teen or young adult become more successful at processing the shame he's confronting.

First, keep in mind that troubled teens trapped within thinking they'll never be good enough to be accepted, that they'll never stop messing up, often perceive threats where none exist.

For example, Austin frequently assumed people were talking about him, even though he had no evidence. When young men struggle in this way, especially when their home dynamic has become confrontational and the parent-teen connection tenuous, it is not uncommon for a teen or young adult to feel as if he's under continuous scrutiny.

These suspicions, real or imagined, can then cause him to remain on "high alert" at all times, hypervigilant and bracing himself whenever a parent is around, the fear being that whatever he is doing will be observed unfairly, his motivations misunderstood, and that a negative, punitive judgment will swiftly follow.

As you've already learned, the likely result is for your child to protect himself from this perceived threat of being shamed or humiliated by you, his parent, the one person in his life who is supposed to accept and love him unconditionally. Until these defense strategies are diffused, almost any "parenting" you do will likely be viewed as supporting his assumption that you are a threat to his identity and self-worth.

Often, shame-prone individuals develop an altered persona: a mask behind which they hide in an attempt to distract others from seeing them and all their "humiliating" flaws.

Austin's persona became that of a tough-guy, hiding how worthless and inadequate he felt. These masks come with their own challenges as you begin to bridge the relationship gap with your son. You'll likely find your teen unwilling—likely, unable—to be authentic and vulnerable with you, the same as he is with others. Everyone may seem like a threat.

Parents frequently tell me they want to know what is going on with their son but he refuses to talk with them. "If he talks to me at all, he tells me everything is fine, but I know something is going on." Their intuition is often right, but it can seem like an insurmountable challenge to get shame-prone sons to honestly communicate and relate their problems.

In the table that follows, I've included Parent Playbook skills for you to practice as you work to bridge this gap with your own teen or young adult.

> **NOTE:** Remember that there is no endgame to this step and that no two parent-child relationships are the same. You're establishing a solid foundation, merely beginning your journey.
>
> For now, your job is to recognize how these relationship tools work best for you and your teen and to practice using them.
>
> More specifically, you are working to help him lower his defenses, to show him you understand his struggles and want to join him on his field of play.
>
> That stronger place of connection will be the bedrock from which the rest will grow—even though there will still be ups and downs.

Trust that with every attempt at connecting, you'll become more aware and accepting and successful at having an active presence in your son's life as the loving parent he needs and wants you to be.

Skill	Intent	Practice
Stop pushing him to talk with you. Start listening.	Diffuse the defense mechanism causing him to withdraw and avoid you (because he doesn't want his unhappiness discovered). As his fear of exposure becomes a genuine threat, your son may employ even more disturbing defense mechanisms. As he withdraws and begins to avoid you, look for signs that he is beginning to attack himself or self-destruct. This coping mechanism can present in a variety of disturbing ways. I have heard parents quote their sons as saying, "I just can't get it right. I might as well go kill myself." The logic being if the son feels that bad about himself, his parents will be less likely to continue to push or humiliate him. While we must always take these threats seriously, keep in mind that they often can be an attempt by your teen to control his environment by getting you to "back off." **NOTE:** If you believe your son is suicidal, get him professional help immediately. His safety is your highest priority.	**Recognize the negative cues that reveal his altered view of himself.** Whenever possible, reflect back an understanding, accepting, and more "realistic" view of his circumstances. Wait for him to hear you because of your steadfast consistency rather than attempting to force him to talk to you before he's ready. Convey an understanding of just how difficult his reality is. Reflect back a hopeful assurance that there is always potential to improve regardless of his circumstances, without sacrificing your honest understanding of just how difficult his reality is.

Skill	Intent	Practice
Stop fighting. Start relating.	Diffuse your teen's seeing your concern and attempts to help as personal attacks. Studies have shown that shame prevents individuals from repairing relationships after interpersonal disputes. Shame often prevents individuals from believing that a relationship can be repaired after a fight. Don't allow this assumption by your teen about your parent-child relationship to fester.	**Proactively understand, and then share your compassion with your teen.** Take the first steps to repairing your relationship and convincing your teen that no matter how much fighting there has been, you'll always be there— ready, willing, and able to be a part of his life. You'll always be on his team, fighting alongside him no matter what. That is your steadfast message.

Skill	Intent	Practice
Stop shaming. Start empathizing.	Shame has been linked to significant risk-taking behaviors. Research has found shame-proneness to be related to drinking problems, drug use, and hypersexual behavior. Interestingly, those who engage in hypersexual behavior also tend to be more hostile toward themselves. Studies have found being shamed, ridiculed, or humiliated by others to be related to violent and aggressive behavior. Young men can turn to risk taking for temporary relief from their circumstances, even though these behaviors often make it harder to succeed at the very things they most want—relating, belonging, and acceptance. Understanding these behavioral trends and the motivation behind them can be a valuable asset to parents. Your son's disturbing actions are a cause for concern. But always keep in mind that they are motivated by pain. Of course, you want to keep him safe, but it's essential you focus on the root cause of his actions rather than repeatedly beating away at a behavior pattern you likely cannot—at this point—control. Don't add to your shame-prone son's perception that you find him a lost cause.	**Practice a more empathetic approach, modeling healthy interpersonal choices.** People who are shame-prone have difficulty navigating relationships and feeling empathy toward others. They create unwarranted interpersonal conflicts. And they are so focused on their own situations, they tend to overlook or discount the pain of others. With your deeper grasp of the source of his aggressive or emotionally disconnected behavior, make your concern for where your teen's coming from and your acceptance of him, despite his actions, your focus. **Make certain he regularly hears "I'm always here to talk" louder and clearer than whatever version of "Stop doing that! What's wrong with you?" has become a too-frequent mantra in your relationship.**

Stepping into a Position of Strength

I am NOT suggesting you surrender your boundaries, beliefs, or principles, or that you condone your son doing whatever he wants.

Furthermore, I am assuming your son *does* in fact need your help and that you possess the knowledge and experience needed to guide him toward a healthier path if he'll let you. Your role in helping him find his way is vital. In later steps, we'll address a more proactive approach to engaging your teen and influencing his behavior.

It is essential, however, to first grasp that reflecting empathy and compassion for your son is an active role.

You are now relating to your child from a position of strength rather than weakness. Parenting approaches that focus on a more punitive, domineering method of controlling behavior omit this essential step.

> *In order to rebuild credibility and trust—the cornerstones of influence—your son must first feel seen and heard and understood, flaws and mistakes and all, and he must know he's accepted by you regardless.*

To be clear, I am assuming your son's behavior actually *does* need to change. In no way am I suggesting you approve of the destructive decisions he's making. You are, instead, accepting him as he is and learning to rebuild your relationship.

Understanding does not suggest approval.

Your goal is to recognize and understand the motives underlying your teen's choices and actions. Reflecting your understanding of his circumstances and related behavior is a powerful invitation to connect, which your child *will* respond to. Over time, and with your careful, consistent practice, he will make room for you and this new approach in his reality.

YOUR NEXT PLAY

You are one step closer to being an influential, on-the-field leader in your teen's or young adult's journey toward making better, safer, more successful choices for himself.

Your Game Plan in Step One	Reflect understanding, empathy, and compassion toward your teen or young adult.
As a parent, you will continue to	relate to your son from a position of strength rather than weakness. Instead of playing defense all the time, you are now proactively offering acceptance and belonging regardless of his troubling behavior and poor choices.
Your teen is beginning to	be aware of your change in approach, and some of his defensive posture toward you is softening.
Your relationship dynamic is changing to	your becoming an on-the-field team leader rather than your son's opponent.
Your Next Step	You must regain your teen's or young adult's trust so you can reconnect on a deeper level.

STEP TWO: RECONNECT
Repair Your Relationship

Your Game-Plan Challenge	Establish fresh credibility with your teen or young adult.
You, the parent, are	gaining empathy with and compassion for your son, but you have not yet reestablished your credibility as a parent.
Your teen or young adult is	noticing your internal shift—he wants to connect with you—but he does not yet trust you or the initial changes you've made.
Your relationship dynamic is	still disconnected but becoming more authentic.
Your Goal for This Step	Reboot your parenting approach. Let your son know of your commitment to making better parenting choices as you help him make better decisions for his life.

You need to establish fresh credibility with your teen.

In Step One, you practiced gaining empathy with and compassion for your son. Chances are good you're already experiencing a positive impact on your relationship. He *is* noticing the internal shift you've made through your words and behavior. Trust this progress as you move forward to Step Two and strengthen the new, more authentic foundation you've established.

Next, in order to repair your relationship, it's vital you more clearly express to your teen your commitment to a fresh start. As you read our seven-step game plan and realize the importance of making better parenting choices, this next step is essential, wherever you are in your relationship.

Without this component, so much of the negative relating the two of you have experienced will follow you forward into the new connection you're building. As a parent, you are looking for what computer professionals call a "hard boot": a total refresh of your son's perception of your intent and approach to partnering with him and his approach to his world.

The two of you must deal more directly with all that has happened between you up to this point.

> Sadly, sons of all ages have expressed to me a desire to reconnect with their parents. But they grapple with the stumbling block of doubting their parent will ever change enough for that to be possible.

You must do your part to reverse this perception—to establish authentic credibility with the child you've unwittingly pushed away in your desperate struggle to help him.

Often this means addressing how the same parenting style affected you when you were young—how, when you and your worldview were dependent on your mother's or father's choices, the things they said and did made you feel. It can be quite painful for some of us to do this kind of reflection. It means returning to the vulnerable state you were in when you were your son's age or younger.

It can also be difficult to stop making excuses for what you were truly going through in your youth—and for the pain your parents caused *you*. For me, it was most definitely a challenge to recount some of what I've had to recall in order to share the memories I share later in this chapter. However, honesty is key. You must first better understand yourself and why you were reacting the way you were during your son's formative years in order to more clearly process your son's responses to his life and the choices you've made in it.

When you take this next step, you're offering your son the gift of knowing *exactly* how important he is to you and what you want to change about your parenting approach. You are expressing your goals for your relationship and setting clear expectations for how you see your parent-child relationship improving.

I observe many parents digging in their heels, refusing to consider that their parenting approach must change.

Parenting style is a very personal and often "generational" thing—we do as was done to us. Some of us cling to these "learned" patterns as dogmatically as others cling to religion. We're doing what's right for *our* child. So many things have already gone off track. Much is at stake. Surrendering the hard-and-fast "rules" of parenting we've assumed or been told are the "only way," can seem akin to forfeiting the last of our dedication to being the very best parent we can be. Questioning which type of parenting is the "right" is an unsettling place to find yourself in—and exhausting work.

Trust me. I can identify.

But consider the cost of clinging too tightly to what isn't working.

> *Being unbendingly certain about your parenting approach, or too stubbornly sure you know best can come at great cost.*

Steadfastly refusing to change your day-to-day approach to dealing with your son's choices will ultimately stifle the growth you're longing for in your relationship. First and foremost, you must admit where you've been off base and then be committed to not make those same misdirected choices again.

I am not asking you to throw away your principles and beliefs.

What I *am* asking you is to make your relationship with your son your highest priority. This will take the healthy relational foundation you've reestablished to the next level. As a result, you will be surprised at how solvable your current disagreements become.

We are all fallible.

No parent is perfect.

Despite my turnaround as a parent and the intensive psychological work I have done in my own life, to this day I make mistakes that need to be acknowledged, apologized for, and corrected. And I have learned to value and respect my son's need to hear me verbalize this.

> *Your goal for Step Two is to "reboot" your parenting approach and to let your son know of your commitment to making better parenting choices as you help him make better decisions for his life.*

THE PARENT-CHILD DISCONNECTION

In Step One you accomplished a change of heart: you began to better see your son through a lens of empathy and compassion.

Though everyone's situation is different, young men who exhibit bad behavior, make poor decisions, and are on a self-destructive path almost always have a negative self-image and develop defensive strategies to protect themselves from humiliation. Yet at the same time as they're expending considerable energy isolating themselves, they're motivated by an innate desire to belong and be valued.

As you've learned, parents often struggle with the same internal conflict—just as we once struggled to cope with our own mother's and father's parenting styles.

Our experience with relating to *our* parents can often be the source of much of the dysfunction, frustration, and anger we perpetuate in our own child's life—no matter how hard we work to develop more empathy and compassion for his journey.

> *Before we can move forward, we must look back to those things that shaped us in the very beginning.*

Austin and I are taking a step back with our Step Two stories to show you the origin of so much of what we became as Austin grew more troubled. As you'll see later in this chapter, I'll soon be calling on you, as a parent, to reflect on the same type of shared experiences between you and your child so you can better understand the evolution of your own relationship.

Austin: Before Things Got REALLY Bad

Dad got bent out of shape easily.

Once, when Alex was eight and I was around nine, Dad took us to Six Flags over Texas. The heat outside was insufferable—nearly one hundred degrees!—and my brother and I started bickering long before we arrived at the park. By the time we got there, we weren't anywhere close to enjoying what my father had intended to be a fun day.

The lines were way long. The day was a scorcher. My brother and I weren't digging standing outside, waiting endlessly, or dragging ourselves all over the place with thousands of other sweaty people. Six Flags was a place we usually loved, but that day Alex and I were two miserable kids trying to distract ourselves.

So we kept arguing, and Dad finally yelled, "All right, guys!"

When you hear a parent say that, you know they've had enough of your shenanigans.

There was a certain sharpness to Dad's voice I knew not to mess with. Alex and I stopped fighting. Dad finally looked away and walked ahead of us, so things should have been fine.

But you have to understand that my little brother was a master at getting under my skin, and I hated it. Just the fact that he could bug me that way was enough to set me off. He would either make a face, which for some reason really angered me, or he would mumble something and then point at me and laugh. Nothing major. But he knew how to make me mad.

That day he executed one of the dumb little faces he'd mastered, throwing me straight into a furious bucket of pissed off. When Dad wasn't looking, I mouthed off to my little brother, "I'll get you later!" then called him a stupid baby.

We started physically poking at each other, at which point Dad turned around and let us have it with both barrels. "Enough, guys! I try to show you a good time, and this is a bunch of baby crap. I am sick and tired of it!"

He stomped off the path toward the next ride. We followed, dreading another ridiculously long wait. Dad stopped under some shade and turned to glare at us. We were in for it, and we knew it—two young brothers acting the fool, because that's what brothers our age did. Was it that big of a deal? Not really. But here came another of Dad's ridiculous lectures.

Then, in the midst of his threatening to take us home right then and there, a bird landed in the tree directly above us and proceeded to take a massive shit on Dad's head. This was no ordinary bird. I mean, my dad wore his thick, dark hair combed straight back. Imagine the volume of feces it would have taken to soak through that as quickly as it did—with Alex and me wide-eyed and trying not to bust a gut while Dad rubbed his head to determine what had happened.

He stared at the substance on his hand, realization dawning. Alex and I looked at each other and burst into uncontrollable laughter. Dad lost it too and headed for the bathroom to clean himself up. Or at least try to.

Alex and I dodged a bullet that day. But we weren't always that lucky. Back then, Dad could be a real asshole.

He had short fuse, getting mad at things that seemed insignificant. He often blew up at my brother and me as if we were why he was so pissed off a lot of the time instead of whatever was really bugging him.

And then there were the beatings.

One summer early in the late '90s when my brother Alex was eight and I was ten, we had been outside shooting baskets in the driveway, one on one.

I admit I was acting like a little prick that day. I'd dropped the basketball goal to its lowest level, giving me the ability to dunk. Alex was smaller than I was. I had a significant physical advantage over him at the time, and I lived to make the most of it. Each time Alex went for a shot, I blocked it. He held tough until the third consecutive block, followed by my scoring with the stolen ball, which took our game to four to zero.

He was mad. But what made the situation worse was the high pitched "Phew!" I yelled each time I swatted the ball away from him—and, of course, I was laughing at him. His resolve not to let me get to him crumbled when I began "commentating."

"Wow. We don't know much more Alex can take against the best player in the nation, Austin Fall," I crowed. "Wouldn't you agree, Phil?"

My little brother threw the ball at my head, missed, and then started crying. I laughed harder. He chased me down and tackled me to the ground and started hitting the back of my head. I just laid there and laughed even harder. He wasn't hurting me, and I made sure he knew it.

Finally, when I'd had enough, I shoved my crying brother off me, called him a profanity, and then turned around to see my father five feet away, staring me in the face.

"Get your ass up to your room, Austin," he said.

I stomped upstairs and left the door open, but the windows were open and a gust of wind slammed the door shut.

My father yelled after me, "You little jerk!"

He was carrying a worn, thick brown belt when he got to my room. I'd been lying on the bed on my stomach. Before I could get away, Dad was beating my butt over and over. It hurt so bad. I didn't have a chance to tell him I didn't slam the door on purpose.

"You keep your sorry ass in here until I tell you to come out," he yelled when he was done. "You can use the restroom, get a drink of water, and that's it. I'll bring your food up!"

Yeah, I'd been awful taunting my little brother. But had that deserved a blistering ass beating? And even if I had slammed my bedroom door, so what?

That was the point in my life when I started wondering who this guy was. Was my dad my friend or my enemy? Could I trust him? Why should I if he was going to come at me like that and not even give me a chance to explain?

I did my best the rest of that visit to avoid him. I may have been young, but I already saw myself as a man. I couldn't physically take the guy yet, but war could be waged in other ways. I retaliated by shutting him out until it was time for Alex and me to go home.

After my parents divorced and my father moved away, Dad tried his best whenever my brother and I visited.

He really did. Don't ever think because of all the other stuff I'm sharing that my dad didn't make my brother and me feel important most of the time. Summers with him were hands-down the best part of my childhood.

Not many grade-school kids from a small, rural area like ours got the chance to travel as unaccompanied minors from the

Midwest to the East Coast for summer-long vacations. It made Alex and me feel special. We flew to Maryland to see Dad so often that even now the smell of burning jet fuel conjures up the image of my father's loving face.

Traveling without a parent made me feel like an adult, doing adult things, and you know how important that was to me when I was a kid. My brother and I grew closer on those trips too. A three-and-a-half-hour plane ride plus a layover between Kansas City and Baltimore gave Alex and me ample time to form a deeper friendship than I think we would have had otherwise. And I'm grateful for that. We were busy kids with our own agendas. At home we spent most of our free time with our own friends, maybe hanging out together less than other brothers. On the plane, we talked. We were excited and couldn't wait to see Dad again. On those trips, I remembered that I loved my little brother. I'd do anything to protect him.

When our plane touched down at BWI Airport with my dad waiting for us at our arrival gate, I was the big brother making sure Alex and I got to Dad okay. I was important. As important as the president of the United States arriving at a leadership summit on Air Force One. Those are the kind of thoughts that go through a young kid's head. It was so cool!

We'd walk down that Jetway toward the terminal. Our dad would be so excited. He'd pull us in for a group hug. We were his whole world; we were valued. I knew in my heart that his house in Maryland was my home too. That meant more than I'll ever find the words to say.

⌒

Fatigue brought out the worst in my father.

Picture my tired father in heavy traffic with his kids complaining the whole way.

Back then he hated when people drove like morons in congested traffic, and you've already seen his disapproval of Alex's and my complaining and bickering. If I had a dime for every time I heard him curse at another motorist, I'd be set for life. All it took was for the cars in front of us to slow down for a vehicle parked on the shoulder—no accident; just people being nosy.

"Damn it!" he'd say. "What's this horse crap?" Then we'd pull alongside the parked car, and we'd see, say, a guy puking his guts out his open door. Uncaring what the other man's problem was, my dad would yell out of the window something along the lines of "That's what you get for hitting the sauce last night!" as we drove past.

He got louder when he was irritated, swore more. Everyone within earshot knew when he was mad. I always hated how different he became—I mean, drastically different. Like you wouldn't have known he was this cool dad I was once so proud of if the only time you saw him was when he was angry.

His punishments could be swift and confusing.

Once, Alex and I were in Alex's room playing a game that was pretty much about swinging a plastic coat hanger at each other. I don't remember much more except that I swung the hanger too close to Alex, nailing him in the shin. It was an accident, but I knew it hurt like hell. And what was the first thing I thought about? Keeping Alex's whimpering quiet so we wouldn't interrupt Dad, who was working in his study. I offered to let Alex hit me back, which instantly shut him up.

He hit me back with gusto. The plastic cracked against my shin so hard that *I* was the one who yelled out loud. One minute I was nursing my wound and complaining, the next, there Dad was, glaring at us from the doorway, fuming mad.

"What in the hell are you two doing?"

I didn't hear what Alex told him, but whatever it was, Dad freaked out and started screaming. For over an hour, he made both of us stand with our noses in the corner and not move. At all. Because we'd been playing and maybe roughhousing too hard in my little brother's room.

Maybe my brother and I went too far at times, but so did my dad.

That same summer I began losing trust in my dad, something else happened that sticks out to me now.

Dad and my brother and I were outside. It was hot again, and Alex and I were bickering about what game we wanted to play. Dad was already tired and in a foul mood. I don't know why. But when my brother's and my argument once again unraveled into name-calling—the kinds of things brothers say to each other, nothing too bad—but Dad blew up.

"I will tell you what you two are going to do. You're going to sprint up that hill. Not like a bunch of pussies, either! Your asses are going to sprint up that hill and then jog back down, and then turn around and sprint back up again. And you'll keep going until I tell you when to quit!"

It was hot. I hadn't had anything to drink in a long while. And we ran for so long I was about to pass out—seeing little black dots everywhere I looked—before my father noticed.

"All right," he said without admitting he'd pushed us too far. "I hope you two have had fun. Go take a shower and go to bed."

In bed that night, I couldn't sleep for thinking up ways I could hurt my dad back. It wasn't just resentment seething inside me. I wanted to get in his face and scream "Screw you!" If he could have a bad attitude every time he felt like it, so could I.

I avoided my father for something like three weeks that summer. Which is a considerable chunk of time for a noncustodial parent whose kids were about to get on a plane and return to the other side of the country. To my way of thinking, he'd become the enemy for the rest of our visit.

I was young. He had power over me. But did that give him the right to scream and curse at me and run me into the ground?

Words. Hurt. Badly.

One final story about all of this. I swear I'm just about done.

I remember once when I was ten or eleven, sitting with my dad while he rooted for the Utah Jazz during game five of the NBA

Finals. Alex and I were behind the Bulls. We kept good-naturedly taunting Dad, playing with him, and he was giving as good as he got.

The Jazz forced a game six, which irritated me. But I was still in a good mood. It had been a great night, and I liked joking with my dad. He was rubbing it in, of course. I walked up and shoved him into the couch, the way we liked to wrestle around back then. But for some reason that night, he thought I was shoving him because I was mad.

He picked me up and slammed me down on the couch and yelled, "Don't you ever shove me. I'll always be able to kick your ass! Do you understand me, bud? Huh?"

I was sobbing too hard to answer.

He'd hurt me physically. But what he'd said, how he'd made me feel, was the worst of it.

One minute we were playing around and joking, the next I was in pain and afraid and sadder than I'd ever been—and my father had done that to me. He'd threatened me and talked to me like some stranger on the side of the road who'd pissed him off. I'd seen it before, that look in his eyes when he was mad. He appeared foreign to me, like the enemy, *nothing* like my real dad. I hated that side of him. And that night, that guy he became when he lost control had hated me back.

He'd always be my dad, but how was I ever supposed to really trust him after that?

Especially as things in my world kept getting worse and worse.

Kevin: How Could I Have Messed It Up So Badly?

I want to offer a bit more context before we dive into my stories.

When the boys' mom and I divorced and she moved back to Kansas with Austin and Alex, I relinquished my role as full-time father. To make up for lost time, for two short summer months each year, I tried to cram a whole year's worth of fathering into their trips to see me. I held superhuman expectations for myself.

I would build up Austin's waning self-confidence, deepen my relationship with both boys, and influence them to follow in my footsteps, creating successful careers—all while we had nothing but fun the whole time they were with me.

But no matter how hard I tried, I always seemed to fail.

And I mean *fail* spectacularly.

Austin and I really went head-to-head at times.

One summer night, we were in the backyard playing football the way we often did back then.

That summer's trip was nearing an end, and everyone's emotions were starting to show strain. The boys had been bickering the entire evening. No matter what I did to diffuse their arguing, it kept building, with Austin seeming to be the primary instigator.

His bad attitude had gotten worse as the summer wore on, and by then he seemed more interested in causing trouble than having fun. I grew angrier, thinking to myself, "Why can't he just get along?" Finally, I'd reached my limit, and my action—my overreaction—was unforgiveable. I didn't plan it. I knew better. But impulse got the better of me.

I grabbed Austin by the shoulders and began shaking him as hard as I could, yelling at him. I was so angry. So frustrated. I was failing as a father. I'd spent the entire summer busting my ass to create a fun experience for my boys, and nothing had worked. Not for long.

I continued to shake and yell at him with everything I had. In that moment, it was all his fault. It couldn't *all* be my fault. And my son had to know that.

Then I noticed his eyes. They were dead, as if nothing I did would ever again get through to him or hurt him.

"Yeah?" they seemed to be communicating. "I've been here before. Do what you have to do, Dad. Just let me have it. I can take it."

It was as if he were broken. As if *I'd* broken him. The spirit of the Austin I'd known was dead to me, so I couldn't break it anymore.

It hit me like a ton of bricks. I had just done to my son what my mom had always done to me when she was determined to "shake some sense into me."

I instantly regretted my actions, as well as the effect that similar treatment over the years had had on his flagging self-confidence. I knew I'd blown it again and that it was all my doing. Only it would take me years to realize the full extent of the damage I'd done.

A Father's Shame

The 6:00 a.m. Baltimore-Washington International Airport concourse was a blur as we sprinted to the departure gate. This was pre-9/11. Back then the security gate was our family-style starting block. And each time my boys headed back to their mom's at the end of the summer, it was as if we were trying to set a new four-hundred-meter world record. Frankly, I badly needed the distraction. Those annual good-byes killed me.

That morning, we arrived at the gate winded, and then a kind stranger caught up with us.

"I think these are yours." He handed me a neatly folded stack of my seven-year-old's clean underwear that had somehow been dislodged in our race through the terminal. Luckily, those particular tightie-whities had been washed the night before.

Thank all that's holy for the distraction of having to repack the rogue underwear, as well as all the paperwork required for unaccompanied traveling minors. Otherwise there's no way I'd have been able to hold back the tears. Austin and Alex kept looking sideways at me, trying not to be obvious about knowing that a flood of emotion was imminent. It was always the same when we finally said good-bye: their preemptive "I love you, Dad," as if hearing that would heal a father's breaking heart, followed by my husky echo of "I love you too" as we exchanged hugs big enough to last until I got to see them again at Christmas. Watching those two little boys walk down the terminal with a flight attendant was the worst pain I'll know in this life. I'm certain of it.

After the plane pulled back from its gate and flew off, the pain would shift. Guilt gobbled up the grief as a montage of everything I had done wrong all summer passed before my eyes.

Don't get me wrong; I had busted my rear to show my boys a good time. Each of those two-and-a-half-month visits seemed to evaporate overnight, overflowing as they did with nonstop activity: trips to New York, Philadelphia, and Boston, along with more backyard football games than are held in a typical NFL season, but it was never enough to make up for how I'd failed them by not keeping our family together. Next came the sadness, eclipsing the last of the memories of the time we'd just shared. And, finally, there was the shame.

At the beginning of each visit, I always set unrealistic expectations for myself—for the time and money I'd shower on my boys. No expense was too great. But there were deeper undercurrents to my parenting style back then that I only seemed to be able to recognize after the worst of my impulsiveness surfaced.

Simply stated, there were times I was abusive to both Austin and Alex, and those were the memories that haunted me as I drove back to my Maryland home—a home I'd bought for my boys, determined to demonstrate my worthiness as a father and as a man, no matter my busted-up marriage. This same cycle repeated itself each year, and I couldn't seem to get a handle on it.

I loved my sons—until they acted up. Then those deeper emotions that were more about control and domination and showing them who was in charge would take over, and my focus would shift to yelling, spanking, and intimidation.

Back in the Day

Austin was about four when his mom and I separated and later divorced, ultimately living in different parts of the country. If you would have asked me at that time, "What is your top priority, Kevin?" I would have said, no hesitation, "Austin and Alex." But while I did dearly love my sons, I can honestly admit now they weren't my primary focus as I picked up the pieces of my shattered world.

I was hurting from the divorce. I was lonely and missed the boys terribly, but that was more about me than about them. I had no confidence in my ability to create a new life for the three of us. I was obsessed with still being their hero and perfectly doing every *dad* thing I could still do. It was a painfully insecure time.

When my boys (doing what all boys their age do) complained or fought or otherwise made an annoyance out of themselves, my only thought was to get things back under control, to bring them back into silent compliance using the only parenting tools I knew of—the ones that had been used with me. I yelled and used corporeal punishment until everything in the house was once again "peaceful."

Alex was easygoing. Austin was always more sensitive to when things weren't fair. Every time I tried to smooth things over and sweep our growing dysfunction under the rug, he'd have no part of it, always pointing out the least injustice. As his resistance increased, my abusive discipline tactics would ratchet up: yelling, spanking, shoving, whatever. Not only was this approach totally ineffective in modifying my son's headstrong behavior, I was doing long-term harm.

Each summer, Austin arrived seeming less confident in himself than the year before.

It bothered me a lot. Just as both my father and I had a negative self-image, now my son did as well. My goal at the outset of each visit was to bolster Austin's self-esteem. *This year when he leaves* (that's what I'd say at the start of every summer), *he'll know how important he is to me and how proud he has made me, and his belief in himself will soar.*

But as those fun-packed summer months wore on, fatigue would set in, we'd all wear down, and Austin would let his discontent be known. And there I'd be, yelling and physically bullying and punishing him in my need to reassert control.

After each of my meltdowns came the shame and scrambling to repair our relationship. Austin would be always eager to "get over it," which somehow left me more worried. His "It's okay, Dad, I deserved it" terrified me. I was scarring him emotionally. I could see the hurt in his eyes. I knew he was internalizing my punishment as his fault—because I'd been there with my own parents—but I just couldn't stop myself the next time things got out of control. The next time *I* was out of control.

Austin would tell you now how much fun he had all those summers—all the weekend trips and sports and camping out. But when I look back, what I see are the times I yelled and punished him undoing everything else—all that good screwed up because there were times when healthy, loving parenting was the last thing on my mind.

My son had to have sensed he wasn't the most important person in my life. Of course, he was right. I was too wrapped up in my own problems to get myself under control.

And Austin . . .

He paid the most, emotionally, for my selfishness.

Final Straws

What neither Austin nor I have mentioned so far is that I'd gotten married a second time in the midst of the boys traveling to spend their summers with me, which added the confusion of a new, blended family into the mix. Plus, from pretty much the start of it, that new marriage was fragile, heightening my insecurities and anxiety, leaving me even more on edge no matter how glad I was to have my boys come visit.

And after my second marriage irrevocably ended, I was left devastated, knowing I needed to make drastic changes in my life and my relationship with my sons. Since I'd split with their mother, all I seemed to be doing was causing my boys even more confusion and pain.

WHAT HAPPENED?

Kids don't come with instruction manuals. Ask any parent.

We all have regrets for how badly we've botched certain things while we keep trying to figure this gig out. I don't think we'll ever know everything we need to about being a "good" parent. So we do the best we can until we know how to do better, and then we make a change and try again.

Most of us would give anything to go back and change the worst of the mistakes we've made with our kids. But let's dispense right now with the idea that there's a guidebook out there—a one-size-fits-all primer—on how all parents can succeed if they only follow rules A, B, and C. This book certainly isn't about that. We're all different and were raised differently ourselves, and those origins make all the difference.

> *The best we can ever do as parents is accept what we've done wrong, make whatever amends we can, and do everything within our power not to repeat those mistakes going forward.*

From the Psychologist

Like many others I've known and counseled, I arrived at parenthood with a preconditioned parenting style.

I adopted my early approach to raising my children from my memories of how my own parents dealt with me. Many of our "modern" parenting styles and methods are generations old.

Occasionally I will have the privilege of talking with a parent who came from an abusive or neglectful home who has somehow developed an awareness of the surrounding dysfunction they faced as a child and who has made a commitment to be a better parent than their parents were. I've watched these parents with admiration, as I believe they are rare.

Over the years I have had the opportunity to develop closer relationships with my own mother and father.

I've also gotten to know their stories intimately. Both of my parents came from abusive homes.

Mom has shared that her childhood environment was one of frequent screaming, yelling, and physical fighting. She tells how her mother's nickname for her was "shit ass." Mom also talks about being an unwanted child born during the Depression, only eighteen months after the death of an older sister. She recounts her mother often telling her, "I wish you'd never been born."

My mom worked hard to create a family for us that "got along with each other." Still, she used some of the same abusive parenting methods on my brothers and me as had damaged her. Until she died at age eighty, Mom continued to express regret for the way she parented.

My dad has been equally open about his childhood. Also born in the Depression, my grandfather consistently expressed dislike for my dad while showing open favoritism toward my dad's older and younger brothers. My dad told me how his father used to threaten to "slap the dog piss" out of him and berate him in front of others. Often the threats would become actuality, with my grandfather physically slapping my dad across the room.

Unfortunately, my dad learned to view himself with the disgust his father expressed toward him. Remarkably, and with the help of some loving aunts and uncles, Dad developed an approach to life that allowed him to be extremely skillful with relationships. Yet his damaged sense of self was easily detectable and easily triggered.

It's mostly from my mom, I think, that I adopted my abusive parenting style. I loved Austin and Alex dearly (just as my mom loved my brothers and me), but the disciplinary tactics I used on my sons were the same ones employed by two previous generations in my mom's family. My educated guess is that this abusive approach to discipline likely extends generations before my grandparents.

Austin was twelve when my second marriage broke down.

Having to tell my boys about it gutted me. For years, my hasty, ill-advised "new life" with their stepfamily had been negatively affecting Austin and Alex. And now I hadn't been able to make even *that* work. I'd rushed into a new relationship to cope with my own pain and fears that I couldn't make it as a single father.

The dynamics of a new, blended family were not always friendly and welcoming to my two young sons. Imagine that. And as things went from bad to worse in my new "family," so did my control over my reactions to Alex's and Austin's understandable complaints and other behavioral issues when they were around. They were entitled to their own feelings and reactions to an increasingly difficult home dynamic, not to mention that this was where they had to spend their summers as part of their mother's and my divorce settlement. But instead of making room for their experience of what they'd been thrown into, I'd yell and use even more corporeal punishment. Anything to "keep the peace."

It was finally over—after I'd made things even worse, desperately trying to fix things with a new family. I found myself flying to visit my boys, who were back with their mother in Kansas, needing to give them the news in person.

I sat Austin and Alex down in a Taco Bell.

I'd already told them we needed to talk, and I think they knew it was something serious. Pearl Jam's *Last Kiss* was playing on the overhead speakers. I sat beside Austin, with Alex across from us.

"Guys," I told them first, "I haven't been a very good father, and I want to tell you both that I am very, very sorry." Thank God they were too shocked to respond, because I had to finish the rest of what I'd been rehearsing for days. "There have been so many times I have screwed up and failed you as a father. I have yelled too much, I haven't been close enough, I have gotten way too angry at you guys when I shouldn't have, and I want to sincerely ask you boys for your forgiveness. I am truly sorry, and I am going to change things moving forward."

Silence followed. I could tell from their expressions that they didn't understand. I'd never come right out and talked to them about my feelings before. But something was driving me that day. Somehow I knew things would never be right between us if I didn't.

"You guys don't have to forgive me right this second," I continued. "But I want you to think about it. I regret the way I have handled things with you two, and I am sorry."

"But you're a good father," Austin blurted out, "and we love you."

I was so grateful to hear that—and so sorry my boys had no idea how badly I'd been handling them. "I love you too. And we're going to have a better relationship. I promise you guys I am going to be a better dad."

I'd always longed to be my boys' hero. And I knew they still wanted to see me that way. I was confusing and scaring them, and I regretted that. I regretted everything. But I had to finish what I'd flown to Kansas City to say.

"There's something else," I said. I was shaking. My stomach was churning. No way was anyone eating their tacos tonight, I realized. "I am getting a divorce. We made the decision after we dropped you guys off at the airport in August."

I went on and on about the details. I tried to be calm and genuine and to explain how broken I knew things between us had become. I was going to do whatever I had to do to fix that, I assured them, while in my own mind I was praying it wasn't too late.

I loved my sons no matter what I'd done to them, or failed to do for them.

All that was important in that moment was letting them know how sorry I was and how committed I would be from then on to making things right.

Austin Checks In

I was looking at a totally different dad than I'd ever known.

And I wasn't certain I liked the change—or that I knew what he wanted me or my little brother to say about his new divorce. I kept telling Dad that Alex and I loved him, and he kept saying the same thing back to us. But he was so upset. So calm but freaked out at the same time. He was so sure he'd been a bad dad.

I'd been telling myself for years that everything was okay in spite of how mad I sometimes got at him and in spite of whatever negative things happened when we visited for the summer. What was I supposed to think now?

It hurt, hearing my dad say he'd screwed up. And now, the stepfamily we'd been told had to be a part of our lives was going away too? WTF? For years he'd been forcing Alex and me to put up with this blended family BS. When I was around his "new" family, it was as if I were an outsider playacting like I belonged. And now that life was over too?

By then I was already screwing up so much of my life on my own, I didn't need extra help feeling as if I were going nowhere fast.

Dad didn't know yet that trouble was becoming a bigger part of my life. With all his beatings and tongue-lashings and how badly all my "bad" times with him already hurt, no way was I volunteering how messed up the rest of my world was. Home, school, and, hell, I'd even had a couple of run-ins with the law. My life was for shit. I was learning to accept that maybe it always would be. I didn't need my dad's grief making it worse.

Only now he was dumping a new truckload of his own problems on top of mine.

He kept going on and on about the details of his new divorce and how he was going to make everything up to me and my brother.

Sure, my dad loved me.

And I believed him when he said he wanted to be a better dad. But would he really change?

For years each summer, I'd start my visits with him with childlike optimism. But, frankly, by this point I didn't trust Dad anymore. Could he really be a better parent? We'd just have to wait see.

WHAT TO DO?

Kevin: Your Story with Your Son Will Be Different Than Mine.

You may not have made nearly as many parenting mistakes as I did, but allow me to continue deconstructing the decisions I made at this huge turning point in our lives. Stick with me as I explain how and why I arrived at the moment when I finally knew there was something positive I could do to improve my relationship with Austin and Alex.

I couldn't keep messing up this way.

Austin was almost a teenager, and Alex wasn't far behind. As I relayed in Step One, my oldest son was by then having an increasingly difficult time in school and dealing with his peer group. And there I was, yet again making life harder for him to navigate. They needed a better dad. A new dad. We all needed a fresh start.

Before the trip to Kansas City I described above, I did a lot of praying and meditating. I kept searching for answers, until finally an internal voice spoke to me in a way I had never before experienced. "Move to Kansas City" it prompted—close to where my boys lived with their mother. That was how I'd prove to them and myself that my commitment to being a more active, present, supportive part of their lives was the real deal.

For the first time in years, I would really, truly put my sons first.

We'd have our clean slate. I would change the way I parented. And I would make certain Austin and Alex knew that this—doing better for them—was my goal.

But I realized none of that would be possible without two things happening.

First, my boys needed to hear me say something that would have meant the world to me at their ages, had my parents found a way to express it to me. I had to apologize for the mess I'd made of everything: my abusive parenting and dragging my boys through my second failed marriage. And I had to find a way to achieve both of these things and to express my heartfelt regret without overburdening my boys with the shame I felt.

Second, I needed to verbally commit to them my intention to change the way I parented.

Going forward, they needed to know that the abuse would stop.

I recommend to all parents I work with that they make the same verbal commitment to their sons that I did to Austin and Alex:

- There would be no more yelling, shaking, shaming, or spanking.
- From that point forward, I would talk to them like young men, since that's what they were.
- As adults, they got to make their own decisions. I would offer advice and guidance, but my days of being a controlling, domineering parent were over.

Again, your list of changes will be unique to your parent-child relationship. Your parenting style will need to be overhauled in its own way. But an apology for your mistakes is imperative, as is sincerity when you talk from your heart about what, specifically, you plan to change.

Did I keep my word, move to be closer to my boys, and change my abusive ways? Absolutely. Did it make all the difference in the world and fix everyone's problems, especially Austin's? Sadly, no. Life isn't nearly that neat and tidy when we commit to solving problems that have been allowed to rock on for as long as I ignored my issues with my kids.

> You will likely still have a long road ahead in repairing your relationship with your troubled son and helping him with his issues. But from now on you will be working from a stronger foundation.

Along with this commitment to making things right and changing your parenting style, time and consistency and a promise to never, ever give up fighting for your child are going to be key. The changes I made with Austin and Alex couldn't in an instant undo all the damage that had been done. I had to deal with knowing the pain I'd caused. But I also had to keep fighting for my relationship with them.

I continued to be angry at myself for abusing Austin and Alex. Worse yet, they continued to suffer the consequences of having lived through that kind of parenting as long as they had. I changed my behavior going forward, but I couldn't change the past.

For several more years I would carry the guilt and shame of how deeply Austin had internalized the rage I'd spewed at him.

A Note from Austin: Were Things Really That Bad?

Yeah, they were.

I talked a little in Step One about how hard that time in my life was, and in Step Three's stories, I'll hit rock bottom. There was a lot more going on with me than I shared earlier in this chapter when my dad's second marriage crapped out and he moved to Kansas City.

My life hadn't gone well for a while, not since my parents' divorce. Their split had been my fault somehow—at least that's how it seemed to me. And then when I visited my dad, he was all over Alex and me, trying to force us to believe that our new crappy family situation was for the best, while it *really* wasn't, which made it feel as if my problems were once again all about me.

I couldn't be okay with any of it; in fact, it felt as if things were getting worse by the day.

So I was a worthless piece of shit, making trouble where there wasn't any and not doing a better job of being okay with how things were going to be. Remember that by then, things were going from bad to worse for me back home. I couldn't get anything good going for myself. No matter how hard I tried, I felt awkward everywhere I went.

I didn't like school. It didn't like *me*. I didn't fit in with the other kids there (except for the ones getting into trouble all the time, like me). I was well on my way to building my reputation for doing destructive things. That kind of behavior became my outlet. I fought. I bullied. I made people at school laugh.

That's who I was becoming, and the rest of me was just fading away, as if I'd never be anything else again.

Sure, my dad was apologizing, and I wanted to believe him.

I wanted a second chance with him. But even if he could change as much as he said he wanted to, how was that going to help me? He didn't have a clue how bad things back in Kansas had gotten.

That night at Taco Bell, I knew he was serious about what he was saying to us, and I knew he was doing the best he could to make things right. But there was too much to fix that couldn't be fixed. And at the time, I didn't see how many of my problems had to do with my dad and the way we were relating to each other. Kids just don't think that way. At least not the ones like me.

My dad did change.

He started communicating more. Even before he moved to Kansas City, he started calling a couple of times a week instead of a few times a month. And I changed, at least where he and I were concerned. He set the example, and I noticed and started reaching out myself.

And then he took a new job in Kansas City. He called to say he wanted to live close enough to watch Alex and me play sports. He wanted to be a bigger part of our lives. He was doing everything he said he would. He still wanted us to visit and stay with him in his new place, which was a few hours from my mom's. He was changing everything about his life so he could keep his word to Alex and me.

Still, things weren't perfect after that.

Far from it. And Dad and I would keep making mistakes and missteps, solo and together. But my dad and I *had* grown closer.

And soon, sooner than either of us could have known, that closeness would save my life.

WHAT'S MOST IMPORTANT?

This step is NOT about making everything in your son's life better.

It's about making sure he knows how important he is to you and how hard you'll fight to improve the closeness between you. Remember, your ultimate goal with your teen is connection.

> *In Step Two, you're making a deliberate effort to reestablish your credibility as a parent and to regain your teen's or young adult's trust.*

Once you start down this new path with your son, consistency is your mantra—despite the trials and turmoil and, yes, anger and frustration ahead. Keep practicing your new skills, keep your Step-One and Step-Two goals in mind, and keep up your awareness and acknowledge both your *and* your son's progress.

Your Parent Playbook

By owning up to my mistakes and moving to the Midwest from the East Coast, I started my sons and myself down a new path of healing and closeness.

As you work to create a fresh start with your son, consider the following tools I utilized in my fight for a better relationship with Austin and Alex:

Tool	Purpose	Goal
Own your mistakes.	Let your teen or young adult know how much it hurts you that you've hurt him.	**Shine a light on issues you know your son is aware of** but which he's likely blaming himself for or thinking you don't see as problems. This frees both of you from the pressure of pretending everything is all right or trying to make everything seem perfect.
Apologize.	Apologizing is not a sign of weakness. True strength lies in one's ability to be comfortable as an imperfect, vulnerable human being. An apology can be one of the most transforming relational exchanges a parent can have with a child.	**Apologizing to your son moves you from a position of power in his life to that of a human being.** You become someone who wants to "relate," more than being in control or being right or being someone who is unquestionably obeyed.
Take the first step.	Be the one to break the stalemate first. Extend an olive branch, even if he doesn't expect one. *Especially* if he doesn't expect one. Prepare yourself for surprise and perhaps suspicion. But get there first.	**Leave no doubt in his mind that this new path to put your child first is your choice, your goal, your mission.**

Tool	Purpose	Goal
Be authentic.	Our kids are perceptive. They'll spot a superficial, empty apology from a mile away. This step is about leaving no doubt of your empathy and compassion toward your son. Our boys never forget, and many sons grow old longing for a sincere apology they believe they will never receive.	**Employ the empathy and compassion you developed in Step One.** The sincerity of your apology will deepen your connection with your son.
Be specific.	Generality (a blanket apology) breeds misunderstanding and distrust. Be specific about the mistakes you've made, *and* the changes and goals you're refocusing on. I apologized to my sons for yelling, shaking, spanking, pushing, and shaming them. I told them how much I regretted dragging them through a bad marriage and for not seeking their input before getting involved in the first place.	**Focusing on specific behaviors and actions clarifies both your regret and your intent to change.** It resets everyone's expectations and gives your son clear milestones to observe as you work your ass off to do better for him.

Tool	Purpose	Goal
Tell your son how important he is to you.	Your son may think he knows you want to be close to him, or he may have no idea. Regardless, make it clear beyond doubt that his well-being and happiness are more important to you than any of the other priorities you've put before him up to this point.	**It's a bold gesture, and you're really putting yourself out there, but the payoff can be priceless.** Austin now talks about how the selflessness of my apology and promise to do better improved our relationship, letting him know for certain how much I loved him. That alone, if nothing else comes from it, is worth whatever it takes for your son to have the same experience.
No strings attached.	Reset your relationship by making this about your heart and wanting to share it unconditionally with your son no matter what he's done or will ever do. No expectations. No need for him to return the gesture or to say he loves you. Accept his response, whatever it is, but reassert that this is your choice, your change, and your needing nothing from him but a second chance to love him the way you always should have, and to make him your top priority.	**Eliminate any doubt in his mind that what's happened between you two is *your* responsibility.** You're the parent; make certain he understands that the buck stops with you when it comes to never giving up on making things better between you.
Be consistent.	You'll continue to butt heads with your son. He may not trust your intent right away. But be where you say you're going to be, doing what you've promised you'll do, over and over, until he believes you'll never stop.	**When your son realizes your commitment can endure whatever next happens (to him or between the two of you), you've reached a major milestone.** You are on your way to more positively influencing his life.

Tool	Purpose	Goal
Be patient.	Your son must find his own motivation to extricate himself from his problems. And until he does, his actions likely will not improve regardless of what you do. Wait him out. If he rebels, be there when he finds his way back. If he acts out, control *your* reaction and mirror a more constructive, accepting way of communicating.	**Rather than reacting in anger or frustration or disappoint-ment, your pride and love for your son will lead the way.** Your son will pick up on your cues and begin to respond to you in kind, likely sooner than later.

Most children, regardless of age, are quick to forgive a parent if the apology is offered sincerely and followed by a patient, consistent approach to reestablishing a healthy parent-child relationship.

But remember, you are resetting your relationship with your son. This is another new *beginning*, not an endgame.

> *By no means will your work on achieving your Step-Two goals end anytime soon.*

While you ultimately want more influence over the behavioral changes your son must make, your objective with your heartfelt apology and commitment to doing better is to reestablish trust and connection and to break your relational stalemate.

If you are anything like me and carry a lot of guilt as a parent, the thought of an apology can tug on deeply rooted emotions.

Including a heavy dose of guilt.

Be committed to dealing with your own "stuff" before, during, and after your apology and parenting recommitment. Work hard not to "dump" your emotional baggage into your son's already difficult reality. That kind of added burden is detrimental to your son and your cause.

I recommend thinking through your apology and everything else you intend to say and then practicing several times before sitting down with your child. If you find you become emotional when you practice, chances are the emotion will be even stronger when you look your son in the eye. If your approach doesn't become less emotional as you practice, consider working with a therapist before you approach your son.

If one of your commitments is to end abusive disciplinary tactics . . .

Keep in mind that apologizing and making needed changes in how you parent does *not* mean you lose your parental power.

This step isn't about giving your child permission to do whatever he wants, and you should assert that as part of your conversation. I did while at the same time promising to stop using physical force in any way as I helped Austin make better decisions for his life. I was committing to no longer make my relating to my son about punitive action. Instead, I would make it about being there for him, sharing whatever I could to help him, and relating to what he was going through as he worked through his issues.

What would that look like to you?

Sometimes it helps for you acknowledge what the relationship has been like from your perspective.

When in doubt, lean into telling your son more, not less, about how you see the mistakes you've made. For instance, I could have stated to my son (and later wished I had) that I saw my yelling and physical abuse as making me seem untrustworthy and unpredictable to my kids. I talked about how I wanted to have better conversations with them so they'd come to me with their problems without fearing that I would get mad or yell. But for that to happen, I knew I had to re-earn their trust.

> *Our sons need to unlearn their bad experiences with us so they can learn to behave differently toward us.*

Give your son a jump start in that direction by being as frank and detailed up front about how you see things have gone off track. Open that dialogue and that direction of thinking for your son, leaving room for newer, better relating memories to make their home.

Who's in control now?

You have one final expectation to set—and it's quite possibly the most important one of all.

If you are no longer going to physically or emotionally assert your control over your son's life choices, then who is taking over?

It's your teen's turn to make his own decisions. Let him know you will always be there to support him and help him but that you expect him to know right from wrong and to act accordingly. You're trusting him to be responsible and to ask for help when he needs it and to be willing to face the consequences of his decisions when they come. That last point is essential to convey.

For both good and bad consequences, you won't be standing in the way of his dealing with the results of his actions. You'll cheer him on and help him deal with whatever comes, but those consequences will come. So he should be doing what he thinks is best, because he'll have no one to pin a bad result on besides the man in the mirror.

It is also key to assure him (and yourself) that you can deal with those bad results without conveying anger or frustration or disappointment. I told my boys that, come what may, I was treating them like men, with respect and understanding, going forward.

Steroids for Relationships

Empathy and compassion are steroids for relationships.

With them and the other relating skills you learned in Step One, you are now ready to create a fresh start with your troubled son. It's time to overcome the obstacles placing you at odds with your child. All Step Two requires of you is a willingness to change and to express to your son your mistakes, regret, and new relationship goals.

An effective apology extends empathy and compassion.

You're asking for reconciliation so that you can work together going forward. By acknowledging our mistakes, we actualize our determination not to repeat them. Making and sharing detailed plans and goals for improving your parent-child relationship (e.g., rebuilding trust, establishing authentic communication, etc.) invites everyone involved to participate in the change that must happen. You are reestablishing connection, clearer boundaries, and appropriate responsibility for behaviors and their consequences—for you, the parent, as well as for your son.

While my sons may have been a lot younger than yours are now when I took this step, I have used Steps One and Two of our seven-step game plan with young men in various environments, and across the board I have found the results to be extremely productive and beneficial.

When we "reboot" our relationship and develop authentic communication, our interactions change from emotion-filled to more matter-of-fact.

We will discuss this dynamic more in our next step.

Remember that therapy may have to be part of your son's recovery.

But as parents, we have an opportunity to fully participate in the outside-of-therapy aspects of what our child is experiencing. After discussing the seven-step game plan in this book with your son's therapist, keep working in every way he thinks is beneficial toward establishing a healthier relationship with your son.

YOUR NEXT PLAY

You are one step closer to being an influential, on-the-field leader in your teen's or young adult's journey toward making better, safer, more successful choices for himself.

Your Game Plan in Step Two	Address poor parenting choices honestly, apologize for your mistakes, communicate clear plans for parenting differently, and follow through consistently, applying more influential, successful parenting strategies.
As a parent, you will continue to	revamp your parenting style, rebuilding an authentic, rock-solid connection with your teen or young adult.
Your teen is beginning to	gradually trust you and behave differently toward you despite the poor parenting choices you've made in the past.
Your relationship dynamic is changing to	a solid foundation of trust, empathy, and acceptance upon which the rest of your relational work can be built.
Your Next Step	**Having positioned yourself to more authentically and compassionately influence your teen or young adult, you are better prepared for the moment when he hits rock bottom and turns to you for help and support.**

STEP THREE: STEP IN

Be There When Your Son
Hits Rock Bottom

Your Game-Plan Challenge	Waiting for your son to make better life choices—allowing him to experience the grave consequences of his behavior—is difficult. Yet your number-one priority remains consistently reflecting your empathy and acceptance of him as a person.
You, the parent, are	no longer powerless. You are relating from a place of more authentic influence, and you are taking the steps to reconcile your relationship with your teen or young adult.
Your teen or young adult is	still behaving destructively and/or making poor life choices. Potentially damaging consequences could result, yet you know "forcing" him to stop is an ineffective parenting approach.
Your relationship dynamic is	still developing. You are waiting for your chance to join his field of play, knowing he must first turn to you and ask for help.
Your Goal for This Step	When your teen's or young adult's issues reach a crisis point and he turns to you for help, work together to help him act on his newfound commitment to change.

Watching a child spin out of control is a helpless place for any parent to be.

At this point, panic is a near-constant state. Your son *is* going to crash; you know that. It's only a matter of when and whether or not he'll recover. The consequences of his actions may negatively impact the rest of his life. "Coming back," isn't always a given. We've all heard the horror stories.

Our troubled teens aren't living anything close to their best lives.

Due to the issues they confront every day, these young people are at a greater-than-average risk for alcohol abuse, overdose, and, tragically, suicide.

Parents want so badly to intervene. But how? When?

Our teen's poor choices are a runaway train picking up steam, roaring toward a certain fate if our sons don't begin to make better decisions. And all we as parents can do is anticipate the inevitable catastrophe that lurks around the next bend. Or the next. We have grown to brace ourselves, anticipating the worst, and with good reason.

Lying awake at night, we ask ourselves, "Why can't he see what's going on? Why won't he just stop before it's too late?"

Yes, you're angry. You're entitled to be.

Your child can't be that blind. He has to know he's wrecking his life and possibly his future. Yet he refuses to ask for help. He doesn't want your involvement when you offer. And before long there will be no turning back.

Watching is your assigned role at this point, until he invites you into his private world to help with the self-destructive problem-solving that's keeping him from making better choices. So far in your Parent Playbook, you have learned to compassionately watch and empathize and to authentically, positively communicate—*while* he makes more trouble for himself. He's in pain. He's trying to dig himself out. But his attempts to reason himself out of the emotional black hole he's dug for himself are too dysfunctional to gain traction. And so he keeps sinking.

> *Thanks to your Step-One and Step-Two game plans, you are no longer powerless. You've taken the necessary steps to reconcile your relationship with your son.*

You are still waiting for your chance to positively influence your child's choices and behavior.
But you are no longer locked into a battle of wills with your son. Rather than an opponent, you and your son are now more often on the "same side" in the complex battle he's waging. With your newfound level of empathy and compassion, you have apologized for past parenting mistakes and expressed your commitment to partnering with your teen in a healthier way going forward.

You've gained a tremendous advantage that will be paramount in the work ahead.
You have proactively realigned your interests with those of your son. You are communicating more clearly and honestly. Your number-one objective, rather than controlling your son's behavior, is now to heal and grow your relationship.

> *You have positioned yourself to more authentically and compassionately influence your son, preparing for that inevitable moment when he does turn to you and ask for your help and support.*

When that happens is wholly dependent on your son seeing change as a necessary goal. Until he arrives (*on his own*) at this behavioral turning point, he will continue down the same track he's currently on.

A former boss of mine aptly, albeit crudely, summarized "motivation to change" in the following way, speaking in terms of what motivates someone to seek alternative employment:

> *In one hand, you carry a bucket of money. Its contents consist of your salary, bonus, benefits, etc. In the other you carry a bucket of shit. It holds all the crap related to your work, such as long hours, conflict, travel, etc.*
>
> *As long as the money bucket weighs as much as the shit bucket, you'll likely remain in your current position. Once the shit bucket outweighs the money bucket, it is time for a change.*

Your son holds these same two buckets.

One bucket contains the payoff for his behavior. These are the core motivators (from Step One) driving him to act as he does: belonging to a group, escaping pain, avoiding humiliation, etc.

Make no mistake, there is a perceived "payoff" driving your son to continue to make poor choices. Despite what society or authority figures in his school or other groups may reflect back to him and you, troubled teens aren't inherently "bad" kids, randomly misbehaving and causing trouble because they don't care about the consequences. In fact, a large percentage of these young men and women tend to be highly creative, sensitive, intelligent human beings.

Your child's other bucket holds the negative consequences he faces as a result of his "troubled" behavior: alienation from the very peer groups to which he yearns to belong; school suspension and/or loss of college prospects; legal problems; potential health problems; family problems; the emotional toll of knowing he's screwing up opportunities to "get it right" while he can't seem to stop himself. Keep in mind that your child's perception is distorted. He feels a great deal of shame due to his failures. He is willing to carry a heavier bucket of consequences, pretending that he has everything under control for longer than you might, rather than admit he needs help.

Like the employee weighing the pros and cons of seeking a new position, your teen maintains a metaphorical balance sheet, estimating the cost or benefit of each bucket he's carrying. And he is making behavioral decisions accordingly.

Unfortunately, due to his limited life perspective and experience, your teen's take on how much loss is acceptable in his "negative consequences" bucket is distorted. Additionally, how much he's willing to sacrifice (or endure) to achieve the perceived payoff he's after can also, in his mind, be a distorted relationship.

> It is important to note that we're discussing his "perception" of attaining the targets in his "gain" bucket (i.e., acceptance and belonging).

There's also the matter of whether the action he's taking is actually *diminishing* the achievement of his goals—a reality many troubled teens have difficulty acknowledging and correcting regardless of how significantly they're struggling.

> In Step Three, your teen reaches a crisis point, struggling with the negative consequences of his behavior. When he turns to you for help, it is your chance to work together to improve his problem-solving skills.

He must reassess not only which "gains" are actually attainable and valuable, he must reexamine which negative consequences he's actually willing to endure in order to achieve his goals.

It's once again helpful to think of this in terms of a cost-benefit analysis of his behavior:

- Which goals/benefits are actually attainable (realistic outcomes that are within his ability to achieve and control)?
- How much trouble/cost is he inviting into his present and future as a likely result of pursuing each goal?
- What is his *actual* status in achieving each goal?
- Will attaining a goal actually bring him happiness?

Regardless of what your son may say or even realize, on some level he understands these elements.

When he's ready to turn to you for help (because of your new-found "relational" leadership approach and improved commitment to successful communication), you will finally have an active role on the playing field of his life. You will find yourself fully in the game in a position to help him better reason through his available choices, set attainable goals, grow his problem-solving skills, and reposition himself toward the success he craves.

You will be in a powerful position to influence his decision to build a better life for himself.

THE PARENT-CHILD DISCONNECTION

I'd worked hard to have a better understanding of Austin's weaknesses and vulnerabilities.

I'd done the work to recognize and overcome my own defenses. More self-aware, I'd begun to encourage my son to work through his behavior and relationship issues. I'd also moved closer to my boys, taking a job in the same state as their home with their mother—though I was living in Kansas City, over three hours away from their rural hometown.

Austin knew without a doubt that I loved him unconditionally. I'd stuck to my commitment to allow him to make his own choices—and face the consequences of his behavior. And yet, I could sense things racing toward another a crisis if Austin didn't find some way, on his own, to embrace the necessity of change.

He wanted to belong, to be loved, and to feel valued. His greatest desires were to be successful, admired, and respected. I truly believed my son could achieve all of that and more; he simply didn't yet know which "plays" to call to get him there. He was still settling for a cheap, hollow version of the happiness he deserved.

Unfortunately, it would take Austin facing even more harsh realities before he arrived at his "rock-bottom" decision. As a parent, it was excruciating to watch. But deep down, I trusted my son. I believed in his capacity to commit to the changes he had to make. I knew that experiencing the difficult consequences of his continued bad choices was an essential component of Austin finally embarking on the healing path he longed for.

Austin: Let's Get Crazy

At some point, no matter how hard my father tried to reach me, I pulled away.

Having him move closer was great. He wanted to be there for my brother and me as often as his new job allowed—also great. He could be more involved in our lives, and now we could spend every weekend together.

Dad and I loved each other, but by the time I was thirteen, the rest of my life had begun to consume everything. I was failing at school—literally. There were numerous suspensions, plus the occasional brushes with the law that were becoming more frequent. And with each screwup, it became harder for me to look my dad in the eye.

The weekends with him I'd once looked forward to became just plain awkward. It was easier to find reasons to be "too busy" to go. Even sharing a meal, when I forced myself to see him, became excruciating. When Dad was around, I'd press pause on my noxious routine. But as soon as I could escape, things would go right back to "normal." The older I got, the harder it became to be around my dad.

I was a troublemaker, and everyone in my small hometown knew it.

I continued to spend time with people who, like me, were going nowhere. My friends and I, a toxic group, related to each other by making fun of each other and everyone else. I began drinking at age thirteen. Consuming alcohol made me feel like a man. Its effects made me feel invincible. The tough-guy reputation I was forging became my identity and my future. The people in my small town had already labeled me, using my prior conduct as a frame of reference. Who could blame them?

I worked hard at building my reputation. My circle of friends began to shrink as anyone with a positive, healthy outlook on life distanced themselves from me.

Dad talked to me a lot.

Even though his advice and encouragement had no effect on my behavior, I still listened to him. His vision for me was positive. He artfully described my potential future in a way that was inspiring and made me want to change.

As I watched his success and listened to his suggestions, I saw and heard things I wanted. I wanted to be well liked, to be important, to be successful, but I didn't know how to get off the out-of-control train I was riding. I wanted to change, but I didn't know how. It was all too big for me.

My inability to change confirmed what I'd known all my life: I was powerless and worthless. And in the end, if I gave up my tough-guy identity, what would be left of me?

I was quickly becoming overwhelmed.

Every morning, I woke up thinking about someone or something that had pissed me off.

Before I rolled out of bed, I was furious, and the tone for the day was set. I stopped smiling, though I laughed a lot. Mostly *at* someone, making fun of them because I'd exposed a defect I could exploit. Then, for a while, the focus was off me and my own insecurities and the sorry-ass state of my life.

I honed in on my victims. I brought them down to my level with practiced ease. Disparaging others was a low-grade fuel. But it and my anger were the only "hits" available to an outlier like me (the way I saw myself back then), so they propelled me through life.

I played football during my freshmen year of high school.

I requested my dad's jersey number from back when he played. I wanted to follow in his footsteps. But the thing I remember loving most about football was using it for unleashing my rage. Inflicting as much pain as humanly possible on my opponents— that was my goal.

I liked practice so much more than the games. In practice, I could hit my classmates; *so* much more satisfying than going after strangers. I reinforced my tough-guy image by dominating my peers. The harder I hit, the more the coaches liked me. It was a bully's dream come true.

During team scrimmage, because our center kept missing his blocks, they placed me at nose tackle to teach him a lesson, as if I were some enforcer or something. The guy was bawling his eyes out after the first three plays. The more he cried, the harder I hit him. Punishing someone else made me feel more masculine, which was a nonexistent state in my "real" life.

School didn't exist for me to learn; it was where I had fun, played football, and made people laugh.

My grades sucked. I managed a C average so I was eligible to play sports. But I was a walking wall of fuming frustration. Surrendering—because what was the point, anyway?—I quit turning in my homework and projects. My grades plummeted.

Three days before the final game of my freshman year, one of my coaches pulled me aside in the hallway. If I couldn't get my grades up before the end of the week, I would be ineligible for the last game of the season. I was gutted—not that I let him know. I'd been exposed as a dumb slacker by someone I was dying to have respect me. And if I was yanked from the team for grades, my teammates' parents would find out I was dumber than a sack of rocks.

I was finally motivated to get to each class. I asked to talk with each teacher, telling them I'd do anything to pull up my grades. I volunteered to do extra work—something I'd never have offered otherwise. But all year, I hadn't put any effort into any of my classes. I didn't deserve their consideration. The most common response I received was, "Sorry, it's too late now."

It was my fault. I deserved it. But that didn't make it any easier to stomach. Rather than cry like a baby, I went into the locker room before practice and, as usual, made a joke out of it.

"Well, boys, they said I am too stupid to play. The ole grades aren't good enough; I'm just too stupid!" I'd have said anything that day to cover how ashamed I felt about losing my spot on the team.

My freshman year was the last time I played. So my grades improved because I had more time to study and get my work done, right? Hardly. Sophomore year, losing total confidence in my academic ability, I surrendered once again to the inevitable—and dismantled the last of my already low self-esteem about my academic ability.

I longed for someone to talk to. Anyone who could understand. And there my dad was, trying to get through and be there for me. Just like I'm sure you're there for your teen or young adult, trying to get him to let you in.

But that's not how it works with troubled kids. They'll go down swinging, setting fire to everything they care about in their lives, before they'll admit how totally in over their heads they are.

I opened up to my closest friend.

He spun my plea for help into a joke—with me as the punch line, of course. It felt like a slap in the face.

With no one to talk to about my problems, I spent more and more time isolated in my room at home and chewing over the mess I'd made of my life. I know now that I was grappling with depression that grew worse the longer I left it unchecked. I drank more, sneaking booze into my room when I could. I still went out with friends, but the party scene suddenly seemed like another place where a loser like me would never fit in.

I guess I'd pinpoint my junior year as the time frame when hopelessness sunk its fangs into me, determined to bleed me dry. My friends were still important to me; in a hometown as small as mine, they were all I had. But other kids my age, some of them in the same behavioral spiral, had no idea how to help. Their specialty, like mine, was making fun of other kids, not building them up. And it wasn't as if I was being completely honest about everything I was going through. No way was I taking that kind of risk.

Things finally grew unbearable. Thank God. Because that's when I reached out to the one person to whom I should have known all along I could entrust each gory detail: my father, who'd proven he'd be there for me no matter how low I sunk.

During those junior-year conversations with Dad, everything finally came out, and he listened to every awful bit of it.

I felt like trash. I was a total loser. For the first time, I verbalized how badly my life truly sucked. I'd taken so much pride in convincing everyone that I was perfectly content with my life. I was doing just fine. No one could know that a strong, tough guy like me was, deep down, a mental defect.

The topic of my friends came up. I didn't really care for them, I was starting to realize. "Bad breath is better than no breath," I remembered someone saying somewhere. That was me and my friendships: it was better to have rotten friends than none at all.

I had become a disgusting monster, and I hated it. I hated me. And I didn't want to live anymore. I finally asked my father for help, and that weekend he drove over three hours from Kansas City to see me.

As I saw my father's car pull into my mom's driveway, the emotion of seeing him swamped me. I did my best to collect myself. Damn, I hated crying. My jaw clenched, I opened the screen door and headed outside. He waited beside his car. I avoided eye contact. There's something about my dad's tender, brown eyes . . . even back then he could see through the garbage I'd packed into my life, straight to my soul.

When he finally said, "Hey, Aus," I just lost it and came completely undone.

And instead of judging me for being the weakling I hated being, he pulled me close and held me, whispering, "It doesn't have to be like this anymore. You are too valuable and talented to keep going this way. I know you have so much to offer, and it's time for you to start believing it. You need people in your life who love and care about you, and right now you don't have that."

I stepped back, our gazes met, and I realized I was nodding.

"Why don't you get out of here?" he asked. "I have a room waiting for you at my place. It's time for a change."

Out of options, a total failure at everything I'd tried so hard to make happen on my own in my hometown with my mom, I said, "Okay, Dad. I'll come live with you."

That next Monday, Dad and I informed my principal and guidance counselor I would be dropping out of school and moving to live with him. Both administrators supported our plan, saying they hoped starting over with my dad was the change I needed. I spent the rest of the week "drinking" good-bye to my friends and feeling like a loser for having to leave. Starting a new life in a new place with all new people scared the living hell out of me.

The devil you know . . .

At my mom's, I'd been in constant fight-or-flight mode, anticipating threats everywhere I turned, every time I left my house. It was the only life I remember living. When I moved, I packed my fears and took that mindset with me to live with my dad.

I think the possibility of succeeding at my dad's maybe freaked me out more than the thought of everyone there rejecting me. He lived in a large city instead of the small town where I'd grown up. I'd spent most of my life surrounded by the same few thousand people. Now I'd have to become a city kid—a tiny speck in a metropolitan swarm. You'd have been anxious too, thrown into such a foreign environment.

I didn't even know how to drive in that kind of traffic. Every time I got behind the wheel, I was a nervous wreck, sweating and talking to myself like a lunatic. People honked at me and my lame driving skills. Each sound was a personal attack, reinforcing that I was still a loser dropout—I always would be, no matter where I moved.

My basement bedroom was the only place that felt safe.

Dad was determined I could be more than a basement dweller.

Higher education was my father's holy grail. Even I knew that I couldn't get any kind of decent job without scoring at least a high school diploma. By then, Dad was working on his master's degree in psychology at the University of Kansas. Countless times, he'd offered to let me roam around campus while he was in class. I think he thought the positive, energetic atmosphere would convince me to finish school. But what if all those older, smarter kids realized what a loser I was? Inviting more rejection was a not an option. No, thank you. There'd be no college campus for me.

Securing my high school diploma, on the other hand, was non-negotiable. I agreed to go with my dad to a nearby high school. He set up an appointment to talk to one of their advisers. Even there, there were so many kids it was insane to think I'd fit in.

My entire class back in my hometown had fewer than ninety people in it. In this new school, in my grade alone there'd be over 1500. There was absolutely no way I was going there. Not a chance in hell. *Hell* was exactly what it would have been like for me. And on the car ride home, I'm not certain I expressed my mounting panic quite that maturely.

So, a high school equivalency diploma became my goal. I attended a night-school program at a local community college, customized for me and other dropouts. With my self-esteem in the sewer, I finally felt at home. I breezed through the preliminary, subject-level quizzes and the final test. Dad congratulated me on getting my diploma, wanting to take me out for dinner to celebrate. I wanted nothing to do with it.

This wasn't a success. I'd failed—taking the loser's way out of high school. If anyone asked me where I'd graduated from, my answer would forever be "Nowhere. I have a diploma from nowhere."

Don't think I didn't appreciate everything my dad was doing for me. But I was ashamed he'd had to step in and dig me out of my mess. I felt humiliated, inadequate. I was *not* the independent, strong man I'd wanted so badly to become. My father, thankfully, got all of this. No matter how much I blew up at him or refused to talk about how I was feeling or do pretty much anything he thought would pull me out of my emotional tailspin, he kept encouraging me.

Dad kept me focused on moving forward.

Finding a job, learning a trade—we talked about all of it. Going to college, too, but the thought of that still made me want to curl up and hide somewhere, or vomit, or both. We visited a couple of junior colleges and met with instructors who taught plumbing, welding, and electrical. The more hands-on work of these trade programs actually resonated with me in a way academic classes didn't. But I still dragged my feet every step of the way. I'd most definitely fail at vocational classes, too. Hadn't I screwed up at everything else?

Dad bought me a cell phone. I was excited to finally have one. He was hoping I'd make some new connections in my home with him in Kansas City. Instead, I reached out to the old crowd in my hometown.

It was just too much, too soon, I think. I couldn't handle the do-over my dad had in mind for me. I would humiliate myself. I'd let him down. Just thinking about everything I'd have to do there to make something work felt crippling. Turning to the comfort my hometown drinking buddies was much easier. I decided to head back just for a visit. My dad wasn't pleased. But true to his word, he didn't try to force me to stay with him. Of course, once I hit the road, I never came back.

I wasted all those opportunities I could have had living with my dad the first time around.

When I think back to all the time and money and effort he put into giving me that fresh start, it makes me sick. Even worse, I know in my heart that I'd hurt him, shrugging it all off and ditching him like that. Even as I drove away, it was killing me that I'd disappointed him. So I went about the business of numbing myself to my latest failure.

I fell right into the old life that had gotten me into trouble in the first place.

For a while, though, even as I dove back into drinking and partying, things seemed to be looking up. I was offered a job by one of my hometown's major employers, a company that produced bricks. The brick plant was one of the better-paying local employers. The work would be hard. But that was okay. It was the kind of honorable job "real" men had. I'd be stacking brick into a packaging machine.

After my first month there, my fingers and thumbs were blistered from the rough surface of the bricks I handled. The constant bending, twisting, and turning left me aching in places I hadn't known a body could ache. And I didn't think I was progressing fast enough to whatever next level I should be promoted to—back then, wherever I was, was never good enough.

I began to mentally beat myself up all over again. This time, because I wasn't good enough at moving bricks from one place to another. All around me, everyone else was dealing with the same mundane, rote, backbreaking work. But I was the only *loser*. If I wasn't the best, I was a failure, no matter what I was trying to do.

I was determined to give it my all, though. I stacked brick on that old machine for slightly more than a year. I drank and smoked cigarettes with my coworkers, determined to fit in. Having the steady job and pay started to feel good, but working with a team of people who liked me was the real reason I stayed. It was almost like being back on the football team. A lot of other people in that small town would have given anything to have that job. I must have been doing something right to have gotten my position and kept it for so long.

I was finally promoted to production forklift driver. The job description said I'd be unloading brick from two packing machines at a time. But like lot of other manufacturing facilities, that brick plant padded their bottom line by pushing employees to do more and more. Soon I was expected to help unload trucks in addition to keeping up with those two packaging machines. I did everything I could to keep up, working my ass off, but it was more than one person could handle. I was good with a forklift by then, but the better I became at my job, the more work I was expected to do.

I wound up driving faster and faster, determined not to get fired. But I also knew how reckless I was being. At some point, I knew I'd cause an accident. Nevertheless, I kept going.

Like an emotional cancer, the stress and the anticipation of failure gnawed at my insides.

How did I cope? By adding even more stress to my life.

Drinking after work became a daily highlight. I looked forward to the beer or vodka buzzing through my system, making everything lighter and brighter. My weekends became a total haze. Morning to night, my goal was to numb away how totally out of control the rest of my life had become.

My friend Rick and I fed off each other's ignorance. It was as if we wanted to "out-crazy" each other. When we weren't working together, having fun was our number-one objective. And when you're numb, you fail to notice how hard-core and reckless the things you're doing have become. All I cared about was feeling good in the present. Consequences are for later—and you make yourself believe that later won't ever catch up with you.

One night, Rick said there was a party down by the river. There'd be live music, part of some local festival, which sounded just fine to me. I was too young still to drink in public. But when I picked Rick up, I was working my way to the bottom of a bottle of whisky. Driving slowly, already trashed, I took the back roads to the party.

Pretty wasted, I had a decent time at the party. But it was mostly a crowd of thirty-somethings. There was no one I knew to talk to. Rick was chatting plenty of people up, though. The only way I could get him to leave was to agree to chug more whisky with him.

He pointed at a mark on the bottle and said, "Fine. We're drinking this bottle down to here." He started and nailed the halfway point. My turn. I followed suit until the amber liquor was level with the mark. Then our friend Jason called, wanting us to meet up in a nearby town. Drunk off my ass, I somehow got Rick and me there in my old diesel truck.

Jason had been looking for reinforcements to go kick the ass of some guy who'd been picking on his brother. Sure, I thought, not knowing or giving a damn about Jason's baby brother. Why not? It was something to do. And, besides, Jason's crew had plenty of alcohol. Score! Rick and I squeezed into the backseat of their already full car.

I kept chugging beers the whole way to the next county. We never found the guy they were looking to ass kick. Around 3 a.m., Jason stopped next to an abandoned farmhouse. Long story short, while I was in various stages of passing out in the backseat, everyone else piled out and did some serious vandalism. I remember there was a tractor with a key inside, and I remember not bothering to tell anyone to leave it alone. Having worked for farmers when I was younger, I knew how much damage was being caused. But what business was it of mine? Some guy named Paul used the tractor and its bucket to knock down one of the farmhouse's walls. Several bales of hay were set on fire.

"What in the hell?" I yelled, causing everyone else to laugh harder than they already were. "You guys are insane."

More and more bales of hay were ignited.

It was inexcusable, and I knew it. When Jason dropped me off at my car, I guess he realized how worried I was. He asked me not to rat him out. I grudgingly agreed. Back then I wanted friends more than anything. Loyalty to anyone who'd accept broken, stupid me was deeply ingrained in the messed up "code" I lived by.

Rick and I crashed at my house. The next morning, when we finally talked, I realized that in my drunken stupor I'd slept through even more destruction to that farm than I'd realized, including an attempt to break into the farmhouse and steal things. Thousands of dollars' worth of damage had been done, and I was a part of it. But no matter how worried I was about getting caught, I was determined to keep quiet. Real men didn't rat on their friends.

Too bad for me, as it turned out. Another guy turned us all in. It didn't matter that I hadn't personally perpetrated the vandalism. I had been there, and I hadn't gone to the authorities. That guy, Paul, who'd done most of the damage, had come right out and said I'd participated—landing me with a felony conviction, a $10,000 restitution, and a bunch of weekends in jail.

"Finally, Austin's rock bottom," you may be thinking.

Unfortunately, not so much.

We were shit-faced again, Rick and me, and it was only seven on a Friday evening.

In my flatbed Ford diesel, we turned into a nearby town for the ice we needed for our too-warm beer.

"Screw that piece of shit," Rick yelled out the window as we passed a local bar. "Dude, that guy is a piece of shit." He was talking about some guy whose truck was in the parking lot of a local bar we'd passed.

Ice secured, we rolled back out of town to cruise the surrounding dirt roads, getting our drink on, making fun of people, laughing like the bored rednecks we were.

"This place sucks," I said, nearing that same small town again. "It's always the same shit."

Rick agreed and then said, "Holy shit. I know what we're doing!" He laughed hysterically. What a blast. He was going to steal that guy's truck—getting the guy back for whatever past transgression the guy had committed to earn Rick's disdain.

I was drunk (noticing a trend here?) and went along with it—as long as Rick promised we wouldn't get in trouble. This time I was totally in on it, even though Rick was the one who stole the guy's ride, pulling away like it was no big deal. I watched him do it and waited a few minutes before following. We parked my truck behind an abandoned farmhouse and headed out for a joy-ride in the stolen vehicle.

But before long, the truck started overheating. The engine was actually catching fire by the time a deputy sheriff drove up to us, lights flashing. The truck lost power before we could get away. We ditched it (the engine *was* on fire by then) and took off running, hiding in a nearby cornfield—two drunk kids thinking we were invincible, only having to evade one small-town deputy. Then we heard sirens coming from every direction, it seemed.

Rick and I crawled on our stomachs for half mile or so before we felt safe taking a look. There were several state troopers, a fire truck, an ambulance, and the still-smoldering truck. The troopers were using spotlights to search the field we'd just left. We had fooled them! *What fun*, we thought after we headed for Rick's house on foot. Until I realized I had messages on my phone. A cop had left a voicemail, asking if I was okay and telling me to call him when I got his message. My mom had called too, crying and broken up and worried about me.

They must have found my truck behind the old farmhouse.

We were so screwed.

Rick's father nailed us with questions as soon as we arrived at Rick's house. We lied. Bad lies. But we bought ourselves enough time to crash for the night. The police came knocking first thing the next morning. We were still wearing the same clothes from the night before. The police talked to Rick and me separately. Our fabricated stories didn't match up. The officers left, but I knew they'd be back—or waiting for me at my mom's.

"Either you tell your parents, or I will," I told Rick. He refused, so I came clean to his parents, who made us call the police and turn ourselves in.

The result? More "fun." More felony charges and fines and weekend time in jail. More pressure to stay in a job I hated, where it was harder and harder for me to keep up. Because if I didn't stay, how the hell was I going to pay my fines?

Four months later, I started to lose it at work, still driving a forklift under increasingly impossible pressure.

I was a nervous wreck. My life was filled with so much trouble it felt as if I'd never get out of it.

The last thing I needed was to be screwing up at work, too, stopping production because I didn't get everything done fast enough. It was like drowning in anxiety, and then depression, and, as always, the anticipation of public humiliation. I was going to fail. Everyone was going to think I was lazy, a loser, a screwup, just as I'd been in high school. I couldn't control it—the certainty I felt that I would forever be broken.

I came home each afternoon, sat in the house, and thought of all the things I could mess up before the next workday. I couldn't sleep. I couldn't stop the panic and hopelessness of the life I kept torching every chance I got. I was sad. And I think the harder I tried to quietly tough things out, the more of me broke. But I got my ass to work every day, crumbling but determined not to let people down any more than I already had.

"You need to slow that damn thing down," my supervisor screamed at me one day after flagging me down as I rushed to meet my next impossible deadline. Everyone was watching. "You're tearing the hell out of that machine, and it needs to last us awhile. If you can't do the job, I will find a guy who can!"

I responded with a nod and drove off. Fast. It was my only option to keep up with my workload. That was when I started fantasizing about beating the shit out of my boss. I'd beat him down and humiliate him in front of everyone. This was personal now.

I dreaded the job I'd once been proud of. I hated everyone and everything about it, but it was the best-paying job around, and I had legal fees to contend with. I suddenly hated the small town I'd been so happy to move back to. Yet I'd pissed away my opportunity to dream and do better somewhere else. I'd come slinking home with my tail between my legs. Now I couldn't even make things work at a brick plant.

I'd be twenty-one in a couple of weeks—I'd be a man. Like I cared. Nothing excited me anymore. I was exhausted. Everything hurt.

Most people are afraid of hell. I figured I was already there. Hopes, dreams, believing I could make *something* work—all of it was gone, along with the loser friendships I could by then see as the superficial diversions they'd always been. Not a single one of those guys, even Rick, was there for me when I went looking for support. *Good-time* Austin was done, so our friendships were as well.

I had a serious issue with alcohol and how I used it to get me through my loser life. I had a criminal record that would haunt whatever future I might be able to scrape together. I was a worthless piece of shit, just as I'd always known.

And then one day, I opened a file on my computer and saved it as "MSN": an acronym for *My Suicide Note*.

I wrote one sentence and then deleted it, repeating the cycle numerous times, until I grew increasingly more frustrated. I slammed my forehead down onto the keyboard, leaving unintelligible text in the file. I couldn't even document the end of my hopeless, sad existence.

But in a way, feeling that sad felt *good*. For so long, I'd lived in a constant state of rage. It was almost a relief to feel something, anything else. Even if that *something else* was giving up.

I couldn't handle the pressure anymore—of my job, my legal troubles, the hefty fines I'd be paying off for years. *If* I kept working, which I couldn't, I might as well end things on my own terms.

First I officially cut ties with my job. And then I crawled back home and under my covers. Lights off, totally alone, I thought about what I wanted the people I'd leave behind to know. One by one, I pictured their faces.

What would I tell them? And I was fine, honestly, until my father's image appeared. This was going to crush him. He'd put so much into rebuilding our relationship. It would crush him, my throwing all that back in his face, but I desperately needed everything about my hopeless life to end. He'd blame himself. And he didn't deserve having to live with my last official screwup for the rest of *his* life.

Deep in my heart, I knew Dad would want to know how I was feeling. I knew I couldn't deprive him of that, as if it didn't matter how hard he'd fought to be there for me in even the worst of circumstances. I also knew my mother would go insane, spending the remainder of her life thinking I went to hell for killing myself—and that would torture my dad too, even though they were divorced.

I called my mom first, asking for help for the second time in my life.

I started crying as soon as I saw her.

"What's the matter, baby?" she asked.

And once I told her, she was crying too. Then she called my dad. Before the dust had settled, the plan was for me to go live with him again. This time in Iowa, where he was pursuing his PhD in psychology.

The day I left my hometown to move in with my dad for the second time was the day my life as I know it now began.

Kevin: A Parent's Endless Wait

By the spring of 2005, when Austin was still in high school, I was pursuing my master's in psychology.

I was jumping through hoops in attempt to enter a graduate program at the University of Kansas. I had to get a good score on a general admissions exam (the GRE)—not easy for a guy eighteen years out of school. But I was determined.

I'd also kept my promise to Austin and had changed the way I parented. Our interactions had become loving and direct.

Fruitless talks and lectures were less and less frequent. My focus had shifted to deepening our relationship so that when he needed me most, he'd know I was there for him. And he was going to need me. Nothing anyone said to him at that time was making a dent in his seeming determination to continue spiraling downward.

Austin was flunking his high school classes and getting into increasing amounts of trouble in his hometown. My heart broke for him. And when he finally called asking for help that first time, he sounded so trapped and exhausted and out of options.

He was about to fail his junior year of high school, and he took responsibility for that. Vulnerable may not sound like the right way to describe a kid who's told you the stories Austin has. But that's what my son was despite all his faults. He was a vulnerable kid who desperately wanted his life to make sense.

I thought to myself, *Finally. He is ready to make some changes.* I knew it would be a painful and difficult challenge, but I was so eager to help my son I didn't assess just how difficult things would be for him when he moved in with me—or exactly what kind of help he needed if he was going to be successful.

I had been waiting for this chance for years.

I was going to give my son everything he needed for his new life. My parents were living with me at the time. I planned a "Welcome to Kansas City" party for Austin on the Sunday after he arrived. He'd love that sort of thing.

Or not.

I could tell almost immediately how embarrassed he was. I hadn't counted on how sensitive he'd become to what others thought about him. He felt ashamed about dropping out of high school and moving away from his mom and little brother and friends. In one sweeping move, I'd exposed him as a loser. He was humiliated.

While I'd crammed for the GRE, I had been certain Austin would get excited about his fresh start in Kansas City. He'd passed the high school equivalency exam, and my thinking was

Great! One success under his belt; he was ready to move on to the next step. I told him I was proud of him, that his classmates back home were still going to class, and look, he was already done with high school. But Austin remained uninspired and nixed any discussion about college. There were trade careers that would have made wonderful alternatives, but none of them appealed to him either.

Getting a cell phone had sparked his interest. Besides that, nothing. So I began to ask him, "What do you want?" to which he'd answer, "I don't know."

After weeks and weeks of the same response, I was, frankly, pissed that he refused to try. I stopped attempting to engage him. His attitude whenever he didn't immediately get what he wanted became nastier by the day. The whole situation turned into a nightmare.

Honestly, I was more worried than angry.

By then I had already worked with several men who were mired in bad, repetitive, no-end-in-sight life dynamics. None of them had ever seemed as *stuck* as my son.

Was Austin doomed for failure?

It was killing me to think that. Anger, sadness, worry, hopelessness . . . I felt it all. Sleepless nights, and days filled with his negative energy made connecting even harder. I loved my son, but I was losing patience.

I regretted getting him that phone. He was texting nearly all the time, and I knew he hadn't made any new friends in Kansas City—he hardly left the house. So this kid who'd said he wanted a fresh start was right back where he was, talking with his bad-news buddies from his hometown. He finally approached me one day about heading back home just for a visit. My heart sank.

"Okay. Have a good time," I responded. I'd failed as a dad yet again. Once he walked out that door, I knew there was no way he was coming back.

What I didn't have a clue about was how big a mess he'd have to make of his life before he finally committed to getting the help he needed.

It took two-and-a-half excruciating years before Austin's downward spiral bottomed out.

Alcohol, legal problems, fines mounting with each new screwup, dead-end friends . . . all of it added to the load of guilt and shame he was already carting around.

"I did it," he kept saying. "I can handle it." He was a tough kid, but even the strongest of us have our limits.

I let his cell plan lapse, significantly diminishing our ability to communicate. But I refused to abandon him. I'd stay as focused on our relationship as he'd let me, for as long as it took. The relationship we'd formed when I'd reconnected as a parent was the ace up my sleeve. Actually, it was all I had left. I was banking everything on my son still believing that I'd love and support him no matter what.

There were glimpses of hope.

During one of my visits, he drove me out to his workplace and showed me around the brick plant. He seemed passionate about his success there and knew a lot about the operation. I was proud of him and made sure he knew it. But his response was "It's just a brick plant." It was as if as soon as he saw my excitement for what he was doing with his life, he had to piss all over it just to prove to me (and himself) just how worthless he still was.

By 2008, I had completed my master's degree and was accepted into the Counseling Psychology doctoral program at the University of Iowa. For the next four or five years, I would move away from my family again so I could do research and study my field on a deeper level. Iowa was the third-ranked program in the United States at the time I entered. I'd be working myself to death while I was there, and my reading disability caused me to work at a much slower pace than the average student. Top that off with my being forty-three when the next oldest student was fifteen years my junior, the two part-time jobs I'd be working to pay the bills, and my parents' failing health, it would take everything I had to make a successful go if it.

Not to mention Austin, who only contacted me at that point because his mom had made him. It was easy to feel as if I could do nothing more for him—not until he was ready to do better for himself.

It was the end of my first semester.

I was facing finals and several big papers. On a cold, dreary day in December, Austin's mother called me to say Austin was suicidal and that they both thought his best option was for him to come live with me in Iowa City. Cue a shocked, Kansas City PTSD flashback.

After I recovered, I said, "Okay. Have Austin give me a call, and we'll talk about it."

I panicked. Of course I was going to help my son.

But I was running on empty with everything I was already doing. There was absolutely no way I could repeat the same efforts I had made when he'd come to live with me in Kansas City. It was time for both of us to get real about what exactly *he* would do to contribute to a second try at living with me.

When Austin called, we talked for a long time—about his commitment to change, about why his trip to KC hadn't worked, and about what would make this move more successful. He was finally out of answers and earnestly asking for help.

I said, "You are not going to come up here and do the same things you have been doing at home. You have to start thinking differently, deprogram old ways, and learn new ones. Reengineer your life. You're going to have to work for the change you want. I can't help the way I did in Kansas City. You're driving this time."

He agreed to all of it.

And so we both got a second chance to do better.

WHAT HAPPENED?

As long as Austin was determined to pull away, there was no stopping him.

From the Psychologist

Your teen may not be talking to you at all.

Consider a couple of potential reasons for this.

First, he may need you to prove yourself to him.

You've reset how you relate to your son, but earning his complete trust in your unconditional support is an ongoing battle.

Continue working on empathizing with his situation. Reflect back compassion and understanding (again, this is not the same as condoning his behavior and actions). Honor your commitment to be there for him no matter what, when he's ready to turn to you for support and help.

He will come around. He does need you. He knows that, and deep down he wants to trust you to help him find a way out of his problems.

There's a second likely reason for your son's distance.

There is a good chance he feels a great deal of shame for his behavior.

Regardless of what he's done, he wants to succeed in life. But for some reason, he's not yet doing the work.

"Belonging" has been illusive for him. It's as if he can't feel at home anywhere, no matter how hard he's tried. His "outlier" status has taken a toll on his self-worth. When a person feels he has no value to anyone in his life, the urge to address this core motivator (belonging) often drives destructive behavior and circular reasoning.

At some level, your son knows he has fallen short of what he truly wants to achieve and is currently settling for a cheap substitute.

He feels inadequate. He's hyperaware that he's not pursuing the path *you* were hoping he'd follow. He's likely ashamed of the fact that he can't extricate himself from his problems. Withdrawing from you and anyone else whose expectations reflect the worst of how he sees himself relieves him temporarily from dealing with how he's falling short.

Rather than internalizing your teen's distance as rejection, consider that his behavior is a desperate attempt to postpone dealing with the harsh realities triggering your support and concern.

Will he ever be ready to change?

Therapists are in the business of helping people meet their goals.

However, we learn that helping people achieve what they desire and helping them feel better aren't necessarily the same thing. Not at first. Often, what's required for someone to fully commit to a new behavioral path is for them to feel discomfort and sustained unhappiness with their current choices. For some, the necessary changes that need to be made must become the only available option to end their pain—otherwise a true commitment to change can't be achieved.

For instance, someone saying he wants to lose weight, quit smoking, or improve his marriage doesn't necessarily translate to that person doing the work required to make any of those things happen. We want a lot of things in life, but our minds have a way of doing that cost-benefit analysis we discussed. Subconsciously, we're deciding every day which of our goals are *really* what we want, and which merely sound good (and possibly offer us temporary relief from our guilt and shame) when we say them to ourselves and others.

Part of my job as a therapist is to gauge a patient's level of commitment to the work required to improve his life. This is also now part of your job as a parent.

> *As a therapist, evaluating my client's readiness for change helps me more effectively approach him during our sessions.*

If a client is thinking about change but is not yet committed to making that change, our work at first is focused on helping him *motivate* himself—until achieving his goal becomes a top priority. For the client who is legitimately ready to do whatever work is needed, my focus shifts to supporting that client through the changes he must map out and make for himself. It can be helpful to approach your role as a parent from the same two-pronged perspective.

> *First and foremost, it's essential for your teen to deal with the things motivating him not to change. Only when those obstacles have been confronted and disabled will your son be ready to accept your support as he moves forward, fully embracing the better choices he can make for himself.*

Understanding change becomes more complex when you're dealing with a young adult.

The same as I did with Austin when he moved to Kansas City, you can likely see the changes that, once made, could dramatically improve your teen's life. However, even if your son is aware of and has begun communicating with you about his problems (and has even asked you for help), other factors may still be blocking him from being fully ready to change. Getting him over that last "motivational" hurdle of fully committing to overhaul his life can be a complex, lengthy, painful process.

To give you a frame of reference, in the late 1970s, two alcoholism researchers, DiClemente and Prochaska, created a model for the "readiness for change" process. They broke change into five stages psychologists use to this day.

Stage	For your teen . . .
1. Precontemplation	**Change is not on his radar.** He has no plans to change. Why would he? It will take something significant (or the prospect of losing something important to him) to move his awareness to the next stage.
2. Contemplation	**Change is now a possibility and verbally discussed when prompted** (by either circumstances or the person providing assistance), but internal conflict and barriers remain in play. The person is still unwilling or unable to fully commit to change at this time. He is likely to continue with the same unwanted behaviors. **NOTE:** It is common for your teen to cycle back and forth between the precontemplation and contemplation stages until a significant enough crisis forces enough discomfort and dissonance for true change to be the only alternative.
3. Preparation	**Change is now the primary focus.** Plans are made. Emotional and behavioral barriers may still exist, but he has taken the steps necessary to move toward change.
4. Action	**Action is taken to create sustainable change,** away from destructive behaviors.
5. Maintenance	**Habits and behavioral practices are created** so that change becomes a routine part of life—the person embraces their new "normal" reality.

When Austin was in high school (his precontemplation stage), I beat my head against the wall trying to get him to apply himself in school and to stay out of trouble. It took the prospect of him not being able to graduate with his class to shake him from his "What's the big deal?" stance. He would have been humiliated if that had happened (one of his core motivators). What would his peers say to him if he were to flunk and be held back? He couldn't stand the thought of that, so he called me for the first time, asking for help.

He felt an urgency because his world was crashing down (his contemplation stage). He had begun to "think about" making changes in his life. He was willing to move and complete his GED. But due to a variety of factors, he was at first unable and later unwilling to continue moving in a positive direction. So, craving "normalcy" and a place where he felt less challenged (and less like a failure for not yet possessing the skills to successfully meet those challenges), he returned to his old life.

Just before Austin's twenty-first birthday, he faced a greater crisis than ever before. His life was once again collapsing in on him to the point that he planned suicide. Thankfully he asked for help, first from his mother, and then from me (reentering the contemplation stage). Only this time, after his move to Iowa, he was considering finding a job or going to school (his preparation stage). As we'll share later, he still faced some difficult barriers that would at first interfere with him taking full advantage of the opportunities he made for himself (opportunities he ultimately embraced in his action and maintenance stages).

I can't emphasize enough the most important thing to keep in mind while reviewing your role as a parent guiding a troubled teen through these same stages:

> *First and foremost, your teen must recognize and accept that he must change the way he's living his life. Until he success- fully embraces this contemplation stage of his behavioral evo- lution, your pushing him to move forward to any other stage in the process won't produce a successful result, no matter how hard you try to do the work for your teen.*

Austin Checks In: What the Heck Was I Doing?

Nothing.

I was doing absolutely nothing to help myself. I was spinning my wheels in reverse and blazing a trail back to the worst parts of who I'd been before I'd moved in with my dad the first time.

My life was out of control, and I wasn't sure how things had gotten so bad. Little by little, I had "reacted" my way into a dynamic I couldn't tolerate. But there seemed to be no way to escape.

Over the years, teachers, coaches, and parents had often asked, "What were you thinking?" My honest answer had always been "I really don't know." It was as if I had been programmed for an unavoidable, self-destructive collision course that might have ended with deadly consequences.

I was responsible for the things I did and the outcomes of my choices. But ever since I was little boy, I'd been thinking and doing things that made sense to me—even if my behavior was baffling to everyone else. When I was a little kid, that sort of thing seemed to work for me. But as I aged, others expected "better" and more responsible choices from me. Yet I was still me, experiencing and reacting to the world in a dramatically different way than more "successful" teenagers. It was as if a vise were tightening around me and I could no longer wiggle or muscle my way out of the damage I was doing.

I'd flown over one too many cliffs. I was out of options.

WHAT TO DO?

Kevin: You Likely Understand More about "Readiness for Change" Than You'd Like To.

By age thirty-six, I had already divorced twice.

Like my son, I was obviously adept at doing the same thing over and over and yet *expecting* a different result with each new attempt.

I continued to date nice ladies, and I thought we were having a good time. And yet each time they didn't return my calls, it was excruciating. Worse than my divorces. They likely weren't outright rejecting me, but just the *thought* that they might be—that I'd blown it again—was absolutely unbearable. It wasn't logical, but I lost sleep over it and couldn't eat. I was downright depressed. At my lowest point, I sought professional help.

Sound familiar?

Yeah, I get the irony.

I'd reached my own crisis. Pain I could barely tolerate began communicating how desperately I needed help. The journey of emotional healing I undertook as a result transformed my life—much like the emotional work Austin finally committed to has since propelled him toward exciting accomplishments.

"But how can I help my son through the precontemplative and contemplative stages, where he's still resisting change?" I hear you asking.

The anticipated pain of change is what keeps most people stuck in a cycle of precontemplation and contemplation.

Remember our bucket analogy?

This time, think of one bucket holding the anticipated pain of change, while the other contains the actual pain the person's currently experiencing due to poor behavioral choices. A person will resist change until the current pain is severe enough to outweigh the anticipatory pain of doing things differently.

> *In short, allowing your teen to feel the pain (consequences) of his behavior is likely your greatest tool for helping him tap into the needed motivation to change.*

A Note from Austin: What More Could My Dad Have Done to Help Me?

Absolutely nothing.

The guy had given me every chance to get my act together, and I'd chickened out of each opportunity. I'd let him down. I'd let myself down. I'd convinced myself there was no way I'd ever amount to anything, so I might as well quit.

It wasn't that I was disrespecting my dad or even refusing to change. I loved him and believed he was trying to help me. And I wanted to do better. But I was a ruthless, tough-guy fighter, remember? I was afraid of no one. No one except myself and what I saw staring back at me in the mirror.

I was petrified. What would happen if I let my guard down? There was a little boy deep inside me, curled up and sobbing on the couch while my parents screamed at each other. That was who'd be left if I said good-bye to the Austin I'd become. The weakest part of me would be exposed, humiliated, powerless, and defenseless, just like that little boy.

For a long time, I'd rather have died than take that risk.

WHAT'S MOST IMPORTANT?

In a word: crisis

Crisis is an essential component to your troubled teen learning how to more successfully manage his life choices.

I know that's not what anyone likes to hear. Concerned, committed parents are not built to stand by and watch their children endure the degree of consequences that will finally propel an already suffering child to finally change the behaviors damaging his life. For teens barreling down the wrong path, though, the good news, depending on how you look at it, is that the required level of pain and crisis is usually not far down the road.

> *It helps to think of the critical moment when your child eventually bottoms out as an invaluable learning opportunity.*

Because of the new level of pain he's caused himself, he'll be more motivated to accept how much needs to be changed. And you, already working hard on your Step-One and Step-Two Parent Playbook exercises, are ready to help him take that next step.

It's important to keep in mind, though, that it may take more than one cycle of precontemplation and contemplation before your teen or young adult authentically embraces change as the only way out of his troubles.

A troubled teen's early "perceived" crises are often precursors to more destructive beliefs and behavior.

The prospect of failing his junior year of high school humiliated Austin. That was enough to get him *thinking* about making changes but, ultimately, not enough to pursue that change.

Driving that event was a deeper crisis brewing.

> *The underlying behaviors and thinking that had led Austin to fail would continue to bubble and brew and suck more and more of his life away until he was committed to doing the hard work ahead.*

In no way am I suggesting that these "perceived" emergencies and immediate crises are inconsequential.

At times, if the associated consequences are grave enough, they can adversely affect your teen or young adult for years to come—as was the case with Austin's mounting legal problems and crippling fines. Other times, a troubled teen can assign too much emphasis to issues and "emergencies" that aren't really crises, so as not to have to focus his energy on taking responsibility for the underlying behaviors causing his woes.

Determining which type of crises your child is dealing with at any given time is a judgment call. There is no clear formula for making that decision. What I can tell you is that for certain troubled teens, the true "bottom" of their behavioral spiral can be an all-hope-is-lost moment, where they either grab the life vest you've offered them, or they simply see no point in holding on any longer. The hard spot for parents of teens who haven't yet reached that point of no return then becomes how to deal with the "immediate" crises that keep coming up—some of them leaving their son with grave consequences.

> *What if not helping your son means his being evicted from his apartment and not having anything to eat, and he finally turns to you for help?*

I'm a parent. I know what it can be like to say no to your son in crucial moments like these (for his own good, because he's not addressing the behavior that keeps getting him into trouble). Both times Austin called me and asked for help, I responded.

However, a parent whose instinct is to respond to every emergency with "I'll take care of that for you" must ask themselves if there are larger (underlying), more critical problems that need to be addressed.

> *Parents determined to help their son achieve positive, sustained behavioral and decision-making improvements must NOT respond to their son's short-term needs in a way that buffers him from long-term consequences and the underlying behavioral issues that must be confronted.*

As a parent, you must recognize the difference between *core* issues and the more in-the-moment problems that can distract everyone from the bigger-picture work that needs to be done.

Responding to immediate needs and cries for help (in Austin's case, he was flunking out and felt trapped and had no way to support himself at the time) often "saves" your teen or young adult from confronting the more essential changes that need to be made. With Austin, I missed the chance during his first move to live with me to deal with the behavioral issues underlying his poor school performance: his negative self-image, impulsivity, lack of confidence in his ability to navigate through life, and the absence of a positive social network, etc.

In my urgent response to my son's first emergency, I focused on his immediate needs instead (and more than I should have, I still tried to "fix" things for him). Removing him from his immediate situation and softening the blow his behavior had caused not only created a whole new set of problems for Austin to cope with, but my "quick fix" did nothing to help him prepare for the next crisis that would inevitably occur.

Rather than enabling your teen to continue making poor choices, your goal is to empower him to commit to the changes that will *prevent* more of the trouble and pain he no longer wants to cause himself.

Your Parent Playbook

There is an old saying (the exact wording varies) that goes something like this:

> *Give a man a fish, and he will eat for a day. Teach a man to fish, and he will eat for a lifetime.*

No matter how well-intentioned your effort, you can't "fix" your troubled teen.

You can't give him a fish or two and expect that one meal to feed him for a lifetime.

A common problem with the "I've got this for you" approach is that it prevents the recipient of your hard work from owning the problems demanding his attention. Additionally, you have no way of knowing exactly what your son needs at any given time. In fact, he is the one person in the best position to understand his situation and develop a successful resolution to his troubles.

> *As I've said, it is my job as a therapist to guide patients to deal with their issues the best they can. As a mom or a dad, that's now your job with your troubled teen.*

While it may be easier to remedy an immediate situation, the more responsible approach to helping your son achieve sustained behavioral change will very nearly always be *his* facing the consequences of the crises he's caused.

> *Remember that your Step-Three goal is to help your son commit to the changes he must make—NOT make things better for him.*

Often, as was the case with Austin, things must get much, much worse before they can finally begin to improve.

It's also helpful to note that your teen may not always perceive your offers (or insistence) to help as a good thing.

If you try to dominate your child by controlling his environment and prevent him from experiencing his life as it truly is, he may feel emasculated by your intervention.

This approach can leave him feeling inadequate and incapable of solving his own problems. You may be damaging the very confidence you long to instill. And worse, he could resent you for "wanting" to make him dependent on your support, even if that is light-years away from what you intend.

So how do you teach your son to fish?

First, you have some evaluating to do—both on your own and with your teen.

Ask Yourself . . .	Consider . . .	Your Goal
What does my teen really need?	Take the time before acting to be confident you are addressing key, underlying behavioral issues rather than merely putting out "immediate" fires.	**Understand the psychological dynamics driving the behaviors that led to your son's crisis.** **NOTE: If your son's safety is at risk, your first and only response is to protect him before moving on to consider the other questions in this table.**
Is my son aware of his underlying problems?	Is he still in the precontemplation stage, where his only focus is his immediate crisis, rather than sustained change? Is he contemplating change but not at a level that will help him avoid future crisis?	**Understand your son's stage of "change"** so you can plan your approach accordingly.

Ask Yourself . . .	Consider . . .	Your Goal
Are fears and other psychological issues holding him back from making necessary changes?	Is he hiding from the work he needs to do out of a fear of humiliation or failure or loss of acceptance (core motivators that can cause us to behave in ways that seem contrary to our best interest)?	**Encourage your son to consider why he's done the things he's done and why he's asking for your help.** Is it because it feels (artificially) safer to avoid change (and risking failure)? Or facing unwanted consequences that would inspire him to choose a different path?

Then it's time to act—in partnership with your teen, and only with his commitment to the process the two of you agree to follow.

Action	Consider . . .	Your Goal
Set clear expectations for the help he needs and the help you're willing to give.	"I don't know" is not an acceptable answer from your teen when you ask him what he needs, if what he really means is "I don't want to talk about it." However, if he really isn't capable in his current state to tell you what he needs, talk with him and help him set realistic, attainable, positive expectations for improving his situation.	**Focus on your son's potential to improve rather than on the end result either you or he thinks he should achieve.** Help him get a "quick win" so he can begin to build momentum. For example, I asked Austin when he came to live with me the second time to focus on being happy and confident in himself and on building healthy friendships rather than on getting a job or going back to school. He needed to shift his focus to feeling more positive about himself (since his underlying shame and guilt over what he perceived was a "hopeless" life was driving so many of his bad choices).

Action	Consider . . .	Your Goal
Outline a general map that provides direction and gives him attainable goals to pursue. Inspire your son to reach his potential without adding to the pressure he already feels.	Always remember that you are working with a low-self-esteem individual driven by shame rather than confidence. You are asking a lot of him, and he needs to be committed to asking a lot of himself. **NOTE:** Shame and fear of failure should never be used by either of you as a motivator.	**Cast a vision for the future you're confident your teen can achieve.** However, be realistic (and help him understand) how long it may take him to achieve sustained change.
Set expectations for what you need from your son.	Clarify your expectation that he must work hard for the change he wants to make. Support him but let him know that the degree of your support will be set by the level of effort you see him applying toward achieving his goals.	**You are inspiring your son's commitment to relearn how to approach and live his life.** You are helping him rebuild confidence that he can do this for himself—he can fish—without needing anyone else to feed or fix him.

My relationship with Austin literally saved his life.

He felt ashamed asking me for help. Real men don't need anyone but themselves. But he'd grown to trust me enough to make that call.

Once we began working together, I didn't respond with a condescending "I told you this would happen." Instead, we talked about hope. I did my best to offer a positive vision for his future. If he was willing to work for it, any dream he had was still possible.

Austin may not have truly grasped my vision at the time, but he knew how to work hard, he knew he wouldn't have to go through what happened next alone, and he dug in—instead of quitting and squandering his potential.

Making that eight-hour drive to Iowa City had to have been a nearly insurmountable task for him. But his bucket of pain and hopelessness finally outweighed his bucket of fear—at least for a while.

And I was there, with a bedroom and a fresh start, prouder than I'd ever been of my son's strength, and determined to honor his trust and find a way to help him no matter what happened next.

YOUR NEXT PLAY

Your teen or young adult has hit his rock bottom. And you've worked hard to build a stronger relationship foundation between you, which means there is great cause for hope as you move ahead, working together.

Your Game Plan in Step Three	Step in when your son is finally motivated to change.
As a parent, you will continue to	allow him to experience the consequences of his behavior. At the same time, with empathy and compassion, you will set clear expectations and encourage him to make the changes you know he can make.
Your teen is beginning to	commit to change. But he does not yet have the skills or experience to sustain success on his own.
Your relationship dynamic is changing to	that of a team, with your son turning to you for support and guidance.
Your Next Step	Having waited for your son to commit to change and turn to you in crisis, your role evolves fully into that of an on-the-field leader. You are ready to begin modeling better behavior and life choices for your son.

STEP FOUR: LEAD YOUR TEAM

Give Your Son
an Example to Follow

Your Game-Plan Challenge	**Continue to encourage your son on the journey of change ahead, when even you have difficulty grasping what the next milestone should be.**
You, the parent, are	no longer shouting advice and orders from the sidelines. You are now in a position of authentic influence, inspiring your son to continue working toward his goals.
Your teen or young adult is	committed to changing his life's path, but he does not yet possess the experience or skills for his new behaviors to become habits.
Your relationship dynamic is	that of you being an on-the-field, experienced teammate—a leader your son looks to for encouragement, inspiration, and guidance as he takes his next difficult steps toward recovery.
Your Goal for This Step	**Model the types of behavior and choices that will help him achieve success while securing him the professional help he needs to meet his unique challenges.**

Commitment to change is a huge step for your son. Now he must relearn how to live his life.

Step Four is where the rubber hits the road. And your role is to continue to be there for him unconditionally while at the same time *intentionally* modeling the types of reasoning, decision-making, and behaviors your teen or young adult must undertake to achieve his goals.

Your son is in the preparation stage of change.

At this point, Austin committed to restructure his life. His first step would have to be "rewiring" his thought process so that healthy decisions and more successful behavioral choices were possible. Your teen or young adult will face his own unique challenges and an equally long road before his new life approach becomes a habit.

Your son will need your support in this often ambiguous, exhausting, and seemingly endless transformation. The end point or even the next major milestone may seem too out of reach. Doubt will creep in, causing him to question his purpose, his ability to complete the tasks ahead of him, and whether all the effort and difficulties and pain he'll face are worth what he stands to gain. You are in essence asking your son take a leap of faith—a sometimes daily recommitment that you, his on-the-field leader, must help him navigate carefully.

THE PARENT-CHILD DISCONNECTION

My son was an adult. He was also still very much a young man in need of direction.

It was almost as if we were father and son for the very first time.

Austin wasn't the only one frightened of this new beginning. I was scared too, if you want the truth.

My mind was spinning. There was no way I could handle all I already had on my plate if Austin wasn't going to be positive, cooperative, and work hard to change. Yet I had no choice but to welcome him.

He was in an extremely fragile state: at high risk for suicide. I couldn't turn him away, and I couldn't squander this second chance. But was he really 100-percent committed to change? Or was he once again looking for an escape from the latest fix he'd gotten himself into?

Sure, I was studying for my PhD in psychology.

But I'd yet to work with or even study clients with difficult diagnoses, severe mental illness, or who were in need of one-on-one interventions. I felt woefully unprepared and unqualified to help Austin with his issues. And then there was the fact that he *wasn't* my client and never would be. He was my son, and he needed me to be his dad, not his psychologist.

Healthy boundaries between us, and my acquiring him the best medical and mental health services available, were essential to his recovery. We both would need as much qualified, hands-on help as we could get.

And then there was the unknown.

How much trouble would he get into this time? Though I'd been in touch with him and his mother, I knew little about the scope of his drinking, his extreme fear, his sense of constant threat of being exposed, and his aggressive posture toward perceived challenge or humiliation. I was flying blind, and the stakes were incredibly high. On the line was my schooling, our relationship, and Austin's life.

The same as when I'd held him as a newborn in my arms, as excited as I was to have my son with me, I hadn't the first clue how to take care of him.

Austin: Reboot—Redux

I arrived at my dad's apartment two days before my twenty-first birthday.

I spent the day I became an "adult" inside his apartment, sheltered from the brutal Iowa winter and waiting for my father to return home. We'd planned to celebrate over dry-rub ribs—his treat. I set a record at dinner by being the first twenty-one-year-old to not touch a drop of alcohol on his birthday, downing my coming-of-age with a glass of water. Party!

Even more demoralizing was the fact that I now lived mere blocks away from the University of Iowa, infamous for being one of the top party schools in the country. Going out that night and cutting loose called to me like a siren's song. I went to bed early instead, my uneventful "big" day expiring with a whimper. Don't get me wrong, staying home that night was not about me changing. This behavior would be a one-time occurrence only.

When I moved to Iowa, I envisioned leading a clean life, with little to no drinking. But there I was, at the heart of Party Town USA. Friendless. Lonely. Bored. I wanted to step out into the scene. I longed to make friends. Plus, I really didn't see drinking as my problem. My behavior and bad choices were what had caused all my problems. I didn't yet see the link between what I'd done and how much I drank and with whom.

I could handle myself. I'd drink, I reasoned, but I wouldn't get into fights or cause trouble. I'd have fun when I partied instead of making trouble. That life was behind me. There was no reason to deprive myself of having a little fun while I worked my ass off to fix all the rest.

I knew my father had made something special of his life. Even with all the scorched earth I'd left in my wake, I admired all he'd accomplished. I was too much of a "man" to admit it, but I craved a piece of the respectability and purpose and ambition that oozed from his pores.

His ironclad work ethic inspired me.

How could living with him not have made me long to maximize my own potential? My laziness and self-pity were the worst of me, and I wanted to be more. As we settled in together, he burned valuable study time helping me deal with the issues that plagued my life. He made listening and offering valuable insights a priority. I wanted to care and contribute and be more like him. I just didn't know how to get there on my own yet.

And since I didn't know how to move forward, I kept doing what I did best: partying and making easy friends like the ones I'd left behind. None of it meant anything, anyway. It was just good times. What harm could it do?

True to his word, my dad didn't make ultimatums that I had to stop, "or else." But that didn't mean he liked what I was doing or that I didn't know how worried he still was.

One evening not long after I moved in, I brought one of my new drinking buddies to the house.

We'd planned to hit the bars early, so my friend waited out on the couch and talked on his phone. This guy was one of the biggest liars I'd ever met, so naturally I'd gravitated toward him. He'd elevated the term "one-upmanship" to an art form. There was nothing I could do he hadn't already done—and done better than me or anyone else on the planet. He made his "I always have to be the biggest, best, and brightest" stories up on the fly. My dad wasn't a fan, to say the least.

The next morning, Dad wanted to know why I was hanging around such a "dipshit."

He had my best interest at heart, but he was still my dad: a gifted therapist, but he didn't pull punches. If he noticed me veering, he'd offer unsolicited advice whether it was comfortable for me to hear or not. That was one of the expectations he set when I moved in—and one of mine was that I'd always listen.

It was a scary time. My future was on the line, and I had no idea where to go or what to do with myself or how to make healthy friends. How did I make friends with someone who wasn't a totally superficial waste of time?

The relationships I'd experienced so far, except with my parents, had been pretty much one-sided. I'd invest time and energy only to discover nothing coming my way from the other person. Or worse, the other person turned out to be a total user, only looking out for number one and not caring whether or not he dragged me down with him.

So there had to be something wrong with me, right?

"Absolutely not," Dad kept insisting in his direct, no-chance-of-misunderstanding way.

> *I wasn't the problem. My low expectation for the type of people who'd want to be with me was the issue.*

As childish as it may seem for a twenty-one-year-old, I was hyperaware of and tragically insecure about my appearance.

I'd often ask my dad for his opinion, determined to look my best. But how did you know what your best looked like when all you saw in the mirror was a failure?

"Does this shirt look stupid, Dad?" How about my hair?"

Any of my "friends" back then would have laughed at or made fun of me. Not my dad.

> *No insecurity or request for his undivided attention was too trivial an interruption (even though, looking back, I can see how much I must have distracted him).*

I was important to him; he let me know. I was valuable.

Slowly, I learned how to find some of that reassurance and positive reinforcement within myself.

Our talks slowly evolved to more in-depth conversations.

We were becoming friends, I remember realizing one day. I finally had a friend I could count on no matter what. I might still doubt myself, but I'd never have a reason to doubt Dad. And I would return that guarantee, I committed to myself, long before I had the tools to accomplish my goal.

> *My father not only showed me how to feel better about myself, he restored my faith in other people.*

Through his unrelenting "there"-ness and acceptance, he showed me I deserved more than the shitty friends who cut me down to make themselves feel bigger (or had dropped me as soon as something or someone they wanted more came along). I've built on that foundation since then, creating rich, meaningful, long-lasting relationships with him and many others—relationships I've intentionally maintained the same way my father refused to let go of his connection with me.

In case I haven't said it recently enough, "Thanks for that, Dad."

I noticed other fathers and sons bond over physical things: hunting, football, baseball, and other "manly" hobbies.

Which was great. But the "us" my dad and I were creating turned out to be different. Self-discovery became our shared hobby. There wasn't a lot of free time, but whatever time Dad had, we spent enriching our lives. Notice that I said "our lives." Because he was right there with me, always as close as I'd let him be, discovering with me rather than trying to "fix" me. "There is nothing wrong with you," his silent support kept saying.

The marvel of this "new" dad engaging with me was that he really enjoyed learning about me and hearing what I had to say. No one else treated me that way (I hadn't let anyone else close enough to). We talked about the meaning of life, the quality of relationships, and the power of love and good intentions. During these philosophical discussions, Dad gently pushed me toward finding meaning for my life.

> *He wanted me to discover my passion, to connect with the fulfilled life he knew I could build.*

Deeper, spiritual questions bubbled up.

I had profound questions about God and the role He plays in our lives. The more I learned in school, the more questions I had—many of which my father had no answers for, though he was always open to discussing whatever I wanted to.

One of the traits I admire most in my father is his comfort with and confidence in "not knowing."

He never pretended to have all the answers—not this new dad, which, over time, helped defuse my shame about all the things that still flummoxed me.

He was this brilliant guy who was content with concepts and ideas beyond his ability to comprehend. He didn't pretend to be some "big man" who couldn't stand to be challenged. Eventually, I took a hard look at my need to "fake" my way through things and situations that tested me. I began to resist the compulsion to beat myself up whenever I felt threatened. I no longer had to project to the world a phony version of myself just to save face. And as I became more okay with myself, it became more conceivable that others might be feeling the same way.

I marvel to this day at my father's relentless work ethic.

He pushed himself to his limit in a top-five psychology program using a storage room for a makeshift office and spending countless hours grinding away at his work. I remember one semester, he got home from an advanced statistics class, took a nap, and then didn't leave that little office until he crashed in bed that night. When I woke up in the morning, he was back at it. And weekends were no different. Up early, studying every possible minute, coming up for air only to eat or sleep. The guy was an animal. And I know by the way he'd curse like a sailor and toss stuff around (yeah, sometimes it was funny to watch), it wasn't coming easy to him.

He was the kind of man I wanted to be. While I was screwing around becoming the greatest coach to ever play the latest EA Sports NCAA Football video game, he was busting his ass working two jobs plus getting his doctorate. Hell, yeah, I felt guilty.

"Would you mind talking for a bit?" my dad asked one day. It was "What do you want to do with your life?" time.

As if I had the slightest clue. Dad suggested I go out and look for a job so I could have some extra money, which sounded fine to me. Except it would just end the way the brick factory had, right? "What about checking out Kirkwood Community College?" he said next. There was an Iowa City campus. The thought made me want to vomit in my mouth.

Before I knew it, though, I'd agreed, and we were on a campus tour with guidance counselor. I gazed at the happy kids swarming around us and wished my life had that kind of direction. I wanted what they had. If I were a student, I'd have somewhere to belong, yet I couldn't fathom it turning out any differently than high school had, where I'd crashed and burned on every conceivable level.

My father asked which classes were still open—something general that would get me headed in the right direction while I figured out what I wanted to be next. Was he *making* me go to school? I tried not to show how pissed off I was. The man was dragging me back to what he knew would be an emotional roller coaster, *if* I agreed to it. And now he was trying to push me down into the damned seat. To round out my humiliation, the counselor gave us a list of some embarrassingly basic courses I'd need for any degree.

"Is this something you'd be willing to try?" Dad asked. Then came the hard sell. "Austin, I know you can do this. You're smart, capable, and this would be a great way to plug into a network of friends. There're all sorts of activities I think you'd like."

Hiding how pissed off *and* terrified I was, I muttered, "I don't know," which no longer worked with the guy, and maybe I was counting on that a little. He always seemed to know what was going on inside my head, and he never let me off the hook when it was time to dig that crap out and confront it.

"Austin, you now have the perfect opportunity to get an education and make something out of your life. Not many kids get the chance to go to school and live for free. I think you should at least try it."

At which point, still pissed and more excited than I wanted to admit, I blurted the first excuse that came to mind. "I don't have the money to go to school, and it's probably too late to apply for financial aid."

"In that case . . ." My father whipped out his credit card, walked up to the front desk, and paid for my first semester of college. I was going to junior college. Boom!

End of story.

It was hard to hate on the guy. After everything I'd put him through, he still cared enough about my future to fork out the money to cover my classes, housing, books, and supplies. And I was now one of those bright, shiny kids I'd been envying on our campus tour. I belonged somewhere now, with "normal" people who had no idea how badly I'd messed up my "old" life. Now I had a chance to not live the rest of my life off whatever income I could scrape together with only a GED on my résumé. But, yeah, I was still scared to death.

And I was drowning in anxiety at the uncertainty of trying for that kind of life again around a bunch of city kids. Me, the awkward kid whose social skills landed somewhere on the spectrum between rural good-ol' boy and Midwestern hoodlum. I just knew that the first time I tried to talk with one of my classmates, I'd embarrass myself and end up with no friends again.

Why would someone want to hang out with me? What did I have to offer?

I was nothing. That's how I still felt about myself, even though I was dying to do better. I was a bum with only a high school education and no job. I was totally unlikeable—a "me" view my dad seemed totally resistant to my leaning into. It was time to do something about all that crap in my head, I guess. Especially if I didn't want to be that kid I'd been a few years back, screwing up and throwing my dad's help back in his face.

I cashed in my $2,000 brick-plant retirement account, paying the "gotcha" penalty so I'd have some walking around money. Buckle was my favorite mall store at the time. To boost my confidence, I scored some sharp looking threads. Back home, staring at my reflection wearing the tightest, most stylish shirt from my shopping spree, I could almost imagine someone else admiring it and thinking I fit in. But I had nowhere to go and no one to go out with. It was a Friday night, and I'd be sitting home alone again doing nothing

"Dad, would you give me a ride downtown? I want to go check it out."

His eyes lit up upon hearing my request. God, I longed for a life where just wanting to go out didn't seem like a monumental milestone.

"Have fun!" he hollered out his open window after dropping me off, so proud, as if he'd just left me at a playground with my new bike or something.

It was winter, the wind whipping through the subzero temperatures, blasting me in the face like razor wire and finding the manufactured holes in my faded blue jeans. Other than that, all I was wearing was the long-sleeved, pink-pearl-snap shirt I'd been so proud of. I ducked into the first bar I saw. It was only nine o'clock, but the place was packed. It wasn't as bad as I'd expected—not nearly as "big city" or intimidating.

Pool tables were everywhere. Allen Jackson resonated from the overhead speakers. I thought, *What in the hell?* This was just like back home. There were mostly guys, so I ordered two Long Islands and chugged down both. It was just like old times. When I paid my tab and left, I didn't tip the bartender. What did I know? Outside, walking vigorously in an attempt to keep warm, I saw a group of about seven guys heading in my direction. Bolstered by my good-looking new clothes and liquid courage, I said, "I literally just moved here and don't know where anything's at. What bars would you recommend?"

"Dude, just follow us! We've got the hookup. Our boy Pat's workin' tonight. Screw paying full price."

It was astonishing. People actually wanted me around. I'd fit in as if it were no big deal.

Introductions made, they led me to this club with a line of people waiting outside stretching a half a block or longer. I'd never seen anything like it in my life. Brian, the leader of the group, went straight to one of the guys who was checking IDs and collecting the cover charge from everyone. Before I knew it, the doorman let us in for free.

This place was huge. Popular hip-hop and rap music blared over the speaker system. Beautiful local girls abounded, their perfume adding spice to the rich aroma of sugary mixed drinks. I was entranced, standing there with a goofy smile glued to my face. But I was going to downplay how awestruck I was. I *had* to fit into a scene like this.

"Austin, you coming with?" one of the guys, Elliot, asked.

"Oh . . . yeah! Sorry. This place is awesome, dude!" So much for playing it cool.

He laughed. "Glad you like it."

I turned sideways, saying, "Excuse me" to everyone as I sliced my way through the thick crowd of other kids my age—students, I realized, just like I'd be in another week. When we reached a stairway, I asked, "Where are we going? Isn't the bar down there?"

"You're in Iowa City now," Elliot said, not seeming to mind that I was from some nowhere, tiny place in Kansas. "This place has three bars. Two of them are up here."

Upstairs, I bought two bottles of champagne from a beautiful girl wearing a spaghetti-strap top and extra short Daisy Dukes: one bottle for Elliott, one for me. He made a toast, and we drank straight out of the bottle. Since these guys knew the bar back, our drinks were a dollar each. I bought multiple rounds of shots, a gesture reciprocated by the others in group, which left me confident enough to hit the dance floor and even dance with six or seven girls.

Back home in my busted-up Kansas life, most women hadn't wanted to be seen with me. In Iowa, one of the girls I danced with suddenly turned around and kissed me while the DJ masterfully beat-matched songs, blending them together into one seamless track. If this was what belonging with the college crowd felt like, I was hooked.

I soaked it up. The experience of "belonging" obliterated the loneliness I'd felt for so long. I was no longer friendless and desperate to fit in. Suddenly, all I'd ever wanted seemed available to me, and all I had to do was force myself to go to class and study my way through college. Sure, I'd have to make the grades, but I'd party my ass off, too. Like the other "successful" students around me, I'd find a way to handle partying and school together.

No sweat.

Going out all the time drained my bank account.

I eventually had to get a job, which meant even more distractions, even though my dad was supportive of me taking responsibility for making my own money.

I gravitated toward the club scene, naturally. Why not make my work feel like a party? Being a bouncer would elevate my social status, too. I was already a tough guy. And what better way to meet women?

My new "career" was invigorating at first—breaking up fights, kicking out drunken losers who thought they were tough until I relieved them of their misconceptions. It was a rush. And when I worked the door, I was in charge. I got to flirt with girls and let them in for free if I liked them. I accumulated hundreds of phone numbers, most of which I never bothered calling. The thrill of getting girls to give me their contact information was the hit I needed. Actually following up or even remembering their names was unnecessary.

But then I'd wake up the next day and my "job" would feel more like an excuse to party; meanwhile, my dad was busting his ass, dedicating his life to helping others. This guy who'd once made tons of money as a high-level consultant now volunteered at a homeless shelter and talked about how much what he did there meant to him. He put in ungodly hours studying and working two jobs while at the same time taking care of his parents (who weren't well) and me. His was night-and-day different than the "cool" world I was so convinced I had to fit into.

He never bragged about it or talked to me like I should be ashamed about what I *wasn't* doing with my life. This same man who'd once screamed and lost his cool whenever I frustrated him was now humble and firmly grounded, thankful for all he had, and hungry to inspire the undiscovered potential within others—including me.

It took a long time for me to wrap my mind around why others meant so much to my dad.

He'd traded in his "great" life for a small, two-room apartment (that he now had to share with his snot-nosed offspring) and the privilege of jumping through the unrelenting hoops that came with earning a PhD. His reality now revolved around this raw, genuine passion for improving the world by loving others. He talked about how helping others enriched his life.

Meanwhile, back at my bouncer job . . . Besides needing the cash, I'd mostly taken the gig to bolster my life and self-esteem. Like a lot of the decisions I'd made when I'd lived in Kansas, I hadn't put much thought into things beyond what promised the most "feel good" in the moment. Gradually, I started to see things differently.

The students in the bar were making risky choices that could adversely affect the rest of their lives. I'd done the legwork. They were the kind of smart kids who'd intimidated me when I first moved to town. So why were they doing the same dumb things I did? Observing people getting trashed and stumbling around began to bother me, even though I was still doing the same thing myself more nights than not.

I wish I could say there was some lightbulb moment and that the epiphany solved everything. But life doesn't work that way. Not my life, at least.

Eventually, the value my dad's effort, decisions, and determination brought to his life and to others' lives became impossible to ignore. Recognizing the utter futility of my world in comparison was a slower journey for me. To this day, I scratch my head at how long it took for the others-focused direction of my dad's new choices to rub off on me.

One of my moments of "enlightenment" came because one of the bars I worked at had a "No fat women are allowed to dance on the bars or stage" policy. The management vigorously enforced it.

One slower-than-normal night, a bunch of girls who were obviously friends (lots of smiles, coordinated moves, and chatting nonstop with each other) were up on one of the bars getting their groove on. One of the girls was heavier than the rest, but I hadn't had the heart to hurt her feelings and tell her to get down. When my boss noticed, though, he stood in front of the dancing girls, his arms folded and resting over his massive beer gut, and then pointed to the heaviest of the dancers and bellowed, "Austin! Go get that fat girl down. We don't want her up there."

The last thing I wanted to do was hurt that girl, but like the coward I was at the time, I walked over and told the heavier girl that management wanted her down. When she asked why, I lied and said, "One of the dicks in management must not like you or something." The look on her face as she climbed down haunted me for a long time. I knew better than anyone what it felt like to be publicly singled out. No one should ever be humiliated like that.

What was I doing with my life?

I'd finally had enough of seeing smart people do dumb things—and joining in most nights as part of the herd.

My contact with the "bar" friends I'd made tapered off. I realized they'd call only when they wanted to get into a club for free. I would text or call them and wouldn't hear back. It hurt badly once I accepted that they'd never been real friends at all. Déjà vu sucks, man.

My coworkers turned out not to be friends either. They were mostly losers who didn't hesitate to do whatever it took to get something they wanted. When I was seeing a girl, and she was waiting for me to finish cleaning up after a shift so I could give her ride home, one of the other guys would be right there, doing and saying whatever he could to try and get my girl to leave with him instead. It never worked, but I'd been betrayed all the same. It was personal, at least to me. The other guys—what did they care? It all made me not want to care either, but I couldn't quite get to that point. I was ready to knock the hell out of the next one of the sons of bitches who tried it.

I was right back in the soup, pursuing phony bullshit instead of real relationships, no loyalty; in a pinch, it was every man for himself. Maybe they were flaky and didn't have my best interest at heart. Or, more likely, never really thought of me at all. But I would have done anything for those guys.

Who feels that deeply for people who are only using them?

I could sense my anger building to levels I hadn't experienced since I'd moved to Iowa.

Early one Sunday morning, I walked back to my car after helping close the bar, raging inside about something one of my so-called friends had done to dis me. I was getting into my car and pulled off my black staff shirt. I'd managed to spill a drink on it and didn't want to smell like booze all the way home. As I was getting in my car, an inebriated guy with three girls walked up, taunting, "Ha, ha!! Look at this idiot! He thinks he's Rambo or some shit."

My body was rock solid from working out every day. I looked good, and I knew it. And I wasn't in the mood that morning to put up with any shit. "Get in your car, and get the hell out of here before I beat your ass. I am not screwing with you tonight, homie!"

The girls tried to get the guy to shut up, but he kept running his mouth, walking closer. "You ain't gonna do shit, bitch."

One of the girls yelled, "Come on!"

But before she could get the guy out of there, I'd smashed my fist into the left side of his jaw, knocking him out cold.

"I'm calling the police!" The girl began dialing.

I ripped her phone out of her hands and threw it off the side of the parking garage we were standing in. "Go ahead and call the police, sweetheart."

"Way to go, Austin," I ranted at myself as I drove off. "You've come full circle, man."

I'd moved hundreds of miles away from the negativity of my Kansas life, but it had followed me. It was still inside me. I was still doing everything I could think of to make certain that Austin was in my life forever.

Kevin: Drowning in Best Intentions

I'd been told to enjoy my first year of the doctoral program—it would get much more challenging as I advanced.

My first semester hadn't been so bad. The coursework was challenging—the Iowa faculty demanded a lot, but that's why I was there. I could do this. We're talking eighty-hour weeks of class, study, research, and the two jobs I was holding down to pay for it all. It was exhausting. But, really, I could do this. Then, in December, one week before semester's end, Austin was on his way to live with me.

I was committed to helping my son, grateful he'd called for help again. I'd hoped for so long that I'd have this second chance. But could we really do this, smack-dab in the middle of one of the greatest challenges I'd ever faced? Getting my PhD was a dream, a slow build I'd been pursuing for years. And now that it was crunch time, things were about to become astronomically more complicated.

Not taking Austin in and doing everything I could for him never crossed my mind. Like so many other parents of troubled young men, I'd stretch myself as far as I could to help my kid straighten out his life. But reality was reality. And the reality was, I already had a few strikes working against me. My reading disability made studying and research take longer to complete than for my brilliant classmates. And my "out of class" work schedule was already a bitch.

I'd just have to work harder, that's all.

Ah, sweet denial — my defense mechanism of choice.

It was all good, I convinced myself.

Austin would hit the ground running. My drive to better myself would be contagious. In no time he'd follow my lead, jump into school, make high-quality friends, and change his life for good this time. We could handle this new change together.

It was delusional thinking.

But sometimes a little delusion is exactly what we need to shove away from the cliff yawning before us.

I had a month to help Austin settle in and get started before my second semester began.

A whole month.

We talked a lot more than Austin's stories show. About first steps, mostly. Lots and lots of "I don't know, Dad." It didn't take long for me to realize that it wasn't in the cards—Austin jumping into a fresh start, taking healthy risks for a change, and envisioning a better life. Not right away.

My son was still frozen by fear—of screwing up and rejection, and basically of life always being as bad as it had always been. He was scared to death. I'd been oblivious to the extent of the psychological, social, and emotional problems imprisoning him. And it didn't help that his internal dysfunction was pretty much the polar opposite of his physical appearance.

At twenty-one, Austin was six feet, two inches, and 225 pounds of solid muscle. He worked relentlessly on his outer image. The world could never know how certain he was that he'd never fit in, *never* be accepted—not a misfit like him. His tough-guy image had survived his teenage meltdowns. And I could sense his clinging to it as if it was all he had left.

Those core inadequacies kept surfacing, telling him he was nothing and never would amount to anything no matter what I or anyone else saw or said.

Motivation *isn't* for dummies.

For the previous two decades, my son had lived a predominately rural life in a farming community. His role models were stoic, hardworking men like his grandfather. *Tough* was good. *Weak* meant you were a loser. And let's face it, many of my early parenting choices had done their part to reinforce that self-image.

> *The walls my son had built around his emotions were as impenetrable as iron.*

Mine, on the other hand, were buckling under the strain of knowing that if Austin didn't make some serious changes soon, I'd lose him to prison or worse. His poor choices were rapidly escalating to a level where death wasn't an unreasonable outcome.

I'd once thought that my white-collar, money-chasing lifestyle would influence him to want the same for his life. Instead, the environment in which he'd grown up in Kansas had formed who he'd become. So far. But now he was back, living with me. And—please, God—we were starting over from scratch.

I needed to set a new, better example—one full of consideration and alternatives rather than following the instincts that had propelled my son so far off course. No lectures this time. I was no expert. Austin needed a teammate whose lead he could follow. I jumped into the game, trading in my coach's whistle and clipboard for a jersey.

It wasn't as if I had my life altogether either. I was five months into an unknown journey that scared me to death. I was lonely too. All my friends were in Kansas City. I was an old man compared to my classmates. Even if Austin couldn't see it, we had a lot in common. Except I'd lived life's ups and downs long enough to believe I could and would come out the other side of my challenge a better, wiser man.

Somehow that was the hope-filled message I had to get my son to see.

*An intense young man moved in with me in Iowa City, all
scowls and cutting, sarcastic comments when we first began
talking.*

I was determined to model empathy and compassion toward
him and everyone else. I worked with the homeless, walking
alongside some of the bravest individuals you'll ever meet. Some
of their stories were heartbreaking. Careful not to break confiden-
tiality, I shared with Austin the generalities about certain individuals I'd meet.

I hoped he'd see that others faced overwhelming struggles
too, some far worse than his. I also hoped some of my compassion for those whose life had been harder than mine would make
an impact on my son. I regularly expressed my gratitude for the
benefits and security of the life I'd been born into.

*Each time my son listened to one of my stories and stuck
around to talk about what it all meant to me, it felt as if I'd
scored a game-winning touchdown.*

Those weren't the earth-shattering aha moments parents
dream of having with their teens and young adults, but we were
making definite progress.

And I'd been wrong in the past—a lot. I made certain he knew
that I knew it.

I tried to be an example of continued growth.

I shared how opinions I'd once held as absolute, I now viewed
with uncertainty. I'd once thought homeless individuals were
lazy. After researching and hearing their stories in person, I was
ashamed by how ignorant I'd been. We talked about becoming
more flexible in the way he thought too, and about challenging
any convictions that didn't feel right, and about how the only reason he was clinging to them was because he'd been told to.

*There weren't a lot of lightbulb moments between us, but he
kept listening.*

He got to see the worst parts of me, parts I wasn't done working through.

I guess the message there was that none of us is really done.

Every Saturday night around eight o'clock, after an eighty-hour week, I'd start my second job, connecting remotely from the apartment computer. Those were grueling, losing-my-cool nights, often with me cussing and slamming papers around. Once, I broke the glass in a picture frame on my desk. Some model of calm and reasoned coping under stress, right?

Austin was in the living room watching TV. "Dad, are you going all Charles Manson in there?"

I started laughing and apologized, taking responsibility for my bad behavior and not caring that my son had called me out on it. In fact, we had a short conversation about the importance of work-life balance—focused solely at me this time.

On another Sunday night, my son walked by my small closet of an office next to the kitchen. I'd been working all weekend, and he poked his head in, a smart-alecky grin on his face. "Have you taken a shower this weekend?" he asked, making me laugh.

My son saw me fail, too.

One of those times was me coming up short on an important exam.

It was nearly the end of another semester, and I was more exhausted and burned out than I'd ever been. I was spending weekends driving the 325 miles back and forth to Kansas City to care for my ailing parents. When I did have time to study, I wasn't retaining anything. Nothing would stick, so I failed the exam.

This was a doctoral program. You don't fail exams and move forward, so I'd have to retake it. I clearly recall self-medicating with ice cream while lying on the couch and staring mindlessly at the television. Except the next thing I knew, I woke up to my saying the f-word over and over into the empty ice cream container, using every possible variation in my arsenal.

When Austin arrived home after his afternoon classes, I was still moping on the couch. "You okay, Dad?"

I told him what had happened. He sat down and talked *me* through my meltdown this time. At least he listened as I talked and talked. I needed help, I realized.

"I think I need to see my psychologist," I admitted. "I need to work through some of what I am going through." I never hid it from my son, the times when I couldn't sort through overwhelming responsibilities on my own.

I tried to live by the principles I was challenging my son to adopt.

I wanted him to have empathy and compassion for himself and others, so I dealt with the ugliness inside me. Austin had witnessed the impatient, dismissive me of the past. That was part of where he'd learned to behave like an ass when challenged or frustrated or just plain bored. I've worked hard to forgive myself for that. Now there was no way I was hiding the worst of me from a young man who only saw the worst in himself. Besides, Austin was smart enough (and we were close enough by then) to have seen through any excuses I tried to hide behind.

> *I believe in redemption. With very few exceptions, I believe most everyone should be given the opportunity to change — without persecution.*

In the small community my son had left behind, Austin had been labeled by many, including relatives, as a troublemaker, a fighter, and a downright cruel human being. Even as his behavior dramatically improved, some who'd known him for a long time continued to dwell on his past failings.

He had to know I still had work to do, just as he still had work to do. He had to see the potential I still saw in myself regardless of my flaws, the same as I glimpsed the goodness in his heart.

Austin knew how to love, and he was worried about his dad. So I kept talking to him about how I'd changed and needed to change even more. I'd failed him and his brother and a lot of other people, but no more. I could make different choices now, behave differently, and do better. And so could he.

> *I would show Austin that change was possible—by first dealing with myself.*

WHAT HAPPENED?

There are some key themes in the stories Austin and I share in this step.

I ask you to look past the "college roommates" element of how we were living (a father and son doing the best they could under difficult circumstances). There was a method to my madness that I'd like to break down for you in a bit more detail.

From the Psychologist

I made time for my son when I had no time to give him.

In return, he made himself available to me—honestly talking to me (as best he could at the time), perhaps for the first time in his life. Our conversations were occasionally superficial—watching football on the TV or something—but there was deep and meaningful connecting going on too. Plus laughter.

> *Early on, it's entirely possible that the laughter we shared was the most healing thing going on between us.*

When he was particularly down, I made certain to share my fears and concerns too, instead of only focusing on him. We were in this game together. No matter how bad things got, I wasn't losing hope. Neither would he, not as long as I was around. And I would always be there for him.

Our kids aren't just smart, they're streetwise.

They'll smell any BS we toss at them from a mile away. They're also not going to connect with a theoretical lecture. What's happening to them is real and day-to-day terrifying. So I connected with my son by being honest about my own out-of-control reality. I opened up to him about my fears.

I did whatever I could to be authentically relatable.

I talked to him about dreaming.

When he struggled and felt he was making no progress, I'd ask him about his dreams for the future. He couldn't name a single one. So I told him about one of mine: to become writer who motivated others to make significant psychological changes in their lives.

"And, what if," I said, "we were to someday write a book together about being college roommates who both changed their lives?"

That dream is the book you now hold in your hands.

There's a time to gently push and a time to wait and watch and have faith in the journey.

Sometimes we still need to push our maturing kids out of their comfort zones—for example, when I pushed Austin to enroll in junior college when I could tell his confidence and conviction were lagging. There are other times, though, when it's essential that your teen or young adult chooses to take that next step on his own.

When Austin arrived in Iowa, he was quite simply paralyzed—hardly ever leaving the house, hanging out in his room playing video games, etc. The first week he was there, I was preoccupied completing papers and finals. We had conversations during the week about next steps and the options of finding a job or going to school, but no action was taken. After a week of that, we began talking more. He had to outrun his past, and we agreed he wouldn't repeat the behavior that had, during our Kansas City days, led him to fall back into his old, destructive habits.

He was depressed, lacked motivation, and believed he'd messed up so badly he might never recover. Beneath that tough persona was a frightened little boy still trapped and broken and out of options. I couldn't afford to push too hard, but I couldn't enable him, either, by allowing him to sit around the apartment and do nothing.

It's a difficult balance, knowing when to push your child to grow, and when to stop pushing so he can feel safe and supported while he finds his own way.

We talked about the pros and cons of getting an education versus taking another full-time factory job—discussing that he was more than capable of succeeding in school if he agreed to take a different approach to college than he had high school.

When he agreed to visit that college adviser, he was out of his comfort zone. But beneath his resistance, I glimpsed excitement. And I knew that if he didn't enroll soon, he'd have to wait another five or six months before the summer session started. Getting it done that day was a symbol of movement and hope. It seemed right. So I leaned into pushing him to enroll to help him secure the chance he'd said he wanted to better himself.

This time it had nothing to do with me. If it had merely been about what I thought he should do or about making him live up to my expectations, college wouldn't have worked any more successfully than high school had. I trusted that there was no way Austin would have enrolled in college if he hadn't, to some degree, *trusted* me.

Trust was a huge milestone for us, requiring a great deal of patience on my part.

You may be wondering about all that partying my son was doing and how much studying he accomplished at the same time. So was I. Meanwhile, I was working eighty-plus hours a week. I could have blown my stack and demanded he shape up. I was in a position of power, and it was within the realm of reason for me to assert some control over the situation before he screwed up again.

But that approach would have completely undermined all the work we had accomplished together. And remember, there was no longer anything in Austin's life that involved my control. So, in that instance, I continued talking about goals and plans and dreams. I kept our exchanges frank but open and positive. And over time, we learned to trust each other more.

Maintaining a long-term perspective is key.

Austin's trusting himself to truly start over in Iowa was a slow process.

It was tempting for both of us to expect immediate change. But through my own healing journey, I knew that kind of growth takes time. If the changes my son needed to make were limited to responsibility and independence, I would have pushed him harder to get a job. But we'd already been down that road. There were underlying issues we couldn't afford to overlook this time.

Austin needed to make deep, transformative changes to how he viewed himself, others, and his future. The long-term goal was for him to realize his maximum potential—and to believe that the future of his dreams was attainable.

I looked first for maturity in his thought process.

Our kids are good at telling us what we want to hear. Look for consistency in thoughts and behaviors rather than mere lip service to what they want to improve. Is their behavior trending upward? Are there fewer steps back than forward, and is the overall momentum of their work on themselves and their approach to interacting with their world moving in a "net" positive direction?

Slow but significant changes to look for include:

- Showing compassion toward others.
- Gaining insight into the core emotional motivation behind past mistakes.
- Changing behavior because he knows it's right.
- Exhibiting conviction to make consistently better choices, because they will improve his life and relationships.

Falling down merely means getting back up again.

Austin got into a physical altercation, exposing himself to an assault charge, when he busted the nose of some skinhead harassing one of his gay friends. I was furious when I found out. Fuming. Why the hell couldn't he just stay out of trouble?

But a part of me was proud of my son.

He and I had grown up in the same area. He'd overcome a lot of prejudices to make the stand he had. While his actions were wrong, his heart had been in the right place. When the Iowa City police arrested him, he didn't ask me to post bail. I did that on my own. I was still angry, and we talked at length about the anger management and better decision-making he had to master if he wanted to make a new life for himself. But I shared that I admired his compassion for the young man he'd been defending—and how much change I saw in Austin for him to have done what he did in such a public way. Eventually, the charges were dropped.

Then there was the morning I woke up to find the following letter waiting for me in my tiny office:

A Year Today

A year ago today my father blessed me with the opportunity to move from Kansas to Iowa City, Iowa. Anyone reading this will already be able to understand what a mess I was and how much I hated my hometown. I remember crying as I crossed the state line, not because Nebraska is such an emotionally moving region to drive through but because I was scared to death about leaving everything I had ever known in order to create the kind of life I wanted.

I remember how scared, depressed, and hopeless I felt during the first month of being an Iowan. I was scared to even drive around the block for fear that someone would discover me and my botched past. If I made eye contact with someone, it felt as if their gaze was burning a hole right through me. One could have almost smelled the insecurity and shame on me as they walked by.

It makes me want to break down and cry when I think of how my father took time out of his busy schedule in order to keep guiding me in the right direction. He is in the Counseling Psychology doctoral program at the University of Iowa; that's not some kind of lightweight degree. That's elite. No matter how great the amount of energy-consuming work Dad had in front of him, he always took time to talk with me and keep me pointed in the right direction.

After each talk we had, I walked away feeling loved and cared about. He gave me hope; my father, Kevin Fall, gave me my life back. As I say all of this, I do understand that I failed to mention the thousands of dollars that Dad spent on me. All he asked in return was for me to stay on the journey and keep moving forward while growing. I will look any man on the face of this earth in the eye with confidence and proudly tell him that Kevin Fall is the greatest father who ever lived, hands down.

I have plenty of friends up here in Iowa now. I go to Hawkeye football games, stand in the student section, and yell my tail off! I hang out with friends, go on dates, and kiss pretty Hawkeye girls all the time. I have great confidence in anything I do. The difference between now and then is night and day.

In saying all of that, I want whoever may read this to understand: there is not a day that goes by that I don't thank God for my father and take a little bit of time to appreciate all the things he has done for me. I am the luckiest son in the world. It's hard to imagine a year ago today.

Austin Checks In

The help my psychologist father provided me didn't come in the form of therapy.

Sure, we had some serious discussions, but what helped me most was his willingness to listen, his positive encouragement, and my observing the life he led. Living with him wasn't easy at first—not for a long time, actually. But whenever I needed a listening ear, he lent one and provided constructive feedback.

When I needed an attitude adjustment, he was there for that, too. But he was no longer the angry, frustrated, negative disciplinarian he'd once been.

His life in Iowa was light-years from what I considered "normal" back home in rural Kansas. Unlike me, Dad didn't incessantly drink, and he no longer swore much or made fun of others. He had a huge heart, and among the changes he'd made was sharing that heart with others as often as he could.

Dad quite simply loved people.

He was softer and more giving. He was more focused on what others were going through no matter how difficult and overwhelming and exhausting his schedule was.

I remember once, after I'd moved in with him, belittling someone who faced several disadvantages in life. The details are lost to me now, but I recall making several jokes at that person's expense. There was a time when my father might have laughed too. Now he looked down at the floor with a somber expression and said, "We sure do have a lot to be thankful for." And then he walked out of the room.

He didn't lecture me for my churlish, mean-spirited behavior.

But he was obviously disappointed. I immediately regretted what I'd said. If he'd yelled or screamed at me, I couldn't have felt any worse than I did after his few, softly spoken words about how grateful he was for everything we had in comparison to the person I'd been ridiculing.

That moment, something inside me changed. Disappointing my father hurt so badly I began expecting better of myself, because he had first. I'd once felt so down and out I'd contemplated suicide. And there my father had been; there he still was, giving all the energy it required to pull myself out of my tailspin. Who did I think I was, ragging on someone else for where their life had taken them?

The next time I saw someone out of control or crumbling into their own black pit, you better believe I stopped and felt thankful for all I'd been given. The next thought that came to mind was, rather than making fun, wondering if there was anything I could do to help.

WHAT TO DO?

Kevin: Our Parenting Choices Must Encourage Engagement, NOT Disconnection

Once your teen or young adult engages and commits to making the needed changes in his life, he must take ownership of whatever decisions are made next.

However, a great deal of his early success in these crucial next steps will depend on how *you* handle yourself as a parent while you walk alongside, joining in on this still unsettling, often terrifying journey.

FIRST: Walk the walk.

If our troubled kids "check out," it's game over. Again. Possibly for good this time.

If they think we're full of shit, they won't respect or trust us enough to listen when we try to engage and discuss their plans for the future. We have to own our stuff. And we must openly take responsibility (including apologizing and/or seeking the help we need) before our son will respect our opinion about how and why he should deal with *his* stuff.

If we have anger issues, he likely does too. Our teen or young adult often shares our prejudices and our tendencies toward substance abuse as well as our difficulties accepting constructive criticism and responsibility for the negative consequences of our actions.

> *We must have patience to teach patience, and we must share empathy and insight in order to inspire the same, and we must care about and work deeply on our own flaws if we are to understand and impact the underlying causes of our child's behavioral difficulties.*

Our lack of insight as parents *will* have a negative impact on our relationship with our troubled child.

> *We must take advantage of every opportunity to lead by example.*

We must work on our own destructive coping behaviors and decision-making patterns our kids are likely emulating. This calls for brutal honesty about ourselves. And then for compassion and empathy for our troubled sons. For example, the next time your son makes a mistake, pull back when you're tempted to launch into another "controlling" lecture about how he should smarten up. Take your own advice, start living your life "right," and then encourage him to follow suit.

SECOND: Treat your son as if he's fully capable of achieving his goals.

Austin wanted what we all want: success and healthy friendships and a promising future.

Instead he was living a defensive life with the primary goal of not being humiliated. He felt worthless, so he lived as if nothing he did had any worth, regardless of how hard he tried. The chasm between the success he wanted and what little he'd achieved so far in his life created so much discomfort it was all too easy to quit trying, given the slightest possibility that he might fail again.

> *Until your teen or young adult learns how to believe he can be successful, it is your job to believe for him.*

Fear paralyzes. Your son is afraid of making the wrong decisions and of failing. Something as simple as leaving the house wearing new clothes someone might think are the "wrong" clothes can stop him in his tracks, let alone deciding whether or not to go back to school or get a job. Forget about strategizing which courses to take or which type of work is right for him.

He doesn't know how to trust himself. To "get better," he must experience life in a healthy way. He still needs to learn what other kids learned when they were much younger: how to live in the moment rather than see the world only through the lens of past mistakes. He must embrace his latent potential and the possibility that he can indeed succeed at whatever he puts his whole heart into accomplishing.

As parents, it's essential we model a more successful approach.

Your teen or young adult must NOT see you anticipating threats with every turn they take. When he takes a tentative step toward growth, you need to project a calm confidence that he will succeed rather than worry he might once again be humiliated. You must encourage independence rather than project unrelenting fear in the face of each challenging decision and potentially risky choice your son makes.

Your goal: to reflect to your teen or young adult that he is most definitely becoming a fully functioning human being.

In the latter half of the twentieth century, psychologist Carl Rogers offered a great tool I recommend to the parents I work with: the *self-actualization* approach, which any parent can utilize, even those not seeking clinical support from a therapist.

As you work to reflect all you believe your child is capable of, try these self-actualization tools:

Tool		Goal
Be genuinely warm when dealing with your son, embracing his current situation and him as he is.	Your son craves your parental love and acceptance.	**Fulfill your son's "attachment need" and basic desire to be in a loving relationship.** Despite his past mistakes, be his safe place to land and feel good (as well as to explore and trust he will be okay regardless of the outcome).
Support your son's choices.	Your son desires to be valued and honored. He values what you think of him, often even more than he cares what his friends think.	**Build your son's trust that (as long as he's making healthy choices) he will be okay regardless of any short-term setbacks.** Confirm that you will always be okay with him, despite the mistakes he will likely still make (because we all do from time to time).
Whenever possible, share your approval of a decision's outcome— even risky choices and/ or those decisions which end in some degree of failure.	Your son longs for your unconditional support and acceptance, relying on it to bolster his confidence as he learns to support and accept his potential to succeed.	**Be his safe place to land and regroup and "war game" or brainstorm what went right (or wrong).** Be a calm, nonanxious presence as he works through what he may have done differently, as well as his plans for the future.

THIRD: Stop the downward spiral.

It is likely at times that your son is incapable of differentiating between what he thinks and reality.

Remember, for example, how Austin spoke of being angry from the moment he woke up each morning, how he didn't believe anyone in his new "college" town would accept him, and how he at first chose friends who were "not real" and "fake," because he thought that was the only kind relationship he could attract. He was anticipating these types of threats in his new life in Iowa, so these threats became realities he projected into his life.

Paul Gilbert, an expert in the area of emotional defense systems and creator of *Compassion Focused Therapy*, talks about how these "perceived threats" interfere with our sons' ability to solve problems, gain objective insight about situations, and successfully regulate their emotions.

> *In short, at times your son is NOT experiencing his world as it really is. Instead, he is overwhelmed dealing with perceived threats and his compulsion to defend himself.*

When this happens, his fight-or-flight response is out of context with his current reality.

Parents working with their child to counteract this powerful, long-held instinct face a significant challenge. The very act of trying to help can potentially place us in the role of perceived threat. That is why it is so vital you do the work in Steps One, Two, and Three of our seven-step game plan. Before you can successfully reflect a more positive outlook on your son's life, his options, and his potential to have the lasting, meaningful success and relationships he dreams of, you must first redefine your relationship with your son.

In addition to that firm foundation, try the following approaches to counter your son's fight-or-flight instinct and, as a result, help redirect his self-view away from where he's been and toward the successful man he wants to become:

- Create a relaxing, soothing home environment free of threats.
- Project love, warmth, and acceptance in your interactions.
- Offer compassion to counter any perception that you oppose the changes he's attempting to make (or are judging the not-always-successful outcomes he's achieved so far).

FOURTH: Get in the game.

Letting go of the formality of your role as parent (as we've discussed, joining your son in the game as an on-the-field-leader rather than coaching from the sidelines) will help him develop a much greater respect for you—and for himself.

None of us has life figured out. Make certain he knows *you* know that. Also, get right with yourself and with him about who is in control when it comes to your son making permanent changes in his life. And the answer to that question is, unequivocally, him. Ultimately, your son is the only one who can change his situation.

Given what you've been through as a parent, these are advanced perspectives of your relationship with your son. It takes a great deal of faith to get yourself where you need to be so you can, in turn, lead your son.

> *Ultimately, your goal is to allow* him *the chance to see you as the more experienced player and then wait for him to seek out your experience as an asset in his journey toward a better life.*

Trust that your son will recognize, respect, and rely on the new, deeper relationship the two of you have formed. Be patient, practicing with all the tools and techniques you have learned so far, and you will find yourself in a position of tremendous power and influence.

No longer will you have to try to gain his attention. He will begin to offer information about his life and even seek your thoughts, opinions, advice, and support.

Shifting your role from "coach" to "teammate" transforms your relationship dynamic to one of influence and respect.

FIFTH: Model the behavior you expect.

Your son is looking for a leader. That leader can be one of his peers, an adult he meets elsewhere in his life, or it can be you.

The flip side of your newfound influence in your son's reality is that he is watching how you think and act. Embrace the reality of your own problems. Face what still needs work in your life, and take the extra step of discussing with your son how "normal" it is to have problems. If you want to give your child a real boost, consider from time to time asking *him* for advice whenever you genuinely think he can contribute to your latest challenge or goal.

Normalizing problems, making them a shared reality, generates even more trust, as well as your son's hope that he can work through his issues, the same as you do your issues.

The goal is for the two of you to begin talking each other through various options, potential outcomes, successes, and even failures on your way to improving your separate and shared lives.

Be engaged on the same field of play as your teen or young adult. Make certain he knows you respect all he is doing and going through because you're in the trenches too.

NOTE: While sharing the difficulties of your life, you don't want to overshare your problems and create an additional burden for your son to carry. Carefully select the challenges you choose to relate to your son.

The following will help you stay focused on a positive, healing message:

- Reveal weakness while at the same time modeling confidence in being able to work with your flaws.
- Reflect that there is no shame whatsoever for men (or women) to have problems or to need help dealing with challenges.
- Tolerate your own issues and deal with them calmly and constructively, being flexible with yourself as you work through them.
- Model active and proactive problem-solving as you strive to achieve better results.
- Talk authentically about your hopes and dreams despite the challenges you face—particularly if the issues you've chosen to discuss (or the dream you're struggling to achieve) parallel those of your son.
- Make a point of sharing the disappointments and roadblocks you face along the way, encouraging your son to help you talk through a situation in which you're emotionally exposed (and in which you trust him not to humiliate or shame you with his reaction).

Above all else, remember that not everything should be disclosed to your son.

Authenticity does not entail offering your son an unrestricted view of your inner life.

Some things should remain private. For example, it would have been inappropriate for me to have shared that Austin coming to live with me was almost more than I could handle. I lost sleep worrying about him. Much of my very limited free time was spent helping him—none of which he needed to know, and none of which I would have changed, not for a minute.

Never forget that you are the parent.

Your child should never be made to feel as if he must help you get through your day or he is a burden to you. As the adult in the relationship, you have other avenues through which you can receive the support you need: friends, counseling, etc. Restrict personal revelations to those most constructive to and appropriate for your son.

A Note from Austin about Dads and the Things They Say

There were still many days when I felt gloomy and unsure of myself.

But my father went out of his way to encourage me with truthful, positive messages.

Whenever self-doubt crept in, he had my back. There were many discussions when he'd say the equivalent of "Austin, you're a smart, capable man worthy of greatness. There's nothing you can't do, but I need you to believe in yourself."

He wasn't a "helicopter parent," hovering and stepping between me and my choices or the consequences that came my way (good and bad) because of them. If he had been, I wouldn't have listened. We'd have ended up with a result similar to when I moved in with him in Kansas City. But don't think he let me off the hook about important things, either.

My party-to-study ratio was a recurring topic of conversation.

When it got too one-sided (tilting heavily toward partying rather than taking care of my responsibilities at school), he'd engage. I always knew when something was bothering him. He would calmly say, "Hey, Aus, could we talk for a second?"

He didn't chew my ass or jump down my throat. He knew I'd dig in and refuse to consider his suggestions if he did. Instead, he talked to me, one man to another, about the opportunities we both had to learn and grow into who we wanted to become. This was a guy who was dedicating himself to empowering others and nearly killing himself to get there (and to help me on top of everything else). So, yeah, eventually, some of what he was saying got through. Including, once again, that I had unlimited potential if I'd only decide to dig into the work necessary to achieve the dreams I had for my life.

It was tough to believe him at first.

And he was right when he told me that breaking bad habits doesn't happen overnight. I struggled, and so did he from time to time. But we always found a way to apologize to each other, to support each other, and to keep moving forward together, until eventually I made the conscious decision to believe with all my heart what he'd tried so hard to demonstrate.

> *I learned how to own all those gently, honestly delivered words as my own reality. I really was smart and intrinsically valuable, just as my dad promised.*

WHAT'S MOST IMPORTANT?

We've covered a lot in the last two chapters.

We've moved from reestablishing your relationship with your troubled teen to achieving his commitment to change and leading him as he finally pursues a more positive path. And by now, it should be clear that the best way for you to help is by modeling the approach and changes and behavioral choices he must learn to be successful in his own life.

Now is a good time to review the key areas you need to focus on as you work to show your son a more positive life approach.

Your Parent Playbook

> *Your Step Four goal is to support your teen or young adult and to model positive change he can emulate as he takes control and begins to realize his maximum potential.*

To do this, you must:

- Reflect your confidence that he can achieve a successful future.
- Help him believe that both his fresh start and his dreams are 100-percent attainable if he's willing to bust his butt to work for what he wants.

The following table summarizes several key areas on which to focus as you modify *your* behavior and life approach and place yourself on the field, accepted into your son's journey in a position of influence and support.

Model	Consider	Goal
Self-Awareness	Many troubled young men have difficulty regulating their emotions. Even the slightest problem can become overwhelming, causing them to act out simply because they cannot tolerate the feelings they are experiencing. Perceived threats also frequently cause emotional outbursts. Becoming more self-aware of feelings helps the individual create a space between behavioral triggers and the resulting reaction.	**Illustrate for your son how to make positive, successful decisions even while experiencing sometimes extreme emotional pain or conflict.** **For example:** I talked with Austin about feeling overwhelmed by my workload. At times I even lost my cool. But then I apologized (as needed), pulled myself together before the hopelessness took over, and refocused on my long-term goals. Instead of giving up, I discussed and worked through how to approach things differently, and then I implemented my new plan.

Model	Consider	Goal
Flexible Thinking	Your son, like many others, may interact with his world from a very black-and-white perspective. Young people preoccupied with perceived threats either feel safe or they don't. People are either trying to humiliate them, leave them, reject them, or they are not. It is difficult for your teen or young adult to embrace the value of processing multiple perceptions of the same event or relationship.	**Offer examples of how your son can think in more complex ways.** **For example:** Austin and I regularly discussed being angry with someone we loved. This was an important growth point for someone who vacillated back and forth between the impulses to reconnect with old friends and wanting to beat the living hell out of those who'd betrayed him. And yet he knew how angry I had once been with him, while at the same time I loved him enough to welcome him to live with me again and to support him in every way I could. The more we talked and the more I modeled dealing with our at-times strained situation, the more confident Austin became as he dealt with his own internal conflicts.

Model	Consider	Goal
Dealing with Risk	Another problem for those preoccupied with perceived threats is that their "comfort zone" begins shrinking to reduce the likelihood of their being exposed. Your teen or young adult may become risk averse to the extreme, to the extent of refusing to attempt any of the steps needed to achieve his goals. He'd rather do nothing if it means not failing. If there's no guarantee, why even try? It's better not to take the risk.	**Encourage your son to expand his comfort zone.** **For example:** When Austin first arrived in Iowa, he rarely left the apartment. He feared being humiliated by others who learned his story. He did nothing and went nowhere. I began talking to him about the risk I took walking away from my consulting career to pursue a PhD in psychology. We talked about putting everything on the line for your dreams and about the steps I'd taken to bring mine to life. I talked about trusting intuition and prayer and about aligning my dreams with what I felt God would want and expect of me. "What is failure?" we discussed. "What is the worst that could happen?" If my dream as an author and speaker happened not to work out, I would spend the rest of my life feeling honored to be helping individuals in therapy. And at least I'd know I tried.

Model	Consider	Goal
A Healthy Relationship	Self-disclosure and trust are reciprocal. You get what you give, and it's likely your son has been burned one too many times by people who've betrayed or hurt him when he most needed someone to turn to. It is easy as parents to damage our teen's or young adult's trust and to not be aware we've done so. It's simply part of being an imperfect parent. Because of the trouble he's made for himself and others, he likely feels he's not worthy of anyone's time, including yours.	**Prove to your son that, while your current relationship is far from perfect and you might still become angry with him, you will always respond from a place of preserving and improving your relationship. Make certain he knows your love is a "forever" thing.** Boundaries and expectations are essential (yours for and with him; his for and with you). However, show your son through your behavioral choices how to respond to conflict in nonemotional, productive ways that respect the other person while reasserting your expectations. **For example:** On numerous occasions, Austin and I discussed my concerns about his partying all hours. Each time, however, I kept my response to the point and focused on the expectations we'd set for his behavior and choices. And without fail, each of these discussions proved productive.

Model	Consider	Goal
Help Seeking	The myth that real men (or strong people or people of "true" faith) do not ask for help is ludicrous. There were several times throughout graduate school when I needed help. My son would not have become the successful, compassionate, others-focused man he is today if he hadn't sought and accepted the help he needed once he finally chose to commit to making his life better.	**Emulate for your son your acceptance that you are not afraid or ashamed of seeking help when you need it.** **For example:** On several occasions, Austin expressed his concern for me and my health. His concerns were well-founded, and, in part, as a result of us talking, I made time to speak with my psychologist. Successful and strong people seek professional help and benefit from it. Do everything you can to help your teen or young adult see and accept this.

Model	Consider	Goal
Empathy for Others	"Troubled" kids tend to be more than a little rough around the edges. A lot of them have disconnected from not only their own emotions but from having feelings for and about others. And yet most of them, like Austin, possess kind, loving hearts they are protecting from the potential of more hurt. Shame-based individuals are overly "self-focused" out of their perceived need to protect themselves from more trouble and hurt. They are likely to think that no one else cares enough to help them, so their top priority is taking care of themselves.	**Reach through your son's emotional wall and help him get back in touch with his heart. Model the rewards of sharing your heart and love with others and, specifically, that you don't see this as a threat to your well-being.** **For example:** Without breaking confidentiality, I shared with Austin general stories about some of the homeless men I worked with. My care and concern for my clients made an impact on my son as he listened. I knew this for certain the day my son came home, steaming, after standing up for a homeless man downtown after a bunch of kids made fun of the guy.

And if talking isn't an easy thing for you . . .

I totally understand. I'm right there with you. Therapist or not, learning how to talk with my son and trusting that words alone would be enough (along with my living the kind of life I was asking Austin to live) was a huge leap of faith.

At first, most parents have a difficult time initiating these types of conversations. But once you step beyond your fear and vulnerability, powerful things will begin to happen in your relationship. Regardless of your teen's or young adult's reaction, have confidence. You are evolving into your greatest potential as a parent.

I had many a sleepless night wondering if I was doing the right thing, mining for faith, and obsessing over things I'd said, or what I should have said, and what I'd say next time. So I totally understand your reluctance. But here's the tough-love part, where I'm your coach for a moment. Whether it feels good or not, learning to talk more effectively and honestly with your son is a must. Whatever you say has to come from the heart. And the only way to get better at it is to practice.

Sometimes a good first step is to write your thoughts down. Think of this exercise as writing a letter to your son.

You may never give it to him. He may never read it. But there's something about putting your heart down on paper, spelling out how much you love your child and are trying to help him (no matter how many mistakes and missteps you both may make along the way). Once you release those truths into the world, you'll be surprised at how much more empowered you feel to make your hopes and dreams for your relationship a reality.

Below is a possible example of a letter I might have written to Austin once reality set in after he first moved to Iowa to live with me.

> *Aus,*
>
> *What we are both trying to do is not easy. We both left friends and familiar surroundings to start something new. We are both trying to change our lives in significant ways. Life change is difficult.*
>
> *Until you moved in, I was so lonely. I did not have any friends. I am starting to make a few I can trust and connect with at a deeper level, but it is not easy. I am afraid my future will not pan out the way I would like.*
>
> *Five years ago, I walked away from a well-paying career. I took a huge risk I will never be able to recover from if this doesn't work out the way I want it to. I basically gambled my career for a dream. If I stop and think about it, it scares the hell out of me.*

That is what you are doing as well: you left your past behind to embark on a new and unknown future. I know it's not easy. Like I said, if it were easy, a lot more people would do it.

I'm more grateful than I can say to have you here with me while we both find our way into the new lives we want for ourselves.

Love you,
Dad

Take heart . . .

Your son does not want to be where he is today. He is embracing the need for change even if he isn't yet making all the right choices to get him and his behavior where they need to be. He may not be happy with his current situation, but he *is* trying to improve it.

Your son is looking for a model, someone who is battle-tested and has "lived to survive" the same as he has.

Conversely, life as a parent is not a picnic either. You are a flawed person making your own mistakes.

It is the very struggles that mark you as a human being that will enable you to connect with and influence your son.

Engage him in authentic conversations about your problems and his. Ask for advice, discuss solutions, and demonstrate to your teen or young adult that you are in the game, fighting alongside him.

As a reward, you will increase your trustworthiness and credibility, and your son will soon feel safe enough to confide in you even more. You will become what he's looking for to help him map out the life of his dreams.

YOUR NEXT PLAY

The very hard work completed in this step has yielded promising improvements in your relationship with your teen or young adult and in your ability to influence his choices and behaviors. However, he is only beginning his long journey toward recovery and will need your guidance and support even more as you move forward working together as a team.

Your Game Plan in Step Four	Support your teen or young adult in his commitment to change, modeling the healthy behaviors and positive decision-making techniques he must employ to realize his maximum potential.
As a parent, you will continue to	reflect your confidence that he can achieve a successful future and help him believe that his dreams are 100-percent attainable as long as he's willing to fight for them.
Your teen is beginning to	work harder to reach his goals, though he may still be failing as much or more than he's succeeding. At times he is still making choices and exhibiting behaviors that interfere with him achieving his potential.
Your relationship dynamic is changing to	that of influence and respect, allowing you to talk openly with each other about options, potential outcomes, successes, and even failure. You are still the parent, gently and honestly holding him accountable for his decisions and behaviors. But yours is now a relationship of authentic trust.
Your Next Step	Help your son follow through on his commitment to change by dealing with the deeper problems underlying his continued poor choices and unsuccessful behavior.

STEP FIVE: DEAL WITH DEEPER PROBLEMS
Help Your Son Heal

Your Game-Plan Challenge	**Focus on your teen's or young adult's growth rather than expecting immediate, "magical" gains as he deals with the underlying emotional and psychological issues still causing him difficulty.**
You, the parent, are	authentically trusted by your teen or young adult, carefully listening to and reflecting back the thoughts, emotions, and needs he shares as he continues to heal.
Your teen or young adult is	appreciative of your efforts on his behalf and beginning to make good progress. However, he still struggles with his recovery—not yet capable of sustaining the *deeper* changes he must make to achieve his new, healthier goals.
Your relationship dynamic is	a true partnership, both of you feeling your way and at times continuing to make mistakes. However, your relationship and shared commitment is now in sync and propelling his recovery forward.
Your Goal for This Step	**Support your son's work on "deeper" issues, including securing the professional help he'll need to expand his recovery.**

There's always more to it.

Steps Three and Four took us through Austin's acceptance and commitment to how much he needed to change and my work as a parent to lead him, as a teammate, toward making better behavioral and life choices.

We've talked about modeling, the various stages of change, hitting rock bottom, and the necessity of troubled teens and young adults committing to the long climb back to being healthier. And, finally, we've discussed your role as a parent in dealing with *your* path while trusting that your son is capable of making the choices he must make to improve.

But as I mentioned in Step Three and again in Step Four, some issues facing your troubled teen or young adult may require more help than you can give him.

> *Without additional, professional help, many of our sons will not obtain the skills needed to sustain a healthier self-awareness, a positive life outlook, flexible thinking, and relationships needed to achieve permanent, enduring change.*

Our kids simply need more.

During Step Four's stories, Austin and I worked hard on our interpersonal relating and ability to work together as a team. But what we've yet to share is that, at the same time, my son was also working with a therapist to address various "core" issues holding him back; for example, the way he related to himself, his world, and others. Changes were needed in areas that were at the root of many of the poor behavior and life choices he continued to make.

> *Without additional, skillfully focused analysis and psychological help, my son would not have achieved the progress he made as a young man or the exciting successes he's realized since.*

THE PARENT-CHILD DISCONNECTION

There was so much more going on inside Austin, between the two of us, and beyond the stories being told in Step Four.

So we're taking you back into that same time frame and series of events, now viewed through a different lens. Hang with us a bit longer. With this pass, focus your attention on the "other" part of your journey with your teen or young adult as he commits to a new life.

Envision an even more powerful new beginning than you've thought possible—one no longer bound by mental health challenges at the root of so many of the seemingly inexplicable things your son has done (or, as in Austin's case, may still be doing even though he knows better and has every intention of stopping).

This is the big step you've been waiting for.

Imagine your son getting the help he needs.

Underlying all of Austin's (and likely your teen's or young adult's) troubling behaviors were mental health concerns. His addressing those problems and developing a new and healthier foundation became the cornerstone of the new life he went on to create.

Austin: Better Late Than Never

NOTE: Let me give you a little more history about some of my challenges before we march forward into talking about how I worked with my dad and my doctors to discover the solutions that best fit my situation.

I drank and partied my way through college, basically from the start of my stay with my dad in Iowa, but it wasn't about needing an escape—at least not from my junior-college coursework.

I was taking mostly 100-level courses back then (introductory, for incoming freshmen). The material wasn't difficult. From the start, my issues with completing my degree weren't going to be about the classes themselves.

I remember one of my first junior college friends inviting me over to his place to meet his roommates. When we all went out that night, I got so stinking drunk I pissed their sofa bed. The guys thought it was hilarious. Enter my new best buddies, with whom I spent most of my "hang-out" time (and a lot of time I could have spent on school) drinking as much as we could and creating even more "hilarious" memories.

I had lots of college friends. Check. I was social, attending Hawkeye football games like other students. Check, check. Mostly to tailgate. Hard. Like never-show-up-for-a-game-sober hard, because my "friends" in the student section were all doing the same thing. I learned to drink with the best of them. Triple check. I consumed so much liquor on football Saturdays it took me the entire following Sunday to sleep it off, and then some. Mondays were mostly about hangovers too. And I'd yelled myself so hoarse during games it was halfway to the following Friday before my voice recovered.

> *From day one, junior college as an educational pursuit took a backseat to my social life.*

I was handling myself better than I had in high school (I know, I know, that's not saying a lot). What I mean is, I went to class and did my homework. Okay, *sometimes* I showed up, mostly to find out who was going out later and to which bars. Still, picture me mentally patting myself on the back—at least this time I showed up.

But I wasn't enjoying learning. I turned in my assignments and put in the effort out of respect for my father because he'd paid for my classes. I finished that first semester with a 3.75 GPA. Not too shabby, right? Only, imagine what I might have accomplished if I'd put any effort into the experience besides going through the motions, or at least if I'd figured out how to function effectively on a college campus in classes that would eventually get harder as I progressed through my degree.

All that I've described above, every dysfunctional bit, followed me when I made the switch and enrolled at the University of Iowa—everything *except* for my effortless success with my coursework. The university-level academic requirements awaiting me were light-years more challenging and demanding.

I majored in English at the University of Iowa because I hated math and avoided it at all costs.

My mind simply operated differently than numbers wanted it to, and my ADHD added to that disconnect. It was all crap, anyway, right? What did it matter what my major was?

Except, literature majors get buried under homework, and before long I couldn't keep up. There was so much required reading I'd have had to take a book with me every time I went to the restroom just to keep up with the sheer volume. It was excruciating.

But the one thing that never suffered was my partying, which I shared in great detail in Step Four. There was never a lack of friends wanting to go out and raise hell with me, a new kid from nowhere. How could I say no to that? Even if it meant heading to a bar across from campus to get a few drinks in between classes.

Sure, drinking and partying like a rock star was a distraction.

But it was a welcome diversion for a guy who was merely rope-a-doping through each day without hope.

And speaking of distractions, let's spend a moment talking about the girls I met downtown.

I met plenty while I was partying, and each was this amazing "new" shot of validation.

A lot of girls liked me (I worked out and kept myself up), and I was starved for attention, because, for one, in rural Kansas where I came from, men outnumbered women by nearly eight to one. So more precious time away from school flew out the window. But it was worth it. I was the *man*!

As you might imagine, none of these relationships panned out. I told myself I didn't mind. There was always another smile, another pretty pair of legs, another girl to hang with for another night. Meanwhile, the birth and death of each relationship drained me a little more, stealing emotional balance and attention and energy away from other important things that might have helped me find a more permanent sense of belonging.

I could feel that something was wrong and that it was growing worse the longer I remained at the University of Iowa.

Not that I spent much brainpower on figuring out what "it" was.

I had ADHD and always would. Anxiety and depression, too, but what was there to do about it? I was in a better place and (on the outside, at least) doing better all around. Just look at my friends and girls and good times, and all while I got myself to school when I was supposed to. It wasn't all roses and cupcakes, but I could live with that.

> *Except my mind kept going and going, too busy to cling to any one task when I needed it to.*

And then there was all that reading I mentioned. Keeping up became impossible when after reading a few sentences my train of thought would wander off to other things—*anything* besides schoolwork.

Why pick up a book at all? I'd find myself wondering. Before I even began my homework, I would get sick to my stomach. The only thing worse was the thought of not getting it done, failing a class, and having to face my dad at the bottom of another screwup, admitting that I would never be able to do better.

I'm proud I kept trying (while I kept partying even harder). Only a couple years before, I'd have torched school completely just to be rid of the bother. This time I was determined to stick it out. But my white-knuckle commitment didn't cure my anxiety.

The sheer size of the larger university classes stressed me out—two hundred students crammed into a lecture hall, and I was one of the dumber guys in the bunch. That was the only thing I was certain of. In some courses, I'd have to stand up and speak in front of everybody. WTF? Me, the bumpkin from Kansas, whose ace skills seemed to be drinking himself sick and not being able to hold on to a girl for more than a single night. Booze became my little helper when I needed to work up the nerve to attend lecture. Just a little (or a lot) before class to dissipate the building pressure.

Which worked well enough, I guess, until one day it was my turn to present in front of a large, crowded auditorium.

> *I came completely undone; I had a full-on panic attack, totally mortifying myself.*

I tried to shrug it off and play it cool. But kids aren't stupid; my classmates knew I'd choked. I could feel them all watching me, judging me, laughing under their breath as I stammered. I struggled off the stage, sweating, heart pounding, straining to breathe. I was so embarrassed I dropped the class so I wouldn't have to go back and face the shame of my meltdown.

It didn't take long for my newfound (alcohol-enhanced) confidence to evaporate. I managed to bull my way through to my first-semester midterms, for a change studying as hard as I possibly could. When I checked my grades online, it gutted me to see I'd be getting Cs in every class. I was furious. Frustrated. I was desperate for a rationale to hang my disappointment on. What good had busting my ass to prep for midterms done when my grades were going to be worse than when I'd barely studied in junior college?

Dad noticed my spiraling attitude; he said he wanted to talk.

About the drinking, he said at first. Of course he'd known what was going on. He'd seen it. I lived with the guy. Up until now he'd let it slide.

That day, he mentioned how the only time I seemed happy or excited was when I talked about going out—*not* about what I was doing in school. He wanted me to "discover my passion" and work as hard at school (which he saw as a better life) as I had been at partying and getting ripped at the gym. As if the thought of not having friends and places to go to and the rock-hard gym body that impressed girls were somehow going to magically make my life better. Those things were hard-wired into my brain as the end-all, be-all of life. I was freaking at the possibility of having to give it up.

Which all came burping out.

> *I guess I was needing to say it to someone so the craziness of what I'd been doing would finally be out there, forcing me to hear it as the words came out of my mouth.*

That, and the fact that this was my dad and I knew I could trust him more than any of the kids I spent every day with every minute I could escape.

I spilled my guts about the panic attacks and how I sucked at school because I couldn't pay attention to anything. I admitted that worrying about speaking in front of a class made me physically sick. For me, there was no way to enjoy college. There was only disengaging and getting through it because I refused to quit this time, even if it killed me.

I'd gone to doctors before about all the things I'd felt and done and let bother me earlier in life. Now, fitting in and doing well at the university was harder and more intimidating than anything else I'd faced.

> **NOTE:** Remember that all of this was going on while I continued to live the life I was living. I was still functioning and thriving socially.

Dad said that the confusion and disconnection and building pressure I was feeling meant it was time to get some outside help again.

Remember from my Step Four stories that he didn't lay down the law or anything. He didn't lay into me and demand that I shape up or change my life overnight. He kept talking to me, and he kept living his hardworking life as an example of how I could approach mine. And he always kept the lines of communication open.

True to his word, he left the decision to me about when to lean into the lifestyle changes I needed to make. But when I was ready, he made certain I had the professional help I needed to deal with my thoughts and emotions and body chemistry.

I've learned the hard way that you must find the right fit when it comes to doctors for mental health matters.

It's not a one-size-fits-all thing. Dad first took me to a medical doctor who threw a bunch of antidepressants and a weak stimulant at me. No joy. The psychiatrist I saw next treated the anxiety more heavily and prescribed something moderate for my ADHD.

There are side effects to many ADHD meds, and it can be difficult to juggle those reactions along with other medications. This psychiatrist eventually found the right combination of drugs to help me with the anxiety. He also helped me improve my ability to perform more effectively at school. No more meltdowns.

I was able to better focus on homework. My GPA was back up to a 3.0 by the end of that semester.

So, problem solved, right?
Hardly.

> **NOTE:** I'll share in more detail later, in the "WHAT HAP-
> PENED?" and "WHAT TO DO?" sections, about my work
> with my health-care team and how difficult it was to find
> the right combination of medications to help me.

For now, the key takeaway is that if your son cannot achieve
the behavioral results he clearly desires, it's time to seek professional help. Also, it's essential to find a medical professional
experienced in prescribing the *right* medications, in tandem with
counseling (which we'll also discuss next) to give your son the
fresh start he needs.

Otherwise your son might never succeed in his battle for a
healthy, successful future free from the pain that drives his risky
behavioral choices.

**At the same time as I was working on my medication, my
father requested I meet with a counselor.**

It took awhile, but after a few stops and starts, I found a therapist I synced with. This was another one of those things I did for
Dad. I didn't really see the point.

But after awhile it started to feel a little good: unloading
grudges and fears and anger from the past onto someone not part
of my present life, onto a person who wouldn't judge me or hold
it against me the way my new friends would.

> *I left my forty-five minute sessions literally feeling the weight
> that had been pressing down on my chest lightening.*

It was okay to be a man and still have emotions—that was one
of the first things my counselor helped me understand. Charging
ahead like it was no big deal, stuff down tears, and hide sadness until they came raging out as anger—that didn't have to be

the rest of my life. It was okay just to "be," the way I'd never let myself believe I could.

Until then, being "real" was something everyone else got to be. Me? I was an emotionless machine, and it had damn near killed me once already. If I kept going the way I was, my therapist helped me see I was headed straight back to the same place (even though I was taking a slightly different, more determined-to-do-better path).

Instead of spending all that energy hiding the "worst" parts of me, why not pay attention to them?

That's what my therapist prompted me to ask myself. Why not spend some time searching for and dealing with the things triggering my out-of-control emotions?

I'd been in denial about how bad my anger was.

I think a lot of kids like me are: we're shell-shocked from years of nonstop causing trouble for ourselves and the people we care about. To put it another way, I was a self-absorbed narcissist, too focused on managing (or mismanaging) my broken way of navigating life to pay attention to anything else.

And if you failed to focus on others, I learned, how could you figure out the "appropriate" (or successful) way to behave, to be able to live and work and play better with others who weren't just like you?

No wonder I gravitated in high school and college toward other people acting out and drinking heavily and not taking much of anything else in their worlds seriously.

I had no idea until I discussed this epiphany in more detail with my therapist (and my dad) just how deficient I'd been in seeing and picking up on the nonverbal cues people reflected back to me every day. I'd never understood why, by the time I was saying or doing something that was out of bounds, I was already *all* the way out and maybe careening over a behavioral cliff—way too late to stop myself. Turns out, I'd never learned how to recognize others' reactions and how to stop myself before my actions became too outlandish and inappropriate.

> *In therapy, I learned to more closely monitor my emotions and behavior.*

I pruned back those jagged edges. People began to feel more comfortable around me. I became more *Austin,* and that was enough. It turns out my hell-on-wheels alter ego and the life I was still living was not the only option available to me.

Anger no longer controlled so much of my life.

I developed my awareness of how those darker emotions could sneak up on me seemingly out of nowhere, consuming my thoughts and driving my actions.

My mind would sometimes dredge up an obscure person or memory from the past just to piss me off. Didn't matter how long ago I'd known the person. And off my anger would surge, as if whatever had happened just happened, and I'd want to do serious damage if only I could get my hands on that person again. Sometimes, a lot of the time, the anger would spill over in my present, like acid burning through my fresh start, trashing opportunities and relationships that didn't deserve to be discarded.

> *Slowly, I learned to take back control of my thoughts and the actions they produced.*

I didn't have to bow down to the resentment that seethed inside me. For me, prayer became a huge part of this transition. I began praying for people I remembered from a darker time. Instead of fuming over my long-dead "mistreatment" at their hands, I asked God to bless their lives now, wherever they were.

I also asked Him to forgive *me* for all the times I'd hurt others. A new milestone for me. I refocused my "that's not fair" mirror to the past right back at me and realized what I resented most at the hands of others was often eerily similar to things I'd said and done myself.

My anger began to slowly melt away, along with the past. I was taking one more emotional step toward controlling what my life would become next.

That's not to say that all was better and I'd completely stopped getting in my own way.

The drinking and the clubbing continued. More importantly, I continued hanging around "friends" who reinforced the belief that partying was the main focus of a successful college experience. Because everyone who was anyone did it, and all these cool city people liked small-town me as long as I kept showing up to party with them.

I'd gotten the help I needed to turn my grades around. I'd earned the right to cut loose whenever I could. Except there was an added wrinkle now beyond my not giving my all to the education and opportunities my dad was working his butt off to pay for. Generally speaking, drinking and the kind of meds I was taking didn't mix. In fact, combining alcohol and several of my prescriptions at the levels I'd been prescribed could have resulted in lethal consequences.

My doctors and pharmacist warned me, but I still took my meds before I went out with friends. With pharmaceutical help, the anxiety of approaching girls and making friends evaporated like magic. I became a social machine. Everyone loved me—or at least the Austin I thought I could only be when I took my meds.

Of course, the professionals knew what they were talking about. Just a few drinks into a heavy night, and my booze and meds became a brutal concoction. I couldn't hold my liquor the same as before. But I pushed myself just as hard to keep up. For the first time, I was the guy getting black-out drunk multiple times a week. It wasn't unusual for me to wake up in some insane place and to have no memory of how I'd gotten there. Often I wasn't alone, lying next to some random girl I'd only met the night before.

I was risking everything. My doctors and my dad knew it. I knew it. I was making a conscious decision to keep going, thinking, I guess, that the worst-case scenario wasn't going to happen. Or if it did, maybe that was just the way things were supposed to be for a guy like me. "It's natural selection," I can remember reasoning after another round of cautionary talks with the adults in my life. "Either my body is going to tough this out or I will die. That's all there is to it."

Partying was quite simply my identity.

Except that dark, shadowy bar scene wasn't the happy place I remembered it being.

I was in counseling. A lot of experienced professionals (including my dad) were working double time to give me the therapeutic and medical support I needed to level out behaviorally. Important parts of me were changing, whether I'd admit it or not: elements of my personality and brain chemistry were finally free to respond to the world in a healthier, more rational way.

Sure, there was still the rush of working in hip, cool bars, and drinking my way through the night, and being the guy everyone wanted to get trashed with. Especially after my body finally built up a tolerance for how badly I was treating it.

But when I wasn't immersed in that lifestyle, and when I woke up the next day, I found myself growing sick of the roller-coaster ride.

For me, drinking itself never became an addiction. It was my delivery device for the good times and the validation I longed for. When my perceptions of life and my behavior finally began shifting, subtly at first, and then more consistently, it left me wondering what kind of stupid, meathead bouncer lived the way I did. How did I ever let myself think this was all I wanted, or all I'd ever want, for my life?

One cold, winter night stands out to me.

Deep in the heart of January, I was working at a bar and watched a drunk young woman stumble into the wall on her way out the door, then stagger out into the frigid subzero temperatures, not wearing any shoes or socks. I was afraid she would end up losing a foot to frostbite, so I tried to coax her back into the bar, but she insisted on standing outside on the sidewalk. I wound up calling her a cab and picking her up, holding her like a toddler until it arrived. That was the only way I could keep her feet off the icy pavement.

And the thing I remember most?

That she kept trying to kiss me, and I kept thinking how sad and totally out of it and empty she must be feeling. She didn't know me from Adam, and she wouldn't remember me in the morning, but she was determined to make out with me no matter how many times I politely declined. I had to wonder at how often that pathetic display of oblivious neediness had been me. And how many people had tolerated my drunken antics while feeling sorry for me the way I was for this girl.

I finally got her into the backseat of a cab and returned to my job and my angry boss.

"What in the hell are you doing?" he yelled. "You're supposed to be doing your job, not babysitting morons. She's not our problem! Who cares about her?"

"Yeah," I found myself thinking.

"Who cares?" pretty much summed up the last I-didn't-know-how-many years of my sorry life.

My father wrote his dissertation on how homeless men experience shame.

He chose to complete much of his clinical work at a homeless shelter in addition to everything else he crammed into each week. One day he asked me to transcribe twenty-five interviews he'd recorded with clients who'd consented, under the cloak of anonymity, to be included in his research.

Of course, I said yes whenever he asked me for help (I knew a lot about shame myself).

Diving headfirst into those men's stories was emotionally overwhelming for me. I heard about gut-wrenching, unthinkable human atrocities no one should have to endure. It was a reality check for how close I'd come to *really* hitting rock bottom: spiraling drug use; dysfunctional, destructive relationships; unchecked mental illness; criminal activity; and how leaning into all of it had landed these men homeless, hopeless, and unable to find their way out. It was heartbreaking. I was lucky that hadn't been me. It might have been *me* if not for my father's unyielding determination to not quit on me no matter how hard I pushed him away.

I was blessed; I realized it more with each word I transcribed. Blessed but unworthy. Why was I squandering opportunity after opportunity to succeed after making many of the same mistakes these guys had? Only they hadn't had someone like my dad in their corner, propping them up until they got their shit together and took back their lives.

> *It made me sick, how much I'd taken for granted.*

Meanwhile, others in not-so-different emotional circumstances didn't even have a home to crawl back to at night.

I began to see my bright future as a responsibility to appreciate and work toward rather than an obligation I'd likely fail at.

My mind's tendency to get hung up on negative thoughts began to crystallize as an obstacle I had to overcome rather than a *given* that I might as well get used to. Staying stuck might be easier, sure, but being in a perpetual funk and letting my darker moods dictate everything? That was a choice. An immature one I needed to eliminate while I still could.

> I'd leaned into a mental prison of my own making. And maybe—definitely—it was time to start doing something about that.

One final thing: none of those homeless guys blamed anyone else for their misfortune.

That was maybe the craziest takeaway of all.

They didn't see themselves as victims of a broader, cultural problem. These men had taken responsibility for the actions that had gotten them to where they were, even if they didn't have the wherewithal and support to make the corrections they needed to drag themselves out.

For the first time in a long time, I actually did feel lucky—I still had my chance to live life free of blame and past mistakes and the fear that the mess I'd made was all I'd ever know.

Kevin: It's Never Too Late. Thank You, God.

I was so grateful for my renewed, solid relationship with Austin.

It was tempting to overlook the rest.

He was taking his meds and seeing his doctors, and his grades were improving. There were more and more pockets of him acting like a happy kid. Wanting to believe that was the case became a seduction any parent would want to submit to. Take the fun he always had on football Saturdays as an example.

I remember homecoming day the year Austin was twenty-two. He was up early, and his energy was high, even though he'd been out working and partying until dawn the night before. "Game day! The Hawkeye's defense is goin' to shut 'em down!" he said as he grabbed his keys and headed out the doors to tailgate. "You sure you don't want a ticket? You're welcome to come hang with us."

> *My son wanting me along when he was out having fun was*
> *all the medicine I'd ever need.*

But I was buried in work. "I'll watch for you on television. Go have fun."

"I'll see you later. Love you, Dad."

The door shut, and I turned off the TV and listened to his healthy, 225-pound frame bolt down the stairs outside our apartment. I poured another cup of coffee and basked in the silence he'd left in his wake. And I let the gratitude fill me.

My son was living one of my unrealized dreams. College had never been fun for me. As a parent, of course, I wanted him to have more and better. And I was there, front row and center, watching Austin enjoy the new life he'd found in Iowa, this once-high-school dropout and felon who was now a university-level honor student. He'd come so far.

> *Part of that moment, the thankful part, was about my own*
> *healing journey.*

I'd carried so much personal guilt and shame over being an absent father for most of Austin's formative years. That we'd carved out any relationship at all as adults was remarkable. As was his trust in my commitment to be there for him now, supporting him as he continued to work out his issues.

But beneath the surface of both my contemplative calm and Austin's bright beginning to yet another "fun" day of drinking too heavily and partying too hard, there were still issues.

Serious issues.

He was still making dangerous choices that led to concerning behaviors I couldn't do anything about. He was living up to the agreement he'd made to begin building a better life for himself. All the boxes I could have expected were being checked off: he was working on himself, his health, his education, his social relationships.

But I knew how superficial and precarious these "easy" moments really were. I think my son did too. And the terrifying thing was, there were so many times he didn't seem to mind digging himself deeper and deeper into a risky lifestyle that could ultimately shred his chances for true happiness.

But I had to allow Austin to make his mistakes.

I vividly remember the time when he was a baby, just nine months old, and was taking his first steps. The pride. The worry as he occasionally stumbled and fell. "Daddy!" he'd excitedly shout, running toward me, chubby legs churning, both arms held up to me, waiting, and I couldn't always catch him when he took a spill.

I couldn't keep carrying him around then, either, to protect him from ever again hurting himself. He had to learn to walk. He could only do that on his own. Even if it meant hurting himself a little. But I would always be there to console him, holding him close, comforting him, and then putting his feet back on the ground to give it another go. Because he had to believe that I believed he could do it all over again.

In Iowa, the danger of encouraging Austin to find his way on his own steam was even greater.

He'd fallen so many times, the consequences were mounting with each new failed attempt. But he was trying harder than ever to get it right.

And in a sense, I was doing the same thing. Going back to school, working on an entirely different profession, attending classes with students half my age; my choices seemed crazy to some. My first steps after failing spectacularly myself had been precarious. I'd stumbled more than once. And the only person who had been able to work out the kinks was me. I had to want the success I dreamed of badly enough to keep putting in the effort and to avoid making more mistakes that would derail me.

My son needed the same overhaul of his focus and priorities.

My job at this point as a parent and on-the-field leader was to get out of Austin's way and keep working on *myself* so I could be the father and example he needed.

This time around I taught myself to focus on growth rather than specific results.

Having missed so much of my son's early life like many divorced parents do, I acknowledged daily my gratitude for being present at this important developmental period. Austin was once again exploring and maturing and finding his identity, and I got to be a part of it this time.

Only, my place was a few steps back while he worked things out for himself. My focus had to be on soaking in all I saw and heard and observed and reflecting back the capable young man I knew he was. If I kept his mistakes in perspective and learned to relax, I'd be in a much better position to let my son know how accepted he was, even if his recovery didn't turn out to be "perfect" every step of the way.

Don't get me wrong, those five years we spent together in Iowa were nerve-wracking.

Austin would make progress, then the very next moment, it often seemed, I was afraid for him. My mood was all over the place. I was overworked and dealing with my own crazy situation. That was part of it. But monitoring my son's daily (and sometimes moment-to-moment) actions and emotional reactions was a little like trying to track a stock price on the rolling ticker at the bottom of your TV screen.

The fluctuations are all over the place, your confidence in your investment plummeting and surging with each update. It's nail-biting stuff. If you're not careful, the pressure will have you irresponsibly selling too low or buying too high just to be done with the whole thing. That type of micromanaging doesn't work with stocks, and it didn't work with my son.

Expecting immediate, "magical" gains once Austin was settled and seeing his doctors and therapist was a little overly hopeful.

More like delusional.

Slow and steady progress became my mainstay. From my own healing journey, I'd learned that long-term growth—the kind that was transformative and built on an unshakable foundation—took time and patience. And I would do my very best to provide both for him.

My son was worthy of redemption.

So many people had dropped him along the way. Teachers and other leaders, friends, and even family. Sometimes I dreamed, once Austin had "made it," of taking a copy of his Big-Ten diploma, sticking it up all those naysayers' asses, and saying, "See! You counted the wrong guy out. You gave up on him. You dropped him when he became a problem. You never called him while he was working his ass off in Iowa. You abandoned him. Screw you! He made it."

At the same time, I knew how high the odds were stacked against Austin if he didn't continue to make significant changes. He was attempting to rewire beliefs about himself and the world, beliefs he'd held since he was little more than a toddler. I had a lot of sleepless nights after he'd hit yet another wall, like when he kept heavily drinking and partying even though his doctors warned him of the dangers of mixing his medications with alcohol. I worried that maybe he'd given up on himself before he'd had time to get his fresh start right. And there was nothing I could do to stop him.

Each time I tried to pull him back, his resistance was instantaneous.

So I'd force myself to back off, stop commenting, or stop recommending he change whatever was concerning me.

He said more than once to me, "I feel like you are constantly watching and judging me. I need you to trust me. I'm trying to make good decisions, but it's like you don't think I can."

Those were hard words to hear, mainly because in those moments he was right. A part of me *was* watching and judging, unintentionally, subconsciously, no matter how hard I tried not to.

We lived together, and I'd lived through some of the worst late-night phone calls and come-to-Jesus moments a parent can endure. I wanted so much to spare my son from ever again experiencing anything that terrifying or dangerous. Because I'm a parent, and that's how we're built. And working with the homeless men I spent time with, I knew firsthand just how much worse things could get.

So how did I take all that doubt and worry and turn it into a way of relating to my kid that didn't run him off at the same time?

I learned to listen.

My son wanted to be heard. We all want to be. And by listening, I uncovered a wealth of information about the underlying problems he was still coping with.

He knew certain behavioral choices he was making were still a concern for me. He didn't need to be told that. What he *needed* was someone who loved him, who'd been a part of his life since he was a baby, to slow down and really get to know him. Listen to him. Reflect back and discuss the world and life and the kinds of issues we all have so he had new tools with which to think more deeply about his own circumstances and to uncover his own solutions.

That's not to say I got it right every time.

I remember when Austin dropped a math class he'd been bitching about. I'd been watching him party too much and study too little while I barely slept and all my "free time" away from school was tied up with him or spent at one of my two jobs. He made an A on his first test that semester and a B on the second, but then he began stressing and ranting about how it was the instructor's fault, the help center's fault, anyone's fault but his that he couldn't keep up.

When he dropped the class, it was time for another of my stellar "It's time to get your shit together" talks. And I was right when I said whatever I said to him that night. But was being right really the point?

I will never forget Austin's animated response.

He stood beside me once I'd finished lecturing him, looking down at me with his voice cracking, and said, "Dad, I wish you could be in my body for one day so you could understand what it is like to be me. I want to crawl out of my skin most of the time I feel so anxious. And no matter how hard I try, I can't stay focused, either in class or doing my homework. I know I need to party less and study more, but my body and mind are always racing. How do I make that stop? I wish you could understand what it is like to be me!"

His authentic distress burned through my frustration until all I could feel was his struggling with things he'd been struggling with his whole life. He had psychological challenges that were never going away all while what was being expected of him by school and me and life kept growing. That he'd succeeded in what he had, for as long as he had, was incredible.

He was talking about limitations he'd been dealing with since he was a small child. My confronting him had cleared the air. I was grateful for that. But I also regretted not finding a different way to help him open up.

Austin received the medical and psychological help that has transformed his ability to live his life in a productive, successful way.

> *I'll be thankful for the rest of my life that I learned to listen, really listen, when my son opened his heart to me, even when our tempers were flaring.*

As a parent, it is difficult to hear your son formally diagnosed with social anxiety and post-traumatic stress disorder, both of which were quite severe. I'd had no way of knowing the extent of his psychological problems until he agreed to work long-term with his team of doctors.

Acquiring those diagnoses and the extensive testing Austin underwent gave us a new language with which to relate to each other. So much began to make sense for the first time. It was a game changer.

Here was this rough, tough, towering-in-stature man whose world could get thrown by a friend not returning his phone call or text. But now when these things happened, I could see more clearly beneath that tough exterior to the frightened little boy within. He carried so many wounds from his past, all of them still communicating to him negative emotion and perceived rejection, years after someone else would have forgotten. He was still feeling their negative effect whenever something in his present life triggered a connection, all due to his difficulty regulating his emotions and the behavioral impulses they drove.

> *So many times, countless times after revelations like these,*
> *I thought back to all I'd put Austin through.*

I saw with fresh eyes my own contribution to the emotional fallout he was now coping with as an adult. I'd picture the kid whose father dragged him through multiple divorces, the little boy who was crying while his mom drove him away from his dad. In tears myself, I'd become overwhelmed with even greater gratitude for the health-care professionals who were finally assisting my son in his recovery work.

And then I'd recommit myself all over again, with every ounce of energy and every cent I had in the bank and each speck of a moment I could give him, to be there as he continued fighting for the life he deserved.

So, all was right in our world?

You know better than that by now.

We were learning more by the day about our different roles and responsibilities as we moved forward. But adjusting medications and incorporating therapeutic approaches and the ups and downs of day-to-day life weren't a cinch to navigate.

There were better days. Other times, the various pieces of Austin's treatment seemed to work against each other, doing more harm than good. Adjusting meds and combinations of meds (to better target symptoms or counteract competing side effects) became a revolving door. There was a lot of experimentation. Some changes in medication could take a month or two before we'd know if the desired effect had been achieved. And if we missed the mark, the lengthy process would begin once again all while Austin continued to battle whatever issue the meds were intended to address.

His health-care team was on top of things. They were aces at what they did. But the reality was that there was no perfect fit. Things would keep shifting, and Austin and I would keep adjusting accordingly. You can imagine the frustration. Still, my son had accepted that medication and counseling would be a vital part of his recovery. He'd experienced enough positive impact from both to remain committed to their necessity in his life. That gave me a lot of hope.

His willingness to experiment and try new things in therapy also signaled growth. He was encouraged to use mindfulness strategies to reduce his stress and anxiety. Other approaches, including EMDR (eye movement desensitization and reprocessing), gradually reduced his anger, sense of threat, and the broader swings in his emotional responses. He even agreed to see a female therapist each week, expanding his tough-guy comfort zone—something he never could have tolerated when he'd first come to live with me.

Like meds and therapy, Austin's learning to balance his focus on school and pursing his social life was an up-and-down journey.

As was my handling his continued partying and drinking in a supportive, objective way. I'd push a little too much. He'd be short with me in response. There were still the occasional lectures landing on deaf or frustrated ears. And, yes, I was downright terrified on several occasions that he was regressing and about to "fall off the wagon" and give up again.

He'd stay out all night, not getting home until early morning (by which time I'd typically already have been up for a couple of hours, studying). One boundary I'd made clear was my expectation that he not drive after he'd been drinking, so he'd frequently crash on a friend's couch until he'd slept off a heavy night.

And, honestly, I was happy to see him having a good time. After all, that was part of what I'd dreamed for him when he moved to Iowa and decided to pursue college. But he was taking so many risks (with his meds and his exposure to a party scene similar to that of his past, when his drinking had led to so many poor choices). It was downright impossible after everything we'd both invested in his getting better not to react to his potentially throwing this new opportunity away the same as he had so many others.

In the end, it was important we took breaks from each other.

He needed to live his life to the max if that was how he was going to get through what he was going through. And I, as the parent, didn't need to be watching over every detail and choice, driving myself and my son crazy worrying about things I couldn't (and had promised myself I would no longer try to) control.

I grew to accept that, as with his meds and therapy, there would be no simple, quick fix for his risky life choices.

If I was to continue supporting my son on his path to recovery, my job was to handle the reality before me as best I could. My impatience and frustration were my issues to cope with, not Austin's. The decisions he made and their effect on his progress were his prerogative.

His life was what it was, and no amount of my wanting or insisting that it be better or different was going to change a bit of it for the "better." I kept talking to him, but I did everything within my power to stave off the comments about how unwise I saw some of his behavior to be, which gave me time to step back and reflect and do some reassessing of my own—once again dealing with myself rather than micromanaging my son.

And each time I took that objective look at how far Austin had come, I was rewarded with even more reasons to hope that he was on track toward something amazing.

Perspective is a powerful thing once you make it a conscious habit.

Austin *was* growing. I could see that once I conditioned myself to see the small, incremental signs I'd been overlooking. It turned out that my son *was* able to both party and succeed in school, maintaining a 3.2 GPA at a Big-Ten university as an English major.

Unbeknownst to both of us at the time, Iowa's English Department ranked first in the nation, which made Austin's academic achievements even more impressive. He was a high school dropout who had never studied a day in his life, he was coping with several significant mental health diagnoses, and not that long ago he'd contemplated suicide.

> *Now he was achieving incremental and at times phenomenal success in pursuing a healthier, happier life.*

My kid was a walking, talking miracle. He was living proof that it's never too late to start over and that there's always a way out of what seems like even the darkest pit of failure or hopelessness. Once again, I recommitted to reflecting back to him all the "good" he'd accomplished and all the very real hope I had that there were no limits to where his life could go next.

And, finally, let me reiterate that having Austin as a roommate those years we spent together in Iowa was not all about stress and nail biting.

I could always depend on him to make me laugh. Our conversations were deep and rewarding at times, and then other talks we had were just downright fun.

Late at night when there was nothing left of my brain, I would often flip on the television so I could zombie-out before crashing into bed. I learned to expect Austin to hear the TV and come out and talk with me. And I'd know that what he had to say and my chance to engage that crazy-sharp brain of his was better than anything I could find on the tube. We'd hit the mute button, watch Sports Center highlights, and talk and talk and talk.

> *I will forever look back at those days as some of my best as a father.*

I actually suffered withdrawal after we left Iowa, and to this day I still miss our nightly talks. It didn't matter to me what we talked about. It was that we were having the conversation at all, back and forth, and each of us digging what the other was saying. It was peace and respect and patience and understanding and giving and taking. It was hearing and feeling my son's thoughts and heart and knowing he wanted me close enough to know him better.

As time passed, after the first year or so, I witnessed the evolution of how he thought. He was growing psychologically and spiritually. Austin got around to sharing how he was letting go of the anger he'd carried for so long and how badly he wanted to forgive people who'd done him wrong. He spoke of regrets and the desire to apologize to those who'd been hurt by his behavior. We discussed the existence of God, the unfortunate incidents Austin had witnessed in the bars where he worked, and in general about people living less-fortunate lives than ours.

His empathy for others was growing. Little by little, he was maturing. He was finding his own "right" direction. And I was learning to let him do just that and to better trust him and to learn from him as I grew as a parent.

WHAT HAPPENED?

Remember that each parent-child journey through recovery is unique.

Your focus should always be on your son and relating to his individual experience.

But all the parents I've worked with have shared experiencing many of the same dynamics Austin and I have shared in our stories once their child began working his or her way through the crazy, confusing minefield of recovery.

From the Psychologist

As a parent, I had to learn to let go like I'd never let go before.

My son had to motivate himself to actively seek the help he needed, or he'd never have fully committed to the prescribed treatment laid out by his health-care professionals.

That's not to say I just dropped him off and picked him up from his appointments or that I watched him come and go from our apartment and never invited myself into his life and the choices he was making. When I say in my stories that we worked through the roller coaster of regulating medications and trying different therapeutic approaches and dealing with the side effects and stops and starts, I mean just that. I was there with Austin, helping him cope as best he both could every step of the way. But Austin had to want to do the work, and he had to keep actually *doing* the work.

Mine was a supportive role now. The rest was up to my son.

My involvement was still vital to the process and to Austin's progress. It was essential that I made the help he needed available and that I kept searching for the right combination of professionals and treatments and medications.

But to a very real extent, Austin would either succeed or fail based on the decisions he made on his own.

That was a tough reality I struggled to accept.

How did I convince my son he needed help?

I didn't.

You know that, right? I'm betting you already understand based on your own relationship with your teen or young adult. It's just hard to stop yourself from trying. It was *really* hard to stop myself from trying to convince Austin to think or see or feel a different way about his recovery or about the way he wanted to live his life.

But remember that it took my son dropping out of a math course and my asking pointedly if maybe he'd been partying too much and applying himself too little at school (*yes*, I was lecturing about the party-study ratio) before we had our lightbulb moment as father and son. Austin's subsequent meltdown about how hopeless he felt about never being able to handle school was one of the worst days we'd both had since he'd moved in. But it was also a huge turning point in his recovery. He'd finally arrived at his decision to ask for the help he needed.

He was honest about what he was dealing with in a way he'd never been before. He was so "rock-bottom" defeated by his attempts to keep up in his math class despite his psychological challenges that everything he'd been trying to hide about himself came vomiting out. His defenses came crashing down. And I was there to hear every awful word of it and to let him know that it would be okay. We would finally get him the professional support and medical intervention he needed.

The key thing to remember was that it was Austin's decision.

He was ready. Not to change everything I wanted him to. But he was opening key areas of his thoughts and his life to me. And because of our deepening connection, I was, thankfully, right there with him, encouraging and supporting him when he admitted he wanted to take the next step in his recovery.

Austin admitted he couldn't achieve the success he wanted on his own, but he had no idea what kind of help he needed or how to get it.

My job was to help him figure it out, to stay positive and supportive and encouraging while I was devastated I hadn't done more (or been able to do more) sooner, and to be grateful for the opportunity to be there for him now, whatever it took, and to never, ever again become a barrier to his conviction that he could and would succeed.

Austin Checks In

All kids want to make it on their own.

We all want to believe we can handle our lives without help—me more than most, I'm guessing.

Ever since my parents split and I'd felt so responsible to help my mom, I'd been "the man" who was supposed to have all the answers. And yet I'd kept failing. And every time I got another chance, I was 100-percent determined to make it work, to make it right, and to make my life what it was supposed to be. No way did I want to cause my dad more grief. Just like the last thing I wanted was him breathing down my neck, doubting I could do anything on my own without screwing up.

But let me tell you, when I finally owned up to how out of my depth I was in class, and once I finally started seeing the doctors my dad hooked me up with, there's no way I could have handled all of that on my own.

In this section, let's talk some truths about medication.

Let me give you a better idea of how important it was that I had someone like my dad helping me through what came next—after I agreed and committed to getting whatever help I needed so I didn't screw up my shot at the University of Iowa (and at the life I could have after I graduated).

I was diagnosed with ADHD, PTSD, chronic anxiety, and OCD.

A highly respected psychiatrist prescribed me Clonazepam, Xanax, Adderall, and Prozac. It sounded as if I'd be carrying around an entire pharmacy. But, as my dad and I have shared, that medication changed my life.

The hard part was the experimenting it took to get my dosages right. Again, I had great doctors. But there were times when I felt like a guinea pig. Yet this was my life and my choice, and I was the only one who could really know what was working and what wasn't, and that meant we were going to get things wrong a lot of the time, maybe several times, before we finally got something right.

Adderall badly exacerbated my anxiety (a common side effect of a very common ADHD medication), so my doctors agreed it was okay not to take it before I had to stand in front of an audience to speak. That prescription was more for when I was at home, so I could focus on completing my assignments. The Clonazepam suppressed my anxiety, helping the nervousness dissipate, and lessening the likelihood of further, crippling panic attacks. Prozac addressed my anger. I'd been seething on the inside for as long as I could remember.

> *For the first time in my memory, with Prozac, I was given the opportunity to experience reality without anger's darkness sucking at everything, threatening to rip my world apart if I let myself go.*

Which was all an amazing blessing.

However, there are drawbacks to combining so many pharmaceuticals that alter body chemistry and brain function, some of which you've already read about in my dad's and my stories. But for parents dealing with a similar situation, I want to go into a bit more detail of what it's like taking so many meds and trying to figure out what's helping, what's making things worse, and wondering whether you'll ever get it right.

My body became dependent on the effects of the chemicals. Also, the temptation was always there to use them as a "cure all" to hide behind rather than challenging myself to do the behavioral and therapeutic work needed to readdress my long-term issues.

For example, I can remember at one point taking six milligrams of Clonazepam at once before class (enough medication to knock out a four-hundred-pound man for twelve hours). I liked the way it dissolved under my tongue like a chalky-tasting mint, and I loved how it settled the dust of my anxiety, helping me feel comfortable in my own body. Soon, though, the thought of not having the pills petrified me. Running late for class one day, I forgot to take my medication, and I simply turned around and went home. No way was I even trying to go in without my meds!

At this point in my healing, anxiety still ruled my life. Without my meds, I simply could not succeed with my coursework. Therapy and life changes would later provide me other ways of reducing my anxiety and medications. But at this point, medication was my lifeline for coping.

If you're thinking this means I was abusing Clonazepam, consider that it didn't make me dizzy or sleepy and that it relieved my anxiety, helping me function with more confidence. Was I taking too much? Go back and live three minutes inside my skin during that time and ask me that question again.

Yes, as my body got used to it, I craved more. But I found the need tapered off after six milligrams per day. At one point I was prescribed eight milligrams daily, but I found myself not needing that much. My doctor lowered my daily dose back down to six, and that continued to work successfully for several years.

Which is a lot of detail, probably more than you need or want to know.

But this was just one of the meds I was taking and monitoring and juggling with all the rest—while, you know, I was still trying to do all the other things I wanted to do. I'm hoping my transparency will help you better understand what your own teen or young adult is dealing with if multiple meds are part of his course of treatment.

One final note about Clonazepam.

There were significant downsides to most all the pharmaceuticals I took.

I am certainly not a doctor, but the Clonazepam eroded my short-term memory, and it exacerbated my ADHD, so I had to weigh the costs and benefits of the medication.

Relief from chronic anxiety was more important to me than memory loss and attention span, so I continued taking my prescription. At that point in my life, ripping free from the chains of anxiety was more essential than anything else. Under the care of medical doctors and my therapist (and with my dad's support), I found a way to finally feel free enough explore the world without fear, which made the side effects worth it for me. Your son's experience may be different.

But there will come a moment when a decision will have to be made as to which medication to give priority. That decision needs to be, if at all possible, your son's.

My best advice as someone who's been through this complicated, overwhelming process is to always, always err on the side of listening to your child.

He knows his body. He knows his mind and how it reacts to things. Keep an open dialogue with him and his doctors. Keep the conversation going, and make certain your son is paying attention to all the effects of the various drugs he's taking.

Help him determine the most important aspect of his recovery. What will help him feel more in control?

And then work with him and the right professionals to develop an approach to address his mental health needs. You'll be assisting him in opening a whole new world for himself no matter how daunting it may seem to you.

WHAT TO DO?

Kevin: My Son's Problem Is . . .

We've all tried to fill in that blank with our troubled teen or young adult.

The array of issues he is facing can include drugs, drinking alcohol, stealing, lying, fighting, etc. But what are the underlying causes beneath those behaviors?

Only trained medical professionals and counselors can help your son answer those questions for himself. I couldn't do that for Austin, and I *am* a trained therapist.

The truth is, your child's more likely to open up to a third party.

A mental health professional is better equipped to work objectively with your son and his challenges.

> *Your son needs a clinical diagnosis and a professional treatment plan.*

Meanwhile, you, as the parent, will focus on supporting and observing his journey toward a better life.

Let's circle back to our discussion (in Step Three) of the five stages of change.

Retrace with me the progression of Austin's readiness to change as you consider where your son now falls within the spectrum.

Stage	What this looked like for Austin
1. Precontemplation	In high school, Austin had no intention of altering his behavior.
2. Contemplation	As he became more aware of his problems, he came to live with me the first time in Kansas City, willing to do better for himself (after his "home" world had come crashing down). He obtained his GED. However, ultimately, he was unable to continue moving in a positive direction. Consequently, he returned to his old behavioral and destructive decision-making dynamic (and to his precontemplation stage).
3. Preparation	Austin made changes to his primary focus after hitting rock bottom and facing the decision of whether or not he even wanted to continue living. He moved for the second time to live with me in Iowa, enrolled in first junior college and then the University of Iowa, made friends, and obtained and held down a job. A number of problems still needed to be addressed (drinking, anger, inability to focus, and anxiety). Underlying psychological barriers were blocking the healing progress. But he was learning and growing as a human being, focused on moving forward, and willing to maintain and improve our relationship so I could become a helping and supportive part of his journey.
4. Action	Crisis and crippling anxiety in Austin's new life drove his inability to sustain change and propelled him to for the first time open up honestly about his experiences and internal struggles. He committed to setting and keeping appointments with his doctors, working with them to make careful diagnoses of his issues, and then beginning a complex treatment plan that included intense counseling.
5. Maintenance	In later steps, we'll discuss how habits and consistent behavioral practices are created so that change becomes a routine part of life. We'll discuss how Austin evolved into his new "normal" reality.

But how can you propel your son through the preparation and toward the action stage of change?

Once again, whether it's easy to hear or not, *you* can't change anything but how you approach facilitating your child's motivation to take those necessary actions.

> *There is no therapy, intervention, or magic words or potion that will force your son to embrace change.*

My hundreds of lectures didn't make a dent with Austin. He was only ready to change when he'd reached the point where he was so unhappy with his "hopeless" situation he began to truly fall apart and could no longer fix it or mask the pain. Thankfully, I was there to catch him, listen to him, and redirect him toward the professional assistance he needed.

> *You can be there for your son too, but not by pleading, coaxing, or trying to manipulate or coerce the desired result.*

These more dominating, "positional" parenting choices will backfire and drive your child further away from you emotionally. Remember, your number-one priority in our seven-step game plan is to maintain your proximity and relationship so you are fully engaged once your teen or young adult is ready to embrace change.

Lasting change (the hallmark of the "maintenance" stage) is only possible when it is your child's idea.

Even when you fear he is doing lasting harm to himself and possibly destroying his opportunity to get things "right" this time, you have to remember that this, too, is his choice to make.

How do you do that?

- **Remember (from Step Four) Carl Rogers's theory** of our self-actualizing tendency as humans to strive toward reaching our potential.

- **Remember that your son** does **want to get better** and is working hard to get there, or he wouldn't have progressed to his "planning" stage.

- **Remember that your job is to tap into that drive to heal** and make more positive choices (through conversation and reflecting the benefits of a more healing path, as well as finding and keeping and projecting your hope and confidence that he can improve).

- **Continue to positively redirect your son** (without lectures or threats or humiliating demands that he "shape up," which will be internalized as shame and self-doubt) toward removing the behavioral and psychological barriers keeping him stuck in a destructive cycle, undercutting his genuine desire to achieve and make significant change.

How do you know when your son is ready for change?

It's likely he's been on the fence for a long time, ambivalent toward taking that next step you know he needs to make. And then something changes. A lot of small somethings, perhaps.

You'll notice or even hear him say something to indicate his growing dissatisfaction with the situations he continues to put himself in.

His chosen approach to solving his problems isn't making him happy the way he thought it would, and that's your first key indicator that he's making healthy, significant progress.

This is NOT the time to swoop in with a self-congratulatory "I told you so." That would have a disastrous effect on the emotional improvement in his cognitive awareness of the circumstances he's making. It would also undermine the trust you've established with your son.

Remember, this isn't about you.

It never was. It's about you making everything about *him*—all he's doing and deciding, and the healthy progress you believe him to be 100-percent ready to make.

The empathy and compassion you display toward your son will allow him the loving space to wrestle with his ambivalence and weigh the costs and benefits.

His still-overflowing "shit bucket" (from Step Three) is becoming more agitating for him, making him uneasy. He's in between wanting to change and doing all that is required to change, and he doesn't like it. He doesn't need you to explain why.

Walking the tightrope between hope and too much.

He's already instinctively weighing the cost benefit of his chosen lifestyle. And that's your opportunity as a team leader to influence every opportunity he invites your insight into. For example, remember those late-night conversations Austin and I had? Sometimes about random things? More often, especially as his awareness of his situation improved, we discussed the impressions he offered about his life. *Boom!* You better believe I took advantage of those moments.

When he talked about how the alcohol and going to bars were starting to seem like a waste of time and money, I would weigh in about how I saw his current behavior actually working against him while he battled so hard in school to bring his future goals to life. When he made more negative comments about how often he was going out and getting drunk, I would say, "Yes. I can see your point. I can see your 'someday' talents someday leading you to a very lucrative and meaningful career. But I also see your hanging out in the bar scene as much as you do taking time away from building the important skills you're going to need."

> *The key is to weigh in each time your teen or young adult opens that window or door to your influence.*

But do it carefully. Subtly put your finger on that scale of their ambivalence. Add supportive weight to his or her growing instincts that the gap between the life being lived and the potential life desired may be growing in the wrong direction.

When you meet resistance and pushback, back off.

Again, pushing and arguing and wanting change more (or to come faster) than he does is counterproductive. I see too many parents in my practice continuing to argue with their children, often after good progress has been made, but then some aspect slides back toward less-successful behavior. The result is, without exception, that the child becomes more deeply entrenched in his or her opposing position, at times even when the teen or young adult knows it's to his or her detriment.

As a parent, your role isn't to convince your son, it's to help him convince himself.

You're encouraging your son in the direction of change.

There's a lot of good stuff in that sentence.

Let me break it down a bit more, highlighting your continued work with the strategies you've learned in this and previous steps:

- You're encouraging him always.
- You're aware and positive and reflecting your approval of the direction he's headed.
- You're seeing hope and exciting progress in the changes he's already made.
- You're confident he will arrive at the healthy choices he must make when the time is right for him to fully commit to the hard work ahead.

Don't back off too far.

Keep as open a dialogue as possible with your teen or young adult during this confusing "preparation" stage of change. Consciously focus your efforts on the most effective kind of dialogue.

With Austin, as he talked about his growing dislike for the bar scene, instead of saying, "Well, why don't you stop going, then?" I reinforced my belief that he would make the right choice about how to handle the parts of his life bothering him.

"I know you will make the right decision when you're ready," I'd say, or "When you're ready to make a run for your goals, I have no doubt you will achieve them."

State and restate your belief in your son's ability to change.

Reflect on the successful skills you see him growing. Focus on the long game and on the effort you see being made, even if it's currently not enough to achieve victory. Be that on-the-field leader motivating his transition into the "action" of the change you see coming. And above all, make it clear it's your son's responsibility to decide what to do while you remain part of his growing compulsion to make deeper, more enduring changes in his life.

A Note from Austin: I Mean, Isn't It Obvious?

What can I say other than that I'm one of the lucky ones?

I got more than one chance, more than two chances, and more chances, until I was finally ready to get my life and myself right.

I'm a father now, and I don't know where my dad found the courage and resolve to wait for me to decide what to do for myself.

He knew I wouldn't have been receptive to him "forcing" himself into my problem-solving the way he had earlier in my life: "Get a job, go to school, stop all this reckless behavior because I say so, and I'm the adult, and that's just the way it works . . ."

We've already shared about how much we were talking and how active he stayed in helping me process everything I was dealing with.

But there were no guarantees. And my dad was willing to let me make mistakes and learn lessons while he hoped and prayed I'd pull myself back from the edge before it was too late.

My dad never lost faith in me or in my future.

I hope if I'm ever in the same position with my child, I can be half the man, half the fearless leader my father was (and continues to be) for me.

He let me have my space, and I'm glad he did. He picked his battles and only dug in when it was absolutely necessary. He waited me out, made it all my choice. And when I was ready, he moved heaven and earth to get me the help I finally admitted I needed.

In the end, this was my life. My dad knew that, respected that, and was willing to let go of controlling anything but his reaction to whatever I did next.

The only way I could live and sustain change authentically was if *I* chose the happiness and success we both wanted so badly *entirely* on my own. But whether or not I ever got there, the one thing my father made sure I knew for certain was that he'd be there beside me, fighting with me, never giving up on me no matter what happened next.

And even now, as I look back from over a decade down the road, one central truth resonates: Where would I have wound up, where would I be now, without him?

Thank God I never had to find out.

WHAT'S MOST IMPORTANT?

In Step Five, you're actively engaged in a waiting game, taking action only when the moment is right

You're anticipating the right moment and the right opportunity to influence and make a positive impact on the recovery your son is attempting to achieve. You're aware that he's not all the way there yet and that he's still making mistakes (sometimes grave ones with potentially dangerous consequences), but you're better understanding your role as a supportive, on-the-field leader. You're trusting your son's instincts to care for himself (and to seek your help and influence when he's ready to take the next step in his change process).

Your Parent Playbook

Before we leave this step, Austin and I want to add some new strategies to your repertoire.

Put into practice these new recommendations before and after your son asks for the additional help he needs to achieve sustained change in his life.

Strategy	Consider	Goal
Increase your expectations.	Without projecting a "need to improve" on your son while he struggles with all he's facing and the permanent change he's still resisting, find ways to reflect how much more you're certain he can achieve and do for himself. Work to eliminate from your interactions your expectation that your son will continue to fail (even if he is still leaning into questionable behaviors and choices you see as dangerous or counterproductive to change). Then, work on eliminating those anxious, frustrated reactions from your thoughts about your son's ability to achieve his goals. Trust me, he will recognize and respond to the adjustment.	**Treat your son as if he's smart and capable, encouraging him to reframe his perception of himself accordingly.** Blind studies have concluded that children, regardless of their IQ, perform better when testing if they are taught as if they are highly intelligent. Try talking about your son's future as I did with Austin. Recognize and praise the skills he's already mastered and the areas in which he's improving. **Make the successful elements of his journey your focus, augmenting his acceptance of what he absolutely can do once he's ready to change.**

Strategy	Consider	Goal
Help your son find purpose.	Are our troubled sons really narcissistic, or are they too preoccupied by their own insecurities and perceived threats to focus on the world and others around them? Their self-absorbed behaviors are often a symptom of low self-esteem and an anticipatory fear of humiliation. Self-protection is their highest priority. Most often, these aren't "bad" people who will never think about anyone but themselves (as too many teachers and peers and even family members may have reflected back to your son). Instead, these are emotionally sensitive human beings who've never learned the skills they need to handle life without feeling as if they need to protect themselves from everyone and everything. Encouraging someone with this emotional deficit to reposition their frame of reference toward a purpose that will help others besides himself create a new value system and a broader emotional connection. His world expands beyond the individual experience, making possible a more realistic view of what's happening to him and others.	**Give your son a more clearly defined sense of the world around him.** Help him consider and refocus on others and if possible on the plight of those truly less fortunate than he is; for example, Austin's insight into the lives of the homeless men I worked with. **In his book on overcoming addiction, Dr. Stanton Peele suggests that individuals with defined values tend toward life paths that support those values.** Make those broader-value alternatives available to your son. Encourage a perspective that includes helping others in need, not just helping himself. Give him the opportunity to engage in a broader purpose for his life besides protecting himself and to adjust his behavior and choices to make those others-focused goals possible.

Strategy	Consider	Goal
Look for and celebrate "quick wins."	As you and your son engage in meaningful discussions, look for the signs of change—and mark each milestone. Ask questions that allow him to open up about the things he feels good about achieving (the areas in which he is ready to change). Be careful not to focus your talks on only those issues you see still needing significant work. You're wanting to keep the focus on incremental achievement while maintaining the open, trusting line of communication that will remain essential going forward.	**Your son likely needs more help than you can or should provide.** Your role is not to tackle everything that needs to be done. When the time is right, you need to be there to direct your child toward the professional care required.

Strategy	Consider	Goal
Approach mental illness as a real and "must-treat" issue to which your son needs to commit.	Austin needed extensive therapy and medication management from skilled psychiatrists and psychologists. Encouraging this path for your son may be one of the more difficult roles you'll play as a parent. But it is absolutely essential you remain open to it if he needs pharmaceutical and mental-health support as well. Research has repeatedly demonstrated that behaviorally troubled individuals who receive therapy and/or mediation, benefit more than individuals who receive no treatment at all. **NOTE:** Remember, however, that for sustained progress to be made, the decision to seek treatment must be your son's.	**Offer to pay for professional help once your son knows he's ready but leave the decision about if and when to start treatment up to him.** His responsibility and ownership of his treatment must be your priority, as is understanding that medication without therapy (and more often than not, therapy without medication) likely won't achieve the best results possible for your son's recovery.

Strategy	Consider	Goal
Carefully select the professionals your son will use in his recovery.	I can't tell you where or universally how to search for the right health-care professionals. But I can tell you with confidence how to know when you've engaged with the right doctors. Your son's motivation to work on his problems is the primary indicator of whether a therapist, medication, or a rehabilitation program will work for him. Without his active engagement, if he is being forced to attend, the very best resources will be a complete waste of his time and your money.	**Find the resources that will work for your son by observing those in which he engages and works.** Encourage and expect him to participate in choosing who he will see. If his motivation is high, and he is willing to work, and you've engaged a reasonably good psychologist, psychiatrist, or rehab program, he will be on a path to healing and to achieving his goals.

Strategy	Consider	Goal
Expect change to take time.	Our culture too often takes a "tape 'em up and get 'em back in the game" approach to mental health. Everyone should be able to "suck it up" and get over their issues, sooner rather than later. It would be disastrous for you to adopt this position with your son. If you "quick fix" only the symptoms of his issues (as I did early on with Austin), other symptoms will arrive to fill the empty space. Sustained change takes time when your teen or young adult is dealing with multiple underlying psychological problems that impact an array of life areas: occupational, interpersonal, intrapersonal, emotional, etc.	**Accept (and make certain your son knows you accept) that you are interested in helping him modify the underlying psychological issues beneath his behavior, for these are the genesis of his problems.** Commit (and talk through your intentions with your son) to addressing the foundational issues driving his troubled behavior. Assure him that you expect and understand why changing will take an extended period of time—that it takes time to establish new ways of interacting with the world once the rules you've always played by begin to change.

Strategy	Consider	Goal
Allow him to do his work.	Once Austin found professionals that were the right fit for his personality and needs, I stayed out of the way.	**Don't micromanage. Continue to send the signal that you trust your son and his doctors.**
	I didn't interfere. I didn't second-guess the therapist. I didn't offer a diagnosis. And I didn't suggest interventions. Austin's therapy was between him and his counselor.	See and let your son know you see him as competent. As you've both already learned, reality is a great teacher and motivator. It may sound harsh, but continuing to experience difficulties will continue to benefit your son and encourage him to continue his work to improve.
	Therapy and rehab occurs both in session as well as out of session. It is important you allow your son to continue to live his life and implement his therapeutic changes without your interference—even if he continues to make mistakes while in treatment.	**NOTE: This is not the same thing as withholding assistance when your son asks for help. It doesn't preclude you from continuing to offer him a supporting, safe environment while he works on his issues.**

Strategy	Consider	Goal
Participate in therapy when invited.	Expect your teen or young adult to have unresolved issues with you. It's a guarantee. Forgiveness is a process that takes time to run its course. We've already discussed the importance of apologizing to your son (in Step Two) for any wrongdoing toward him. It's short-sighted, however, to consider that matter closed, even if he gladly accepts your apology, as Austin did mine.	**Encourage your teen or young adult to explore his past and the barriers to his progress in the present—including the times when you've been the barrier standing in his way.** When the time comes, encourage your son to express whatever he needs to with regard to you (and be willing to do so in a family counseling environment under the direction of a professional therapist, if that's what your son wants). **Your child needs to feel supported in what he's feeling and in the changes he must make to deal more effectively with those feelings. Whatever you can do to support him, DO IT.**

Strategy	Consider	Goal
Support your son's healing.	If you are disengaged in your son's treatment, how can you support the changes he is trying to make? Research tells us that 40 percent of success in therapy occurs *outside* therapy. How will you understand how to track his improvement (or any growing concerns) if you are unaware of what he's trying to achieve? I have helped many clients gain significant breakthroughs in session only to witness their growth deteriorate once the client returns to a chaotic, toxic, or unsupportive home environment where those "old," unsuccessful behaviors are essential to his survival. In this situation, it's easy for the client to begin to perceive therapy as unhelpful in his "real world." Too many individuals in this sad dynamic relapse.	**Agreeing on therapeutic goals and collaborating with your son to find solutions (when invited to participate in his at-home therapy work) will produce a more positive outcome.** Your consistent empathy and alliance with your son (particularly in affirming positive feelings and genuinely supporting his work) are more important than ever. Simply by following our seven-step game plan, you have already stacked the cards in your son's favor, greatly improving his chances of success. Don't stop now.

YOUR NEXT PLAY

You are now actively engaged in your son's recovery, playing a supportive but subtly directive role as your son fights for his recovery and sustains changes to his behaviors and thought processes.

Your Game Plan in Step Five	Support your son's more difficult work on deeper issues, including securing for him the professional help he needs, when he indicates he's ready to expand his recovery.
As a parent, you will continue to	display empathy and compassion, creating a loving space for your son's still-difficult journey while at the same time encouraging him to continue making the changes he's capable of achieving, including remaining consistent with his recovery plan.
Your teen is beginning to	own his choices and mistakes and to accept the help he needs. He's becoming more independent in his commitment to recovery, but the increased "risk" of failure this invites into his life means he needs your support more than ever.
Your relationship dynamic is changing to	a true team, where he's calling the plays and you're the on-the-field leader offering direction when he turns to you for advice and guidance for his next chosen action.
Your Next Step	Help your son develop the confidence and realistic world- and "self-" views he'll need to sustain a long-term "recovery" mindset.

STEP SIX: MAXIMIZE HIS GROWTH

Help Your Son Develop Confidence and Feel Success

Your Game-Plan Challenge	**Encourage your teen or young adult to embrace his growth and healing while at the same time confirming that there are no "quick-fix" solutions to the challenges he faces.**
You, the parent, are	fighting *with* your son on a healthier field of play—learning more every day how to let him take the lead while at the same time making it clear you're there to support him whenever he needs you.
Your teen or young adult is	growing in his confidence and skills, becoming more independent in his choices, but still turning to you when he feels out of his depth in his healing.
Your relationship dynamic is	now one of substantial, ongoing change, both of you feeling empowered to move forward in your shared journey.
Your Goal for This Step	**Prepare your son to become "consciously competent" and adopt the vital "recovery mindset" that will secure his long-term healing and growth.**

Your son is not a quick-fix project.

In this step, we encourage you to adopt a *recovery mindset*.

> *A recovery mindset involves approaching your teen's healing and growth from a long-term perspective.*

You've tackled a number of challenging things for quite some time. Hopefully you have sought and are receiving qualified medical and mental health support as you navigate the new demands on your time, energy level, emotional well-being, and relationship with your son. There are still barriers to overcome. Let me encourage you to continue leaning into your understanding of and participation in your son's recovery.

> *Exciting growth and healing are around the next corner.*

You don't want to miss engaging with him in those opportunities. Yet you also want to be there for those still-frequent moments when he'll need your presence and guidance and influence as he emotionally orients himself to the more successful life opening up to him.

In Step Six, we discuss how to approach this shifting, "improving" phase of your recovery work together.

THE PARENT-CHILD DISCONNECTION

Your son's commitment to his continued treatment and recovery is essential no matter the progress he's achieving.

> *None of what you're about to read about Austin's "upswing" into embracing a healthier life would have been possible if he hadn't continued his hard work with his doctors and therapist.*

In today's culture, it's far too easy to treat mental illness as a minor injury that can be stitched up and healed as soon as any obvious scars fade.

If one suffers from depression, for example, we medicate the on-the-surface symptoms as a stand-alone problem. And, don't get me wrong, "in the moment" treatment *is* key. Depression is typically triggered by a combination of biological, psychological, and social factors that *must* be dealt with when a person is in crisis. However, after successfully achieving the reduction of depressive symptoms, there is almost always more work to do to address underlying triggers.

Foundational (beneath-the-surface) issues such as attachment style, self-image, or shame-proneness, if allowed to linger unchecked, can cause a multitude of future problems, including additional bouts of depression.

> *Our current system (insurance, treatment, therapist training, and even research) is typically geared toward a specific diagnosis rather than a broad picture of overall mental and physiological health.*

As a parent on the playing field as your son navigates the next stage in his changing process—he's now evolving into his maintenance stage (as discussed in Step Three)—a greater part of your role becomes advocating for your son's overall treatment and journey of healing.

> *Treating the symptoms of your son's issues isn't enough, even if immediate relief has been achieved.*

I encourage you to push your son's health-care providers to address the underlying causes of your teen's issues: self-image, concerns about interpersonal-style (attachment style), and many of the other factors addressed in this book. Skipping the harder and more time-consuming work of achieving deeper healing can derail your son's long-term success and become a roadblock to achieving his goals.

Work to see his path to mental-health recovery as an ongoing process.

Yes, medication and therapy can offer exciting short-term progress. And you may be tempted to think, *Great! Now we're past all of that.*

However, the deeper issues underlying your teen's anxiety, for example, cannot be treated away with a course of medication or a few sessions with his analyst. It's not uncommon for your teen or young adult to cycle back and forth between feeling better and feeling worse than ever. When he has difficulty with his self-esteem, to offer another example, it's not uncommon for him to experience multiple setbacks, even after he's worked for an extended period of time with a good analyst and psychiatrist.

> *Your son's progress toward a healthier view of himself and his world—like Austin's healing journey that we're about to share—is a long-term endeavor.*

And as the parent, it is your job to mindfully craft both your and your son's recovery expectations.

Austin: Healing

Changing how you see and feel about the world changes your world.

I didn't see my world when I was younger the way you may have. I doubt we'd experience my current reality in the same manner, even if you were to live it as me for a day. Our brains are wired differently. We've been through different things. We each have our own unique feelings, even if we're experiencing them at the same time about the same situations.

When I first moved to Iowa, I was such a narcissist.

Dad would come home after working his tail off to find me bitching about whatever minuscule superficiality was bugging me that day. The poor guy already had more on his plate than he could handle, and most of the time I didn't bother to ask about his day. But then I grew emotionally, as he's shared, into a more aware human being, no longer trapped in the anger and anxiety and fear that had consumed me.

I spent more time listening to the old man. I went out of my way to take an interest in his life. And it wasn't just for show: I really cared. I even went so far as to apologize to him for being a selfish asshole for so long. I did my level best to make our conversations more reciprocal.

There was more to my life because of the mental adjustments I was making through my medication and therapy.

For years, I'd been defensive about pretty much everything. Finally, if I received criticism or negative feedback, I no longer immediately became unglued. Disagreements and mistakes became opportunities to learn and grow. Successfully working on group assignments for school actually became manageable for me—and when you put a bunch of college kids together, someone's almost always having a problem with what someone else is saying. I was finally no longer feeling each pushback and difference of opinion as character assignation.

> *My entire "self" no longer balanced on a knife's edge of whether or not someone else approved of me.*

My friendships didn't go up in flames (in my mind at least) each time someone failed to return a call or text quickly enough. I gradually stopped feeding on a constant diet of perceived rejection and humiliation, which enabled me to hold on to friendships and better value more casual acquaintances.

I was no longer the guy yelling and cursing at someone who was shocked and confused about whatever I was freaking out about. I learned to clearly and calmly and directly discuss the actions and reactions of others that bothered me. I learned how to give others the benefit of the doubt rather than automatically assume people were disrespecting me and then go after them with both barrels blazing. I gave them the opportunity to respond to whatever I was feeling, and I let them know I was listening in return. My relationships matured, as did my emotional understanding and control. The world I lived in fit more comfortably once it was no longer all about me.

> Not taking things so personally set me free of the chains I'd wrapped around myself most of my life.

I've learned to live my way yet respect that others likely have a different approach that works for them. I've grown more accepting of my place in this world, offering unreserved grace and understanding even if people still let me down sometimes (the way I let so many others down in my younger life).

It was an immeasurable blessing that my father was a psychologist.

It was due to his skills and connections that we so quickly found mental-health providers to prescribe me the best medications for my combination of ADHD, anxiety, and depression. The invisible burden of these ailments can be crushing. I'm one of the lucky ones who now knows what it's like on the "other side." I took my medication religiously—another bonus of having my dad there helping me understand how vital consistency is, particularly when you're mixing medications that must be taken at specific intervals in order to interact properly. Along with improvements in anxiety, depression, and focus, my badly abused self-confidence flickered back to life.

Experiencing my surroundings and emotions freely, without worry, was like a refreshing breeze across my skin. I heard and sensed and appreciated things I'd never noticed before: birds singing, people smiling, the beauty of human innovation as demonstrated in the architecture that lined the University of Iowa campus. Living in the present, my mind could settle on what I wanted to see and do next (rather than circling back and back and back to the mistakes and defeats and misunderstandings of the past).

Anxiety can be a silent, screaming distraction, obliterating your ability to deal with anything but making it go away.

Free from that demon demanding my undivided attention, I could now speak up in class and engage in discussion without risking a paralyzing panic attack. Studying became something I knew I could handle and complete the same as my classmates. I could accomplish almost anything, my father was prone to remind me. Now, for the first time in longer than I could remember, I believed him.

The classroom became a new home where I belonged.

College was no longer somewhere I forced myself to go because I'd promised I would, which meant I could stay enrolled at the university and enjoy all the other cool things about being a student (like partying and pretty girls).

I remember a communication-studies course I took. One day in class, a contentious topic about which I was passionate came up for debate. I raised my hand, strongly opined, and was met head-on with a barrage of fierce resistance from several other classmates.

Four different people teamed up to explain in no uncertain terms why I was wrong. They were loud, determined, and clearly had no intention of backing down until I agreed with them. It was a dynamic which, before my treatment, would have ended disastrously for all. This time, though, a more confident, controlled me waited for a pause in their tirade, and with a raised but steady voice, I artfully sliced their argument to pieces, locking gazes with each opposing classmate as I did so.

The classroom grew silent around us, until the professor finally said, "Okay!" and segued into the next topic. I hadn't backed down, but I'd respected my classmates' passion in defending their point of view. We'd all been firm, but there'd been no maliciousness to any of our arguments. We'd debated instead of battling to the death, and I couldn't have been prouder of how far my treatment had taken me in my recovery.

Thank heavens for the medication I was still taking to keep my thoughts and emotional impulses balanced.

Only, after class was dismissed that day, I checked my bag and realized I hadn't brought or taken any of my meds that morning. I'd been in too much of a rush leaving the apartment. I was dumbstruck.

For a while, my dad had been telling me that it wasn't just the pharmaceuticals, that I was changing in my perspective and how I genuinely saw myself and the people and world around me, that I could trust myself to keep changing and keep improving, and that I should be proud of the man I was becoming. And he really was right. I was just as capable as my peers when I put my mind to it.

The issue was, on a daily basis, how to convince my mind of the potential that had always been within me. So I kept taking my medication.

> *My need for treatment* wasn't *a sign of weakness, I learned, but, rather, a biological necessity.*

Accepting that I still needed help to control and regulate my feelings on a daily basis was another in a long series of life-changing moments.

My dad suggested I try "mindfulness" meditation.

You read that right. Me. A "manly" man. Sitting on the floor with my eyes closed, chanting and deep breathing as my cares melted away.

I pictured a monk humming away on the dusty stone floor of some crumbling temple. Like pretty much everything I denigrated at first glance back then, I didn't know what the hell I was talking about, but that didn't stop me from defending my position like an expert. However, my old man continued to bring it up when my mood would shift, or if my emotions ran high, or when life just wasn't working for me and my anxiety was off the charts.

I respected him so much. I'd learned to respect his intuition for what might work for me. So I told him I would consider the idea, and then I ended up "forgetting," the way I did (and I still sometimes do, I guess) when something I agreed to do wasn't my idea. About two weeks later, we were sitting and talking when he asked, "So, have you practiced any mindfulness yet?" He wasn't going to push, because he knew I'd shove back. But he wasn't letting the idea go, either, without doing his best to subtly get his recommendation through my thick skull. He suggested some reputable experts, like Jon Kabat-Zinn and Thich Nhat Hanh, mentioning that I could check them out on YouTube.

Mind-Full-Ness

What would it hurt?

YouTube was my compromise. No classes or in-person instructor for me. If I was going to humiliate myself, I was doing it in the privacy of my own bedroom. I found a mindfulness video—a plethora of them, actually—and clicked on one of Dad's recommended experts. It had bells going off in the background and a male voice giving instructions. For fun, I decided to give it a try.

Listening to the voice, I relaxed my body, sank into my chair, and focused on my breathing while acknowledging, judgment free, each sensation that bubbled to the surface. By the end of the eight-minute video, I felt noticeably calmer and more centered. I wasn't yet a "convert." It wasn't as if I'd be running down the street anytime soon telling people about the beauty of connecting with the inner me. But I can admit now that I was a bit excited.

Mindfulness, at least experimenting with it, may just be a great way to clear out the clutter — the chattering thoughts and feelings and experiences that could still ruin your teen's day.

But proceed wisely.

We recommend initially exploring this option under the supervision of a therapist.

There was also this video of a Navy SEAL talking about breathing and how it is the one thing a person *can* control and how essential it is to be aware of and adjust your breathing, especially in moments of stress (when most of us never realize the physiological effects of whatever challenge we've encountered).

This muscular, ripped, intimidating guy was saying that just by listening to our body and mindfully calming the physical effects of stress, we can re-center our physiological and mental responses. We can pause and choose our next path rather than fight-or-flight jumping into action without thinking first and suffering unwanted consequences. Meditation's perceived threat to my masculinity was lessoning by the second.

Each day, I had a quarter-mile walk to campus from a nearby parking garage. I developed my own form of mindfulness focused on breathing and awareness as I headed to class. I called it "mindfulness in motion." As I walked, I gently released every thought and experience beyond the moment. Arriving at class, I felt calmer, more focused, and better prepared to embrace the material of the day rather than my thoughts being divided between my coursework and whatever else was going on in my life.

I found I increasingly longed for a "natural" way to release excess energy.

It's important to note that the "overactive" part of my mind and body wasn't going away.

Meds and therapy were helping me learn to harness that energy in social settings and when I needed to slow down and concentrate. But I didn't like the idea of being dependent on medication to the degree I was when there had to be other approaches to lean into—natural mind-body work that could offset some of my dependence on chemical intervention.

I ran at least a mile on the treadmill each day. The cardio was a great outlet, not to mention the endorphin hit (calming and centering) the exercise released. I'd worked with weights for years as well, conditioning and toning my musculature. As my mindfulness of breathing improved, that practice became a part of my physical training—the running and the weights, where "core work" and breath control are key and can significantly enhance your results.

My "mindfulness in motion" expanded organically from there, resulting in even more of my life feeling balanced and centered.

> *Within two months, under my doctor's guidance, I'd cut my prescribed intake of Clonazepam in half. That was a HUGE win for me.*

No longer taking prescription meds is something I think anyone in my position longs for.

Some people can, though I'd encourage you to only attempt to wean yourself off your meds under the careful guidance of your health-care provider.

I'd love to cut out the Clonazepam altogether—it leeches my short-term memory even at lower doses. Unfortunately, that hasn't been an option for me. But I continue working every day to achieve better results by modifying my lifestyle choices. This gives the meds I do take a better opportunity to work. It also offers my body and mind the opportunity to learn to work together better.

Nothing can throw your thoughts and your day out of whack as quickly as regret.

While we're delving into a mind-body discussion, let me share the power that comes with forgiveness and how it helped me develop a healthier approach to life.

When I was enduring my darkest times, I hurt and mistreated and publically humiliated so many people. To this day, I'm overcome with resounding sorrow for the damage I've done to others. I was reckless. I'm committed to never again become that lost, angry, raging person. But that doesn't change the reality of what I did or the depth of disgust I feel when I allow myself to look back.

That kind of backward reflecting can damage the success of the positive, more "others-focused" principles I strive to live by today. The residual negative emotion still resonating from my past is that powerful.

Spirituality has become an important element of my recovery.

A personal relationship with God, praying for people I've hurt, and asking forgiveness for my destructive actions has been a journey of peace for me. I learned to forgive myself for my mistakes, as God has forgiven me. Released from the burden of shame, I am committed even more strongly to achieving true change in my actions and reactions and life choices.

Perhaps the most difficult and humbling task I've undertaken so far has been asking forgiveness of those I've wronged.

I made the decision to reach out personally and apologize to those I'd hurt most. Without exception, each of them offered forgiveness in return. But one response to my apology in particular stands out to me.

I received a letter that read, "Austin, you're forgiven. I forgave you a long time ago. You were always a sweet, compassionate guy who was putting on a show. I saw that, but I couldn't figure out how to connect with you."

I was blown away by this guy's grace and concern for me despite my behavior, which helped me realize I had even more work to do.

I needed to forgive others.

Again, I found prayer a mighty neutralizer. The more I focused on and released past slights toward me, the more the hurt and resentment and anger I still carried from those times melted away. "Everyone is forgiven" is where I eventually landed.

> *If there is a hell, no one deserves to go there for anything that was done to me. Just as I hope that none of those I've wronged would wish for me to face eternal fire and damnation for my thoughtless actions.*

A growing peace has been my reward for these practices—that, and being able to work with my father now to reach out to others, sharing as frankly as I can of my experiences and growth. I'm humbled by the outpouring of support I receive as we talk with other families facing challenges similar to ours. But most of all, I see our message as a responsibility now.

Because I've forgiven as I have been forgiven by others, I can now be someone a kid (hurting and lost and seeing no way out, like the Austin I once was) might look at and say, "If he did it, I can do it." I have the opportunity to inspire people to do far greater things than I ever will.

It would be my privilege to help others realize the absolute best of themselves. And if we can achieve that, Dad and I, I will be forever grateful. Absolutely everything I've been through will have been worth it.

And, finally, let me talk a bit about forgiving my dad.

For a long time, I'd been telling my dad I forgave him. But when there's as much scorched earth as there was in our relationship, things are hardly ever resolved that simply. I had a lot of issues of my own, but I knew how significantly my life's course had been altered by my parents' mistakes.

Things might have played out a lot differently if I'd had a more stable family life, a firmer platform from which to become a "normal" kid, without all those gut-wrenching good-byes and being shipped back and forth between my mom and dad and two totally different worlds.

And my dad had once been an angry man who used intimidation (verbal, psychological, and physical) to parent. All of that left its mark on my tendency toward self-doubt and low self-worth and shame. I grew to dislike myself at an early age because I sensed strongly that I was disliked by those who should have loved me most. My parents' emotional and psychological challenges reinforced my innate sense of worthlessness. None of it intentionally. I truly believe that. But the damage was done.

> *I carried into early adulthood an underlying resentment that continued to hurt me. But it also enhanced my ability to relate to the better man my father had become.*

I truly forgave my father when we were college roommates at the University of Iowa. No matter how crazy busy he was or how much I was still testing him, this man always stopped what he was doing to listen to me whenever I needed him. He'd apologized over and over for the past, but now I was witnessing his actions backing his promise to do better. He saw me as valuable long before I could honestly embrace my potential. He'd seen opportunity for my new, exciting life while I was still wrapped up in the damage left in my wake. He'd forgiven me first, unconditionally. And because of that grace, I was healing. Now it was my turn to offer him (and our relationship) the same opportunity to thrive.

I needed him more than ever if I was going to get my act together, and there was nowhere else he wanted to be. But I didn't just want a helping hand. I made sure he knew that. I wanted him close, closer than we'd ever been. I wanted the dad I'd never really gotten to know. A role model. A mentor.

> *I genuinely wanted to move forward together, wherever we'd go next.*

Difficult decisions on my horizon.

Important, often daunting choices still greeted me at every turn, but I steadily improved.

By far, one of the hardest challenges that remained was dealing with the bar scene in which I was deeply entrenched and eliminating the toxic friendships I'd invited into my life as a result.

> *Partying was getting old, and many of the superficial friendships I'd thought were rock solid had begun to disintegrate.*

Some of my good-time acquaintances graduated and moved away. Others dropped out or transferred somewhere less academically challenging so that partying could continue to rock their worlds. Comradery only takes a group like ours so far, and ours seemed to have run its course. At least for me.

I was tired of the same routine: go out and get drunk, tell everyone you love them, then wake up and act as if you don't remember anything that happened. My need for that kind of "guaranteed" but soulless belonging was eroding. I had other goals now, things I wanted to do with my life. I longed for a sense of self-worth that revolved around more than how many people knew my name.

Eventually, I stopped going to the bars. People called, wondering where I was, and I'd say I was staying home for the evening. It didn't take long for the calls to stop.

> *These weren't the kind of friends who wanted to know me as anything beyond constantly "up," or sloppy drunk and stumbling all over the place.*

So there I was, in the same space as when I'd arrived in Iowa: alone.

But this time it was a different kind of alone. I felt strangely comfortable in my "solitude." No longer was I emotionally investing in people who would never be a real "belonging place" for me. I was claiming control over where my life would go. I was focused on building a future that truly excited me.

No longer wasting my time chasing quantity over quality, I began networking and choosing my friends more wisely.

Ezra became part of my new inner circle. His may have been the first "reciprocal" friendship of my life. He wanted me to be my absolute best, and I wanted the same for him. We talked often about deep, meaningful topics. We helped each other work through a lot, celebrating the high points and lifting each other up when reality grew too harsh.

> *I learned to lean into relationships with people who wanted the best for me and who'd push me toward becoming the best Austin I possibly could be.*

I learned to value my time and to value and respect others' contributions. If a friendship wasn't a win-win for everyone involved, I learned to stop being the only one nurturing the connection. I would rather sit alone than have an emotional vampire as my sidekick. You know the kind of friend I mean. Be on the lookout—they're everywhere.

I grew to have my own go-to, inner circle of friends, just like my dad—people I could trust with anything. That's not to say I didn't and don't routinely interact with people I don't connect with on such a deep level. I'm learning more every day about sharing myself with and helping others and receiving their generous, positive attention in return. But I'm more careful now about who gets invited to share my heart and soul.

I've built healthier boundaries, investing my emotional and psychological energy in friendships I believe are as nurturing and uplifting for me as I've always longed to be for others.

I was doing better, but there was more healing to do.

With all my diagnoses, there were so many moving parts. Getting a handle on what was connected to what and the possible interactions between everything wasn't going to be *easy* for a long time to come. Maybe never.

I would be going along feeling good about things, and then I would stumble. Someone would do or say something that triggered a negative response. Or I'd start looking back, after the fact, and worry myself sick about something I'd never be able to go back and change. And then the anger would come, the lost sleep, the anxiety bleeding into the next morning. And the outside world was suddenly a threat again—only, intellectually I knew it wasn't.

Each time this happened, for a moment or two, it was if I'd fallen down a rabbit hole, all the way back to square one.

Except by that point, I'd learned strategies that helped me step outside myself and see the bigger picture.

I'd practiced and become more experienced at taking positive and appropriate action in response to my anxiety. I'd learned to re-center myself more quickly and to avoid destructively acting out my anger and frustration before I could get my emotions under control.

Bottom line, I still had a lot of work to do on my healing journey, but I didn't see that as a burden.

My dad and my doctors helped me view my ongoing treatment and personal growth as opportunities to improve.

I remained committed to my treatment and worked hard on my recovery, and those "back-to-square-one" moments became less and less frequent. I gained more traction each day as I learned, alongside my dad, how to be more positive and productive.

Kevin: A Healthier Field of Play

So much of the unhealthy mental processing that damaged Austin's life had its origins in early childhood.

For years, these ineffective life views and approaches had festered like a silent cancer invisible to everyone but him. His mind became a battleground where he warred against destructive impulses and negative instincts he often couldn't control—some of which were thrust upon him due to circumstances not of his choosing.

> *For years, a continuous battle had been fought to control his life outlook and his relating to others.*

At first, mostly below the surface, and then later in the open for everyone to see, his belief that he could never do or be better eroded.

Therapy and carefully regulated medications were now helping him begin to win more battles than he lost. The enemy was still within: professionally diagnosed mental illness in the form of a distorted thought process and a hyperactive sympathetic nervous system that had for years traumatized him with a near-constant fight-or-flight relationship with his world and the people in it.

He was a man now (no longer a little boy or troubled teen), but he was a man whom some he'd cared about had stigmatized him as a criminal and a threat to society. And those same people, were they to witness his progress, might still judge it as not enough. They'd expect overnight change if he were *really* serious about taking a different path. This was a troubling dynamic I made a careful point of talking with my son about whenever he gave me the chance.

I'd been there since his move to Iowa. I'd seen how hard he'd worked despite his continuing to make certain mistakes. I made certain to reflect that, rather than permanently flawed and irredeemable, my son's potential was blooming to life before my eyes. To hell with those who'd written him off.

I vividly remember one of these key conversations.

It was late (around eleven thirty or so on a Saturday night), I'd finished whatever work I would accomplish that day, and I'd settled onto the couch to self-medicate with empty calories and the second half of a West Coast college football game. As mentioned, after four-plus years, I had come to know well the sound of Austin walking up the exterior apartment stairs. He was back early, pulling me somewhat out of my work-induced stupor. Maybe he'd forgotten something.

"Hey, Dad," he said. "You want a beer? I bought us some."

"Sure, I'll take one," was my instant response. "What are you up to?"

"I didn't feel like going out. I thought I'd see if you were watching a game."

I muted the television, wondering what was really on his mind.

He eventually mentioned feeling as if he were wasting his time and money, clubbing the way he had been. He didn't like that he had nothing to show for all those years. "I should be preparing for my future," he said, not for the first time.

His values were shifting. It was an amazing, rewarding thing to behold.

That night, though, as we continued to watch that game, I reflected on his slow but steady improvement over the past several years. Sometimes this involved inching forward, succeeding in a new area only to slide back again, exhibiting a lingering behavioral pattern or thought process I'd believed he'd moved beyond. But all and all, I saw a steady upward trend.

Grateful anew for our deepening relationship, I steered his attention away from regrets and toward the future.

He'd been expressing a lot of compassion lately and a desire to help others who also struggled with self-doubt and a negative self-image. There was much work left to do, but on this night (one of my favorites from our time in Iowa City), I made certain he knew how immensely proud I was of his progress, as well as my confidence in his ability to bring to life his hopes and dreams for his world and for others.

A never-ending job.

I think at some point all parents tell themselves their job is mostly done once their kids reach the responsible and independent age of eighteen.

I can remember imagining the progression from there: My sons would call me once each week with an update on their careers, families, and vacations. We would occasionally travel together and have regular visits. And perhaps it works that way for some families. Though I suspect no parent is ever free from worrying about even the most "successful" of children. In fact, the older and more involved in life our kids become and the higher the stakes, the more we seem to worry. After high school comes college (for many), employment, school loans, and other debt, marriages, and children.

Our concern for our kids never ends, even as our sons mature and begin to strike out on their own.

Even the best of us stumble and fall now and again.

It's part of life.

But during this stage of Austin's recovery, when he was doing more for himself and doing it better and better, I admit to a bit of panic with each inevitable setback. There would be a brief, reflexive thought that we'd never get past the point where I was worried about what might happen next.

There was an element of embarrassment too, whenever something he'd said or done became public; for instance, when he was arrested for stopping that skinhead from harassing another student. My immediate focus then had been on how big a setback this new legal issue would be for my son and on how Austin's name was in the paper in conjunction with the story. I dreaded my faculty reading about it and perceiving the incident as a negative reflection on my character or parenting.

A part of me perpetually worried that "the other shoe" might drop and smash all the progress we were making.

Austin was unquestionably proving himself. He was closing in on becoming the first on his mom's side of the family to earn a four-year degree—and from the top English department in the country. But as a mentor once told me, it takes only one "Oh, shit!" to wipe out a hundred "attaboys."

I tried my very best to maintain my composure whenever he slipped up.

And for the most part, I succeeded.

We'd talk through the experience and the consequences. Before long, he didn't need to be prompted to reason through what he could learn from his actions, especially his mistakes, and how to best avoid future occurrences of the same issue. We spent five years sharing those kinds of ups and downs, each of us getting better at handling ourselves. Austin had a lot prove to himself and me, but ultimately, he hit it out of the park. I had a lot of growing to do myself as I gained even greater trust in my son's ability and dedication to improve.

Are setbacks or relapses bad?

As parents, we want our kids to progress through life without pain or disappointment. However, mistakes and accidents are often the situations in which we learn the most. Also, our need to see things go smoothly can be perceived by others as a demand for perfection. And how unreasonable an expectation is that for anyone, ourselves included?

> *A habit that has served me well over the years has been to objectively label each mistake as exactly what it is—a setback—and then move on.*

My focus then becomes the subsequent growth that can be achieved. That forward progress secures more and more of my attention, eclipsing the "stumble."

For example, I've mentioned several times my concerns about Austin's continued drinking despite his doctors' warnings and the potential that his continued partying might cause additional behavioral setbacks. But instead of issuing an ultimatum about him no longer drinking "or else," I dealt with each situation that arose as objectively and constructively as possible (within the boundaries of the rules we'd established for Austin successfully living with me, pursuing his degree, and holding down a job). His choices were just that: his to make.

Which is what made the moment he eventually said he was no longer going to consume alcohol even more rewarding. He said that while he didn't crave alcohol, when he did drink, he had difficultly doing so in moderation. So, to build a better future for himself, he would stop drinking altogether.

"When I'm drinking, it is just too easy to get into trouble," he told me. "It seems like someone is always trying to challenge my manhood."

And that's how our fridge became stocked with nonalcoholic beer. To honor Austin's efforts, I no longer brought alcohol into our home. Not because I feared he might start drinking again.

> *I wanted, and still would do anything, to support any choice he made to better his life.*

Did I make mistakes as a parent?

Sure.

I've already discussed several of them. And the longer we lived together in Iowa, the more mistakes I made. That's simply part of being an engaged parent. But remember what I said above. Just as it's unfair to hold our children accountable to some unrealistic expectation of how perfect we want their lives to be, it's equally unfair to expect the same from ourselves.

During my time in Iowa, I pushed myself to my physical and psychological and financial limits, and then some. It's no wonder there were many moments when I wasn't at my best. But I always tried to learn the most I could from each setback, intent on doing better moving forward.

Watching Austin grow has been my greatest joy.

For so many years, I would hear other parents talk about their children's successes and accomplishments. While I was genuinely happy for them and understood why they were proud, in response I felt an alarming mixture of jealously and grief. Compared to how they were seemingly breezing through parenting, I was screwing up left and right. Austin had raw ability and unlimited potential; why hadn't I helped him achieve anything of note?

I know. That kind of pity party accomplishes nothing, and it wasn't often that I allowed myself to indulge. But those short-sighted moments weren't a sign of doubt or giving up on my son. They were honest, emotional responses to not being able to see far enough down the road to where all our hard work would *most definitely* begin to pay off.

When Austin first moved to Iowa City, he didn't even know how to use Google. Now he manages our Google analytics and social media marketing. In addition to graduating from college, he's developed a genuine love for helping others. Once, he viewed people as a threat. Now he's comfortable going out on a limb, risking rejection and judgment, to network with other successful people—strangers, most of them.

He's overcome too many obstacles to count.

And he's probably grown as much spiritually as he has psychologically.

He seeks divine guidance in moments where doubt and rejection were once his gods. He's quick to remind me that our direction will not come from ourselves as much as it will from a God who is at the very genesis of our determination to help and serve others. Austin's life objective has become helping people who doubt themselves grow into leaders who will, in turn, positively help and influence others.

Am I now a proud parent?

Hell, yeah!

WHAT HAPPENED?

Most troubled kids are contending with a number of psychological problems.

For instance, Austin struggled with PTSD, ADHD, anxiety, and depression. Underlying these diagnoses was a shame-proneness tendency that fed and exacerbated his negative self-image and sense of worthlessness. Consequently, he continuously responded to every person and situation he encountered as a threat. He frequently felt humiliated, so he isolated, became lonely, and spent almost every waking hour angry and paranoid, with his body in a perpetual fight-or-flight state.

After his commitment to change and willingness to seek professional help was established, the question became how to go about helping him work through his issues.

From the Psychologist
What if . . .

It would have been interesting to watch the reaction if I'd marched into Austin's psychologist's office during that first visit and said, "My son dropped out of high school, has multiple felonies, and is suicidal. I want you to fix him so that he is a college graduate, he's confident with a bright future, and he evolves into a loving, giving person."

Can you imagine the stammering?

Yet, after years of hard work and support, those are precisely the things my son has accomplished.

How? I have received the best training available for my career as a psychologist, and I can say with certainty that there is no single answer to the question.

> *There is no one-size-fits-all solution for troubled kids and young adults facing similar challenges and circumstances.*

But after working as hard as we had together, Austin and I were well positioned to find our own unique way to heal.

Addressing Austin's problems continued to be a tremendous challenge.

It required the help of a reputable psychiatrist, a skilled psychologist, and several other professionals. But most essential was my maintaining a healing, nurturing environment in our home. Without that "safe place," that supportive base for him to return to again and again, it's unlikely he could have (early on, at least) sustained the degree of change and success he's achieved.

Austin was dealing with a lot at once—and not just because he continued for quite awhile to prioritize partying with his friends most every night (perhaps even more so) as highly as he did his recovery.

> *His work with his therapist and psychiatrist was never straightforward; neither was the guidance I was called upon to offer at various strategies, and about numerous recommended approaches.*

For example, should we have treated his PTSD first? Maybe, but what if his depression was leaving him without hope, motivation, and energy? So, should we have tackled his depression first? Sure, that was a way to go, but what if his lack of trust made that an impossible task? And so on and so on—lather, rinse, repeat.

As you've read, there were setbacks, lots of late-night conversations, and plenty of worry, frustration, anger—not all of it successfully handled in a positive way.

What was key for my role throughout, however, was keeping my focus on the bigger picture of Austin's continued progress.

The challenges we were facing didn't consume our whole lives.

That was the message I tried to model for Austin.

I continued with my schoolwork and jobs. He did as well. He made his own choices about how to live his life outside the schoolwork and recovery work he'd committed to. There were football games and fun with friends for Austin. And for me, there were those magical moments when my son would sit and talk with me about his life and his thoughts and his dreams for the future—not just his problems and fears and challenges.

And at every step, I did my best to balance my reflecting back the very real progress he was making toward his dreams with encouraging him to continue digging deep for the determination he'd need to stay committed to his recovery.

This was a time of significant change and transition amidst a much longer journey of improving Austin's emotional and psychological health.

I had my son back.

Even now, tears come to my eyes as I write that. He was growing and practicing new skills and becoming confident in them and in himself. What he was learning would help him more successfully relate to the world for the rest of his life. And yet we seemed to be tackling new and more challenging things by the day.

Each attempt to try a new approach to handling his issues was an opportunity for Austin to anticipate failure and the resulting humiliation.

> *His confidence in his abilities would improve once he had more*
> *success under his belt.*

But in the meantime, there was still his early resistance to contend with—as well as his "white-knuckling" through his first try or two at applying each new recommended tactic.

So, no, the roller-coaster ride didn't smooth out now that we were relying on various professionals to help us find our way.

Perspective became a key objective for me.

I worked hard to help Austin recognize and celebrate his successes. We also worked together on his coping with the setbacks he encountered along the way. He was changing in big and small ways. That's what was most important to remember.

> *The result of each step we took together was objectively that —*
> *merely another move toward the ultimate goal my son was*
> *inching closer to with each passing day.*

Austin Checks In

My healing journey remains, without a doubt, the hardest thing I have ever attempted.

It has been downright brutal at times.

> *Forever, it seems, I'd had this fixed way of thinking about*
> *myself, others, and life in general.*

I don't think I can ever convey the reality of how hard my negative, shame-prone, what-does-it-matter mindset was to overcome.

And one of the most frustrating parts of my recovery was knowing I needed to change something but not having the first clue what that something was.

I'm sure there were times when Dad didn't think I was working very hard. But I really was, even when all I was accomplishing was spinning my wheels. Is it any wonder I hung around the party scene so long? Hanging with those people, being a part of that scene, was at the time the only pleasure I got out of life no matter the damage I was doing to myself.

I mean, put yourself in my shoes. Going to school—I hated it. Feeling anxious and under attack all the time—hated it. Seeing my dad working his butt off and succeeding while I struggled and felt trapped in the same place day after day—hated that, too. Rehashing abuse from my past in therapy—yep, for a long time I really hated that. I knew my dad was frustrated early on with my lack of progress—and *that* I hated most of all.

But then Dad would encourage me and help me see all the things I was doing right.

He never allowed me to get bogged down in feeling I should just give up.

He was great about pointing out the areas where he'd noticed growth.

He loved a quote from the Rutgers University head football coach at the time, and he used it with me frequently. The coach would tell his players, "Just keep chopping wood." Meaning they should keep working hard, doing what they were doing, and just by that action alone they would improve. Dad would say that to me a lot.

"Just keep chopping wood. Good things will begin to happen, Austin, sooner or later."

And he was right.

My life was on its way to slowly, positively changing.

WHAT TO DO?

Kevin: Mindset Is Everything

You and your son are on the same playing field.

You are fighting together to win, with you as the team leader slowly turning strategic decisions and execution over to your teammate. Your son is now open and receptive, engaged and determined to succeed. And regardless of whatever setbacks may come, he is working hard to use the tools he's learned he needs to make exciting progress.

> *What follows are helpful recommendations for doing the very best you can as a parent to assist your teen or young adult on his continued journey.*

Adopt a "recovery" mindset.

Complicating the matter of "what to do" for parents in situations similar to mine and Austin's is the reality that we're often tackling several problems at once. Addressing one behavioral or psychological issue at a time can seem (and likely can be) futile. Pretty much expect that NOTHING about your work with your troubled son will happen in a vacuum.

Addressing one problem can cause others to pop up. Further successful inroads made focusing on one key issue can create an unexpected crisis that will require immediate attention—and pause work being done elsewhere. You're on a long-term journey with your child. Expecting these sorts of deviations to become your new normal.

Trust your teen or young adult to lead the way.

His intuition will guide you toward setting the most effective priorities.

Remember your recovery mindset. Expect that your teen will always have something to improve on or another area to grow in. We are never "finished" with our personal healing. With each setback we face, we have the opportunity to once more work through already known parts of ourselves, only with a fresh set of eyes, learning even more about how to positively and effectively relate to our world.

> *Shed your fix-it-fast mentality. Accept that your son will be working on his problems for a while.*

There are more mistakes to come. But there will be more accomplishments and successes as well. It is essential to keep a "big-picture" mindset as you lead your team through each challenge and victory. Model for your son that continually working on his problems is the goal. How? As we've discussed, by continually working on your own.

Continue to move forward with your life. Encourage your teen or young adult to do the same.

Healing means living, not merely overcoming obstacles.

Your son's issues don't have to define his life. Instead, as he works hard, encourage him to focus on what he wants to do next and how he will move forward to achieve those goals. Share your experiences as you model the same forward-thinking approach. Encourage your son to discuss the obstacles in his path, but not to the exclusion of also sharing the excitement and pride of the achievements that will be gained during the same period.

Frankly, the work you are doing together is often no fun. Austin and I did not particularly enjoy all of it.

But it is a meaningful investment in your child's future success and happiness, and it is well worth the effort. This is a helpful perspective to pass on to your child. He won't be struggling like this forever. And going forward under the guidance of the professionals helping him and their recommended treatment programs, the challenges your son is battling now will have a significant, positive impact on his future.

Keep those stages of change in perspective.

As your son progresses in his recovery, he will heal more quickly in some areas than in others. He won't universally acknowledge the need for change in every aspect of his treatment.

After five years in Iowa, Austin was still in the "action" stage of change for many of his problems. As he approached graduation from the university, he continued to work with his psychologist and psychiatrist to address his anger and the perception that he was under continuous threat. He was making great progress dealing with a key underlying contributor to these issues: a "worthless" self-image that left him feeling vulnerable to hurt and attack. He was making great strides in creating an improved sense of self: one where he possessed authentic value and strength.

The goal was for him to be capable of perceiving a threat (or taking a "hit" or two) without responding as if his only options were to attack, fight back, or run. This would remain an ongoing battle for my son for years, a continued journey with its fair share of associated ups (victories) and downs (failures). But for our team, the fact that he remained in the game and committed to his goals and objectives for his future despite any interim setbacks made the work he was doing an unqualified success.

> *When helping your son make substantial changes, remind yourself and him that this is an ongoing process.*

Work to regularly express your confidence that his skill and the degree of his success WILL improve with consistency and practice. Focus on each success, attempt, and realized new skill, as well as on its position in the overall trajectory of his recovery.

Gradual change can be difficult to perceive and explain.

A lot of your son's new skills and "workarounds" for problems will be achieved by degree—creating improvements that can be a challenge to recognize in their very early stages. Your patience, empathy, and compassion will be crucial in his continued and sustained growth as you both develop a recovery mindset.

Remember how naïve I was regarding the extent of his problems and how rapidly we could eradicate them in therapy when Austin first moved to Iowa and enrolled in the college? Austin was committed to changing, but neither of us had any idea what change required.

> *When it became clear how out of our depth we were, it was my job to reframe our expectations for his therapy and healing process.*

Deep and foundational psychological change happens in multiple steps.

The path of those steps should sound familiar after the Parent Playbook work you've already accomplished:

- Your child must recognize the areas in which change is needed.
- He must then understand the process required to make the necessary changes and how this will impact his life.
- Sustained results then require a recovery mindset and a continuous recommitment to persevere and practice the changes.

Setting realistic expectations from the onset is important.

Transformation will be *gradual*, and execution will at first be imperfect and require adjustments. Your goal is a slow and steady progression of results rather than a fixed focus on the endgame.

Now is a good time to talk about *Levels of Competency.*

What follows is an expansion of the stages of change material we've already discussed (see Step Four). There, you were tracking your son's intent as he committed to making and sustaining the required changes.

> *Now, you need to better understand his degree of success in his recovery work.*

Your focus is shifting to his *competency* and your understanding of your son's *progress*. In the 1970s, Neal Burch of Gordan Training International developed a helpful model for understanding the process of integration of a new skill. You'll be observing the following elements:

- His level of *awareness* of the need for specific skills (or workarounds).
- His *proficiency* at executing the techniques he is learning.

Again, you do this by tracking your son's recovery path as he works to address his issues.

Level of Competency	Progression
1. Unconscious-Incompetence	**Your son is unaware (unconscious)** he is lacking a key skill. **He is incapable (incompetent)** of achieving his goal due to his limited skill set.
2. Conscious-Incompetence	**Your son is aware (conscious)** he is missing a key skill. **He is incapable (incompetent)** of achieving his goal until that new skill is acquired.
3. Conscious-Competence	**Your son has consciously acquired** (or is working toward) the new skill. **He is capable (competent)** of achieving his goal but only with sustained attention and focus on employing the new skill. **His new approach requires regular, conscious attention.**
4. Unconscious-Competence	**Your son is (unconsciously) proficient** in the new skill. **He is capable (competent)** of achieving his goal without awareness of the skill being employed. **His new approach has become routine, or habit.**

Austin's dealing with his negative self-image and feelings of constant threat is a prime example of this progression.

- **When he first moved in with me**, he knew he had problems and was willing to seek help, but he was *unaware* as to the exact changes required. He continued to make mistakes that undermined his progress and was unaware that his negative self-image was at the core of his problems.

- **After conversations with me and working his psychologist**, he became aware (*conscious*) that his "worthless" self-view and subsequent isolating himself out of fear were underlying issues causing a number of problems. However, he was still *incapable* of changing these underlying issues.

- **Austin continued to work with his therapist**, became consistent in taking his medication, and began to develop new skills and proficiencies in using these tools. For instance, he began to practice mindfulness meditation in processing past trauma. His confidence, ability, and willingness to be vulnerable grew, as did the number of "healthy" risks he was willing to take. He was now *consciously competent*; however, concerted effort was still required to keep him on track.

- **It would take continued work beyond graduation** for Austin to reach his *unconscious-competent* phase. As his career as an IT consultant began, he faced challenging scenarios where he needed to successfully navigate conflicts and confrontations with coworkers and clients. By that time, when dealing with angry or frustrated individuals, he no longer needed to remind himself that he was worthy, lovable, and valuable. Instead, he'd grown to be able to (unconsciously) make decisions from that "higher self-esteem" perspective. Austin would no longer see these challenging situations as threats but as opportunities to succeed and help customers.

A Note from Austin: It Was Difficult to See the Growth

The work of healing takes a long time, especially when you're changing the way you see yourself, as I was.

If it weren't for my dad, it would have been easy for me to overlook or discount completely the incremental improvements I made early on. I was hyperfocused on what was happening, not on the long-reaching value of my recovery.

At the time, I was still experiencing significant self-hatred.

I took risks, but only begrudgingly. Each "no-guarantees" moment I faced, I initially anticipated that I would wind up humiliated. It was daunting to try new things, such as exploring mindfulness or attempting to make high-quality friends.

I still needed help to figure out how to handle myself when outcomes were uncertain, even when I had every reason to believe positive things would happen. And when something *did* go wrong, no matter how minor, I still struggled with not expecting the aftereffects to be catastrophic.

Fast-forward to the present.

These days, because of my and my father's hard work while I attended the University of Iowa, I am much better at managing my emotional and behavioral reactions to the ups and downs of life.

Recently I stumbled a bit, but almost immediately I was back in the game, making the adjustments I needed to move forward.

Initially, I was angry that I'd allowed myself to fall back into an unhealthy pattern. But I was angrier at my initial reaction to the incident—that I'd once again been tempted to beat myself up and stay stuck in a bad cycle. But instead of turning my anger inward and further setting my recovery back, with of my years of therapy and hard work, I quickly reoriented myself. I took responsibility for my actions, dealt with the aftereffects, and moved forward in a positive way.

And the correction was all but instinctive this time. I didn't need to stop and process how my belief in myself and thought processes were affecting me.

We have way too much to offer to allow ourselves or anyone else to drag us back to the past or to insist that's all we'll ever be.

"Wow" is all I can say on this side of the incredible journey my dad and I have been on.

WHAT'S MOST IMPORTANT?

Your son is working toward maintenance, the final stage of change (as introduced in Step Three).

Your focus, as well as his, now shifts to supporting and growing the gains he is making toward his recovery and life goals. Your objectives with the choices you make as a parent expand to include facilitating the formation of behavioral habits and practices that will serve your son for years to come.

> *You're working toward successfully building the new normal that will become his life.*

As always, you cannot force your teen or young adult to do anything. But you've made significant improvements in your relationship and your ability to participate in your son's journey as a compassionate team leader. You are now having direct and meaningful conversations with your son, and he is turning to you for support as he makes difficult changes.

The way you communicate with your son remains a game changer.

Your reaction to and participation in your son's recovery will dramatically influence his success in the work he does. "Outside of session" is where as much as 40 percent of therapy's benefit occurs. A peaceful, loving, and nonjudgmental environment is still essential for him.

Equally critical is your conveying support and trust rather than judgment and scrutiny:

- Make your interactions about "We are in this together."
- Continue to adopt the point of view of "I've been there before," so that empathy and compassion make constant appearances in your conversations with your son.

Your son is relearning and reexperiencing love, trust, and encouragement at home as if for the very first time.

He is working to reintegrate his sense of self, his adjusting belief system, and his confidence in his ability to sustain healthy relationships, often by gauging his "success" in his relating to you.

At all times, model "unconditional positive regard" toward your son.

This is a therapeutic term for genuinely caring for the other person's welfare and being authentic and open with your positive regard for them despite whatever negative circumstances or challenges arise.

Within a therapeutic relationship, it is incredible how healing this approach can be for patients. Feeling and believing that the therapist has compassion for them and is attempting to empathize with them is crucial to forming a successful healing relationship. As a parent, you can create the same environment for your child at home.

Your son craves your acceptance above all else. Be certain you are reflecting that back to him at all times.

How do you do that?

- Offer kind words and compassionate verbal responses and observations.
- Keep your tone and responses respectful regardless of provocation.
- Give as much care and attention to *how* you speak to your child as you do the actual words you say.
- Work to understand how he's thinking and how he learns. Craft your comments and answers to better support his approach.
- Listen much more than you speak so he knows you value what he says and thinks.
- Avoid interrupting him as he speaks, which can be perceived as a hostile or aggressive form of verbal rejection, or at a minimum, that what he is saying is unimportant.
- Talk with your son as if you expect him to be successful. Your positive expectations will communicate the message that you think he is capable.

Above all else, continue to make *positive* changes together.

Remove any "negative undertones" from your discussions with and relating to your son.

Families experiencing what yours is tend to function in an environment where self-derogatory statements are expected. Often it is acceptable to "put someone down" as a part of every-day conversation.

This dynamic doesn't in any way reflect on the participants as "bad" people. Behavioral patterns such as these are often unconscious efforts to help family members feel better about their own insecurities. Many of us learned these habits in our formative years. Unfortunately, we've passed them along to our children.

> *Work to identify and eradicate any of these toxic habits from your home.*

Your troubled teen's or young adult's healing depends on a compassionate, empathetic relationship with you. In fact, your modeling of more positive way for the two of you to communicate and deal with issues will help him build more successful, nurturing relationships of his own, breaking the "negative" cycle you may have been perpetuating from your past.

Deal with relapses as *part of* his healing process.

As part of your son's dramatic growth, distinct steps backward are inevitable—triggering your parental fear that he is relapsing into a dark and destructive place. Your son will likely have the same instinctive emotional reaction. The true setback would be if he allowed a single mistake or failure to derail his progress more permanently.

We've already discussed the importance of you not interfering with his experience of and dealing with the consequences of his poor choices. It's critical as well that you don't interfere with his work with his therapist, who will presumably be counseling him through the aftermath of his setback.

Your involvement is important, however, from the standpoint of supporting (and maintaining perspective on) your son's overall recovery:

- Assure him that one incident or mistake does not mean starting over from the very beginning.
- Remind him that shame has no place in his experience of the consequences of his actions. Shame is the result of anger turned inward. Help your son find healthier outlets for the difficult emotions he is experiencing so they do not become weapons used to rip at the positive self-regard he's developed.
- Whenever possible, call attention to the improvement he's made (and continues to make) in his recovery.
- Help him reposition his disappointment into a determination to learn from the experience and to develop a plan or approach that will reduce the likelihood of further recurrence.
- Reaffirm your calm, positive regard for your son. Extend your hand to help him get back on track, share your continued understanding of how hard his journey has been, and express your pride in the many accomplishments he's achieved so far.

Your Parent Playbook

You and your son have accomplished a lot in your journey together.

As your son grows, heals, and maintains his emotional and psychological achievements, several important tools will help you support his continued progress.

Tool	Purpose	Goal
Focus on authentic conversation with, and interest in, your son.	Even as your son becomes more independent in his efforts and works one on one with his doctors, your influence in his life remains key. Proactively express that you are committed to growing and maintaining your relationship long-term. This is not a time to smother him or force decisions on him. He may make mistakes as he makes more choices on his own, but continue to express your interest. Always make yourself available when he indicates he's ready to talk.	**Make the relationship with your son an ongoing priority.** Let him know by your actions that you continue to want to be present in his life. Grow and foster your relationship as a lifelong team. **You are his ultimate source of support.**
Recognize your son's strengths as much or more than his challenges.	Yes, you are knee-deep in helping him work through all that has gone wrong. But your son is making great progress. Highlight his strengths and make certain he recognizes them. Target conversations that discuss how he can utilize his strengths and the same successful techniques he has used in other areas of his recovery.	**Regularly take inventory of and spotlight your son's achievements.** This approach strengthens your relationship and adds to his resources, confidence, and belief in his future.

Tool	Purpose	Goal
Celebrate your successes.	At this point, you and your son have accomplished things together that few could have predicted. Celebrate these milestones.	**Recognizing hard work, success, and key achievements helps set expectations for continued growth in the future.**
Help your son develop a maintenance-/relapse-prevention plan.	A maintenance/relapse plan includes not "tempting" relapse or even sending a signal that you anticipate your son falling back into dangerous patterns. Look at it instead as a way to protect the gains your son has made should there be an unexpected future setback.	**Involve your son in not only thinking of ways to maintain his progress (despite momentary setbacks) but also in thinking carefully about all that would be at stake if there were a relapse.**
Empower your son.	Elevate his status from someone who is out of control to someone who's worked hard to regain his ability to make healthy and successful choices for his future. Trust him to make those better choices for himself. Allow him to make mistakes and work through his issues independently. Be there for him every step of the way, but make certain he knows you know he absolutely can succeed in his recovery.	**Treating your son as a competent equal conveys respect.** Let him know you believe in and value his abilities, even going so far as to ask for his advice and input when you work on your own growth. Treat him as the success you know he can be, and then watch him grow into making even more successful choices.

YOUR NEXT PLAY

Your teen or young adult is working toward the maintenance stage of change. However, he continues to depend on your vital role in his healing journey.

Your Game Plan in Step Six	Help your teen or young adult adopt a "recovery mindset" toward his long-term healing goals.
As a parent, you will continue to	support and encourage him while expecting him to take the lead in his own recovery.
Your teen is beginning to	become "consciously competent" as he deals with his issues and the complex choices and challenges ahead, even though there will be more setbacks along his journey.
Your relationship dynamic is changing to	a more "adult" and balanced dynamic in which you lean on each other in moments of crisis and difficulty and work together to solve problems.
Your Next Step	**Shift your focus to the next phase of your lives and on creating the best future possible for each of you.**

STEP SEVEN: CREATE YOUR
BEST LIFE
Both of You

Your Game-Plan Challenge	Shift your and your son's focus from targeting recovery alone to striving for broader goals.
You, the parent, are	wanting, for your son and yourself, the very best life can offer.
Your teen or young adult is	coming to "full life." As the result of his hard work, he's achieved increased certainty that with sustained hard work and passion he *can* achieve the healthy goals he's set for himself.
Your relationship dynamic is	now one of pride and excitement for a hard-fought "win"—your son's long-term recovery, for which you continue to work together.
Your Goal for This Step	Reorient your shared perspective of the future toward the next dream you want to achieve (both individually and together) despite the surprises and difficulties and diversions you will face along the way.

Be proud of the work you and your son have completed so far and the recovery he's already achieved.

Continue to foster and grow the healing relationship you've successfully rebuilt as you've implemented the techniques discussed in this seven-step game plan, and practice the methods in your Parent Playbook. And be hopeful as you look forward to even more success.

Once Austin graduated from college and began the independent life he was by then ready to embrace, I could have gone back to being a parent who watched from afar. I could have turned my focus once more to my life. But as I think back to all we've shared since we left Iowa, what strikes me is that I would have lost as much as my son lost if we'd gone our separate ways, emotionally, only connecting now and again for holidays and special occasions and perhaps a shared vacation every now and then.

Now **is the time to enjoy the life you and your son have carved out together after weathering your difficult journey to this point.**

Are you still enhancing each other's lives? Are you, as a parent, continuing to "get out" of the relationship even more than you're investing? If your answer is an unqualified "Yes!" then now is the time to lean into knowing each other better and working even harder to expand on the firm foundation you've established.

NOTE: We're taking a slightly different approach to this last step than with the others. As we redirect our lens toward the "rewards" of my son's and my hard work together, our hope for our remaining stories is to inspire you to continue dreaming of (and working toward) your own bright future with your teen or young adult.

Rather than break out into its own section, this time in Austin's and my commentary on "WHAT HAPPENED?" we'll blend those reflections into the stories themselves.

There's still a concluding chapter to come, but with Step Seven, we've crafted a broader, "bigger-picture" impression, a future glimpse, if you will, framed with a final view that includes an intimate look into Austin's and my relationship.

You'll still find separate "WHAT TO DO?" and "WHAT'S MOST IMPORTANT?" material to review. But for this last step in our journey together, please allow our stories to inspire you to believe once more in the limitless potential you and your son share.

We've also "tweaked" the heading for our "stories" section.

Never lose hope, my friends. You and your son have a bright, limitless future ahead of you.

THE PARENT-CHILD CONNECTION

Think of all you and your son have been through.

Consider the hard work and sacrifices and ups and downs, and now you're at place where things are working better. The world looks brighter more often than it appears in shadow. At one time, setbacks seemed to be lurking around every corner. You are no longer bracing for them.

Ask yourself if this wonderful place of achievement and connection with your son is something you want distance from — or is it a growing dynamic you want to explore the rest of your lives?

If you're anything like me, the exciting future ahead is your daily inspiration to keep fighting and to continue working and, above all else, to prioritize your growing relationship with your son as you plan your next steps.

Austin: Forward and Back and Beyond

Before

So much of my early life was a frantic search for love, acceptance, and deep friendship.

I wanted closeness.

The isolated existence I'd once clung to in order to protect myself from rejection and humiliation ignited an even deeper desire for companionship. For years, partying was my solution for filling the emotional emptiness within.

I was never alone. My veins flowing with alcohol's soothing rush, I was accepted by a string of "awesome" people who always welcomed me. My liquid courage helped me "man up" and take part—until the next morning when its effects wore off. But no worries that my newfound self-confidence was based on a me who was actually more about the "insider crowd" I was chasing. There were never-ending parties on my horizon.

And so grew the hollow feeling of loneliness I couldn't shake, feeding my anxiety that I'd never truly belong. So I found a job to reinforce my place in the party scene that defined my identity at the time: I became a bouncer who ushered in coworkers and even more friends for me to feel connected to. I could flex my "tough-guy" muscles and make a bit of money, too. Sweet!

But I also saw some of the most degrading things I've ever witnessed. The bar scene was an expensive, superficial way of life, distracting college students from building a better reality for themselves. And it was all about the money, not the people and relationships that for so long I'd wanted to be a real part of my life.

For years, I'd held on to a "bad breath is better that no breath" approach to being, justifying my questionable choices and behaviors and unfulfilling relationships, not because I was getting what I needed out of the dynamic but because I was driven by an aversion to loneliness and a fear of thinking independently. I was blessed with a beautiful mind, but instead of using it to construct a colorful future (the result, if I'd taken the initiative and chosen between the positive alternatives available to me), I followed the crowd down a static path that offered little resistance and yet promised few rewards beyond the moment.

My foremost goal at the time was to extract every ounce of fun and laughter from every nook and cranny I could.

I reveled in the buzz and the endless supply of girls.

> *I was a master at throwing obstacles onto my path, preventing me from moving forward emotionally, intellectually, and spiritually.*

Partying didn't allow for building deep relationships, no matter the effort and emotional energy I applied. I remember having deep heart-to-heart, one-sided conversations about issues plaguing the lives of my bar friends. Sure, we were drunk. But I did my best during those talks to listen attentively and to offer my best wisdom. I cared. Only, the next morning, I'd discover that person acting as if our conversation had never happened: gone was the booze that had enabled him to open up to me, and along with it the connection we'd formed.

The lack of reciprocity began to anger me. For the first time, my lifestyle seemed a liability. I was miserable. But rather than do anything about it, I wallowed in self-pity and drank more. What bothered me most, I think, was how long I'd been staggering down the same dead-end road and telling myself I liked it. I still had no one and nothing (except for my dad and our growing relationship). I still felt like a failure despite all my hard work.

It was as if I'd fallen all the way back to square one.

It was a deeply crushing reality check.
My dad already had the life I wanted.
Around this time, one of the things that stood out most about my father was how he lived his life loving people. He wasn't the dad I'd grown up with. I'd never known he wanted that kind of reality—or how much I suddenly did too.

He gave people the benefit of the doubt. He assumed the best until he was given a good reason to think differently. He was writing his dissertation on shame and homelessness and spending countless hours working at a local shelter, passionately trying to improve the lives of the downtrodden. He'd return daily with stories about others' misfortunes and his continued love for them.

My dad's priorities made mine seem more than backward.

By comparison, the impulses and rewards driving me for so long were blatantly selfish and myopic. A hidden desire began to surface within me.

I wanted so much more.
It didn't happen overnight.
I had a lot of recovery work and school and other "life" things going on. But over time, with my dad's example and leadership as my guide, my superficial focus shifted. What would my contribution to this life be? What did I want to be known for when I died besides being a tough guy no one dared cross and who could drink others under the table?

What I truly wanted, I discovered, was to help others.

And shortly after this epiphany, I was presented with a unique opportunity to do just that.

A spark of passion

My therapist, Barb, as she preferred to be called, was a very accomplished woman with a dual PhD in both nursing and psychology, yet she was as grounded and humble a human being as you'll ever meet.

She helped greatly enrich my life. One of her most effective suggestions was for me to begin doing volunteer work. She encouraged me to call several of her acquaintances to find an opportunity that would fit. One in particular had a son, James, who had been diagnosed with an intellectual disability.

James lacked self-confidence stemming from coping with his daily challenges. My task was helping him get into shape for the upcoming football season. Sounded right up my alley.

I talked with James and his mother about goals and how I might be able to help him accomplish them. Although James didn't say much—a common characteristic of those on the Asperger's spectrum—I felt we connected. Emotionally invested from that first meeting, I offered to do whatever I could to be of assistance. I recommended a gym membership so we could work out together, and we scheduled times for his parents to drop him off each week. I became his trainer, a role I relished. For James, my enthusiasm for my job likely resulted in more work than he'd bargained for.

At our first session, I explained, "You're going to stretch, and then run a mile and a half. Do your best, but don't blow a gasket or anything. Your mom will kill me. Walk when you must, but push yourself. We'll hit the weights after your run."

The look on the guy's face was priceless: shock at the amount of work on the agenda, determination to save face, resignation that it wasn't going to feel good. His body language said he wasn't happy, but he got on the treadmill and pushed himself throughout our session. I loved the effort. He worked his tail off, stopping only to hydrate. I was so proud of him and praised him for his commitment to his goals. His smile made me feel like I'd hit the jackpot.

He couldn't stop grinning, and planting that seed of confidence in him meant more to me than anything I had accomplished in Iowa. I'd meant something to someone, done something that made someone else's life better, and it felt good and healthy and better than I could have imagined.

"I can't tell you how much I appreciate what you're doing," his mom said after a later session. "My son never wants to go at first, but once he finishes working out here with you, he's glowing. It's amazing!"

I wasn't getting paid, but I was richer for each minute James and I spent together. I was a leader, like I'd always wanted to be, but this time for real. I was making a difference in someone's life. It was a good, honest, reciprocal relationship (because I looked forward to each time we met and watching him reach his goals, and I was also glowing by the time we were done). I had nothing tangible to show for it, but I'd never felt better about myself.

I not only *wanted* to help people, I *could* help others. I *was* helping James. I was accomplishing something meaningful. I was finally making a difference—a core objective that would become a new lifestyle for me.

Grinding through the work and pushing my way forward

My father taught me that people react to things in the present based on wounds they've experienced in the past. I learned a lot watching and listening to him.

Like how to preserve healthy relationships. I started looking for friendships that closely mirrored my dad's: people who truly cared about me becoming the best man I could be. And I was committed to offering the same consideration in return both in my personal life and in the more public relationships I needed to make and maintain.

Applying my growth in new areas

And then there was my "work" life.

One of my first jobs outside of college led me to a great-paying career. As an IT consultant with a medical technology company, I worked with doctors and other health-care professionals, transitioning them into and training them on our proprietary system. The relationship skills I was learning and my improving self-image became key to my success.

I worked my butt off at that job, but the dynamic in which I found myself remained a challenge. It was intimidating working with the best and brightest, especially since I had no prior work experience in the field. But I did my work well and got along. My nontraditional approach to working relationships, including using humor to lighten tense situations, was an asset. As it turned out, I thrived under conditions that wilted many of my coworkers.

My natural high level of energy, in particular, helped me push through a grueling travel schedule. I was regularly called upon to push myself to work more, not less, and often to teach new software applications to which I'd had little or no exposure. Worry and crash-learning material became constant companions, often keeping me up at night.

I remember once arriving at a client site in New Hampshire and discovering that I'd been given incorrect information—that I was supposed to be training clients on an entirely different application than the one for which I'd prepared. But rather than getting angry, I kept my game face on, found out what I was supposed to be teaching (again, software I had never seen), and figured it out. I was given less than a day to come up to speed.

Then I received a frantic call from a colleague arriving for the same event, scheduled to present during the session before mine, who's prep had been similarly screwed up. She was floundering, panicked, crying, and completely out of her depth, trying to figure out the new material, but was absolutely certain she couldn't.

My heart went out to her. I knew *exactly* how that felt from my days of floundering with schoolwork when absolutely nothing I tried seemed to work.

It was already three in the morning, but I worked with her the rest of the night, learning the material alongside her. That morning I helped facilitate her eight-hour class before my eight-hour evening session began. She was newer to the job than I was, and no way was I letting a coworker (a teammate) choke. Not if I could help in some way. Just as my dad had never let me down when I'd needed him most, no matter how much helping me had stretched his already maxed-out limits.

The importance of that moment with my coworker wasn't lost on me. I'd learned to support my team and its needs, at times prioritizing others' well-being and goals above my own. In very large part because of the challenges and failures (and hard-won successes) of my early life, I'd made significant progress in the way I related to people and my world.

Which sounds like an amazing success story, right?

Well, for a while.

Before long, though, the dynamic began to seem eerily familiar. Remember that brick plant back in Kansas where I burned myself out doing killer work, basically becoming a slave for a salary? Now in my IT career, managers were pushing me to do more than should have been intellectually and humanly possible given the time frame in which I was asked to accomplish my tasks.

Once again, the effort and commitment to completing my work wasn't getting me anywhere. The managerial chain simply kept assigning more work rather than recognizing or rewarding the above-and-beyond results I was achieving. It was a frustrating, seemingly dead-end dynamic to which I'm certain many of you can relate.

I found myself wondering anew, *What the hell am I doing with my life?*

My time as a consultant was tremendously successful—both financially and in my growing confidence of how truly capable I was at dealing with the "real" world. But . . .

I was left with the increasing certainty that my high energy level and passion should be making more of a difference.

Not long after the training trip I described above, I left that company.

I'd grown to be an effective public speaker and had learned to trust myself. So my time in that career was in no way wasted. But I was convinced there was something more rewarding for me to do—something where I could impact others' lives while at the same time striving to become my best.

It was time to shift my focus from solely my recovery to striving for much broader goals.

Coming to full life

In dad's and my new venture, I now use that same energy, vigor, and fail-to-quit mentality to help parents and other young adults like myself.

I want to help people avoid making the stupid mistakes I made. I want to inspire people to go out and grab life by the balls.

We only have one life, one chance to swing the hammer. We need to swing that sledgehammer as hard as we can.

My goal is to help others discover their dreams and passions and turn their goals into reality. I feel so strongly about the path I'm on now I would rather die than turn back. I have made plenty of mistakes. Obviously. I don't shy away for sharing every gory detail if I think my candidness may help someone else. But it's more than that, and I hope, if nothing else, this is the message you take away from my recovery journey so far:

I will not allow my past mistakes to dictate the trajectory of my future.

I have been given so much, which is something my father says I've adopted into my own life view. I feel a responsibility now to lead and help others heal and grow and learn to strive and thrive the way others so graciously helped me.

These days, Dad and I work unbelievably well together. Our brainstorming sessions are fun and productive. Our minds seem to work in lockstep, and maybe they always did. When I was a kid, I was too young to know. And back then, my dad was still early in his own journey to healing and living his "others-focused" life. But on this side of all that pain and confusion and fear, here we are *together*, sharing a common passion to pay forward all we've been blessed with.

Setting and working toward common goals comes more naturally to us these days. Ego is a near-nonexistent obstacle of the past. We understand each other better. We've learned to harness the unique creativity we each bring to the table and to target our shared work ethic toward common goals. We share a business where our sole purpose is helping transform lives.

I can't imagine a better existence.

I haven't had an out-of-control argument with my father in more than fifteen years.

Sure, we disagree, and we both have strong personalities. But we talk those challenging moments out now—calmly. We encourage each other during times of doubt, working toward the common goal of creating a better world.

I can't fully express how my father's love and commitment changed my life. He worked with me and stuck by me and paved the way for me to discover that my true passion is to help people.

And now we're producing this project as a result of all we've been through.

There's still a lot of uncertainty in my life. For one thing, like many others of my generation, I'm contending with bone-crushing student debt in addition to the abundance of other bills there are to pay. Yet I've learned to follow my heart as I navigate these continued challenges to my sense of worth and self. I'm determined to remain on a healthy path.

And my heart now knows its passion: to help others.

As long as I hold on to that truth, to that core intent that has already transformed so much for me and others, I believe without reservation that I will succeed.

Since Dad and I began this journey together, I have noticed a dramatic reduction in my anxiety as well as other symptoms of my mental and physiological challenges.

I find I'm no longer jealous of others' accomplishments.

I've embraced the phrase "A rising tide lifts all boats." I root hard for others now, wanting their success, excited to see them do their best. And that best often means them being better than I am—and I'm still rooting for them.

Because the ultimate *goal* is success—yours, mine, and ours. The *key* is for each of us to be the best we can possibly be, for ourselves and for others. The primary *objective* is to be on this journey together, supporting one another.

We will ultimately achieve more of what is possible if we pursue our potential as a team.

Yes, I'm still hypercompetitive. But going forward, I'm competing with myself and all I know I'm capable of accomplishing. I see myself in my own lane these days, running my own race.

While on the same track, you're in your lane, running yours. If I am doing my best, I see no reason to compare myself to what you're doing as you move forward at your own pace.

We might not even be tackling the same "race." But we share this track of life we're both on. And I want you to get as far as you possibly can as you pursue your dreams.

I want all of us to.

> *It's an amazing new perspective for me to see life as a pursuit of passion for everyone I encounter and to embrace my passion to help you achieve the mindset* you *need to achieve success.*

The best life has to offer

I am a father now.

Not all that long ago, if you'd have told me that a little girl would carry my heart in her tiny hands, I'd have said you were crazy. Fast-forward to now, and my daughter has changed my life.

I'll never forget the moment she entered this earth. In that instant, I knew that reality would never again be about just me. Those first days, I spent every second I could with her, soaking in the sensation of her sweet little body sleeping on my chest. She will never know the profound, positive impact she's had on my life. She's made me want to be a better man. I love her more than anything in the world.

As a beautiful, precious two-year-old, she adores me. She calls me Papa. And even though my short-lived marriage failed (which is a whole other story for different book I have in mind), my ex-wife and I are fully engaged and committed to co-parenting. We live about 350 miles apart, which makes the time I spend with my little one critical. Yes, I get the irony in my parenting situation's similarities to that early dynamic between my father and me after his relationship with my mother fell apart. And, yes, I see this as yet another way that Dad's and my hardest struggles are now helping me better tackle my own challenges.

I travel to see my daughter every chance I get. She has my undivided attention when I'm with her: no phone, computer, or any other worldly distraction is allowed inside our bubble. Our time together is about doing whatever she likes to do and my being there to share it with her. And about my doing whatever I can to make her laugh.

I love her laugh. I live to hear her say "Papa! Papa!" as she reaches for me. It melts my heart. I love her more than she could ever fathom. I am a good father. Pause with me for a moment and ponder how that could be possible given the closed-off, angry, destructive young man you met at the beginning of this book. And then believe with me that the same fulfilling future is *absolutely possible* for your teen or young adult.

> *My dream is for my daughter and I to someday have the kind of relationship I now experience with my father.*

She deserves that closeness, that unconditional acceptance and belonging, and that nonanxious presence in her life that nothing she will ever do can shake. I'll work just as hard to give her that as my dad fought to give it to me.

I know it will be a journey and that she will control her future. I accept that my job is to do all I can to prepare her and then to step back and allow her to grow and learn and become in her own way. I thank God that I better understand my strengths and weaknesses now and that I've grown in my understanding of how to work with them.

I hope to remain strong and enlightened enough to successfully support my child as she steers her own course, but if I fall short, I trust that we'll get through that, too. I also have no doubt

I'll have my own dad to turn to for support if I ever again need to get myself back on course.

Kevin: Thriving through the Unexpected

I recently had the honor of meeting a modern-day treasure hunter, David Hawley.

He's the man credited with spearheading the excavation of the steamboat *Arabia*: a cargo ship that sunk near Kansas City in 1856.

Dave shared with me some of the psychological aspects of undertaking a project that enormous. He grappled with a lot of doubt along the way. One doubt in particular surprised me.

"Once we discovered the boat, uncovered it, and excavated tons of cargo the ship was carrying when it sunk," he said, "that was when we encountered our biggest obstacle. Then the problem became what do we do with all of this stuff?"

He faced the difficult challenge of how to store, preserve, and restore all that had been recovered.

"Do we sell all of it, or do we create a museum and let everyone enjoy it?" he said. "All these questions and obstacles seemed overwhelming, as we didn't have the money to hire an expensive curator, so we would have to educate ourselves on how best to do museum-quality restoration and restore everything."

We discussed the common misconception that once excavation is completed, the difficult part of a project is over. When, in fact, once you've achieved "success," that's often when the harder, more time-consuming work begins.

It wasn't an enormous leap for me to see how his experience paralleled my journey with my son. Austin's and my work was an ongoing process too, even as he became independent and was making healthier, more successful choices for his life. Just as with Dave's story about his evolving excavation, Austin's and my evolving path had become about our journey forward rather than us reaching some mythical endpoint beyond which all our work would be done.

There would be more surprises and diversions and difficult decisions ahead.

That's simply how life works.

"Happily ever after" is a state of mind we can achieve for ourselves each day. However, storybook perfection is rarely a destination that can be definitively reached.

Austin's and my goals shifted from healing and recovering to embracing and taking advantage of any new challenges and opportunities that came our way, maneuvering through and overcoming obstacles as we progressed.

A bit more detail. And, of course, more challenges.

My son and I moved from Iowa in 2013.

My internship assignment (as part of my degree program) took me to Western Kansas. Pretty much in the middle of nowhere, I was assigned to a state hospital to work with and rehabilitate violent sex offenders. It was a rewarding but challenging time for me, and I missed my roommate.

No longer did I have Austin to talk with on a daily basis—he'd helped me survive my time at the University of Iowa, as much, I believe, as I'd helped him. I was instead living in a small house with eight students I had never met, all of them very nice but twenty years my junior.

While there, I was to complete the analysis and final write-up for the last chapters of my dissertation. I was also faced with the difficult decision to move my parents into a nursing home (including the task of clearing out their home, which was four hours away). My exhaustion from those five years with Austin in Iowa began catching up with me, taking a cumulative toll. I battled depression that could have derailed my shot at finishing the final year of my degree, but I was determined to get everything done, or die trying.

Internship ultimately completed, I moved back to Kansas City. I'd been married to my current wife, Marcia, for three years, and for the first time we were able to live in the same town. I completed my postdoctoral year at yet another state hospital. Life should have been on an upswing, but my mental and physical stamina bottomed out. Take it from me—your system can run on overdrive and adrenaline and reckless determination only so long.

Serious heart issues presented themselves in October of 2015 and again in January of 2016. A pacemaker and a deliberator upgrade later, I was back among the living. But throughout that year, my depression and doubts about the direction of my life grew more severe. I made half-hearted attempts to start my own private practice. But the motivation, energy, and sustained interest required to build a successful practice weren't there. I'd accomplished all I'd set out to, but I could feel myself checking out. After surviving all that the last seven years had demanded, it felt as if there wasn't enough of "me" left to take my dreams to the next level.

For Austin too

Austin has briefly shared about his short-lived marriage.

You've also read about his successes as an IT consultant. However, after graduation, he at first had difficulty finding that job and career direction. As the financial concerns that followed grew, he welcomed the arrival of his baby girl. She was a bright, beautiful addition to his life and our family. But along with the stress of being a new father came a resurrection of Austin's former destructive views and beliefs and self-doubt.

But in addition to those trials came a wonderful opportunity.

Austin rose to the challenge despite his inner conflict and stayed home with his newborn, serving as her primary caretaker while his wife worked and he looked for jobs. His daughter's attachment to him and the security he made certain to provide in her life is rock-solid. Instead of filling her life with stress and uncertainty, he was mindful of the importance of her environment and held her, singing to her, for hours. I can't praise him enough for his commitment to making her feel safe, loved, and protected in those critical, formative months of her life as she learned to process the world and the people around her.

Once Austin's marriage deteriorated, his wife moved away with the baby (to live with his wife's family). He and I frequently talked on the phone about the challenges he faced. I could hear the fear and hopelessness in his voice.

He'd been trying so hard in his marriage and in his life. But he was battling a lot of conflict still driven by who he'd once been and who he was becoming, as well as the undercurrents of a growingly counterproductive, toxic relationship. He'd contributed his fair share to his marriage's end, but he'd also done his very best to work things out.

> *Nothing was fitting or fulfilling him or making it possible for him to sustain the positive, hopeful, thriving future he was capable of building.*

A situation not unsimilar to the emotional truths I was facing around the same time.

It was at this time that Austin moved to Kansas City to live with Marcia and me—and to once more start his life anew.

After Austin moved in with us, he bounced back almost immediately.

He knew he could trust me, and Marcia is one of the most loving, nonconfrontational souls you'll ever meet.

Austin didn't feel threatened or rejected. He wasn't on high alert all the time. He could relax and be himself in his new environment, and with that peace came new hope. The fight-or-flight mindset of the past and his former counterproductive "survival skills" no longer ruled his life. He was grieving the loss of his marriage and the absence of his sweet daughter, but the more positive, confident Austin he'd become returned more quickly than I'd expected.

Shortly after returning to Kansas City, he accepted an IT consulting job with a Fortune-500 company: a high school dropout who'd eight years earlier moved to live with me in Iowa, dragging with him multiple felonies and a suicide scare. Now, record expunged, he'd grown to be an independent, responsible leader, confident in his abilities and value to others.

Pursuing our dreams together

As 2016 came to an end, 2017 promised to be better on many fronts. I finally had more energy and more clarity about the future I wanted for myself. For a year, I had limped along with my private practice. But as my depression cleared, I also had to be honest that I lacked the necessary interest to make a long-term go of it. While I love working with clients in therapy, managing the business side of my practice isn't as fulfilling an experience. Which led me to consider my original dream fifteen years before: the one that had first led me to pursue psychology as a career.

> *I wanted to help individuals rid themselves of the barriers that prevent them from creating and maintaining deep, rich connections with others.*

That transformation had gotten me through some of the most challenging days of my life. I'd lost touch with that truth somehow. Revitalized, I began thinking of ways to bring my dream to life on a much larger and more successful scale. And there was my son, also wanting to help others and make an impact on their lives.

We first talked about writing this book while we lived together in Iowa. We even started writing parts of it. But we had a lot going on in our lives—too much to sustain any progress. We've talked about it off and on for the last six or seven years. Austin would bring up the topic from time to time: "I still haven't forgotten about that book, Dad. I still want to do it." We'd agree to get back to it. Someday. But talk is cheap, and books don't write themselves. For a long time, a "great idea" was all we had to show for our collaboration.

We'd see each other over a weekend, and we'd talk about our careers—what we did and didn't like about them. I was lucky enough to be helping people, even if long-term I knew I needed to make a change. Austin was basically busting his ass to line the pockets of his company's already-wealthy shareholders. He too wanted to more meaningful work and to make a difference in others' lives.

Our ideas and plans for this book eventually morphed into the concept for a business all our own: *Life Doctor*, through which we'd help parents better connect with their children. We'd prevent other troubled teens and young adults from struggling with the same sense of isolation and defeat and hopelessness as Austin did.

And so began a new life for us, cocreating a business.

We took the plunge, letting go of our separate careers, and have never looked back.

No, it wasn't easy. We had to learn to relate on an even more effective level as we worked through a whole new host of challenges and as we celebrated successes. We're still pinching ourselves to be certain they're real.

Creative vision and brainstorming are some of our favorite things. We can talk all day about ideas, projects, and strategies. We think a lot alike (which can also be a weakness), but we always find our way through to the right decisions. And taking credit or making money is never what we're about. If we create value for others, the rest will take care of itself.

But then there's the business part—the grind. We cost ourselves a lot of money when we first started out and knew nothing about what we were doing. But we found our way, getting better at critiquing each other's suggestions and not committing to a plan until we had it right. Trial and error is an unforgiving life coach, but we survived as a team. The deeply rooted trust we share kept us committed to our overall goal—helping parents learn how to help their troubled kids.

We're both perfectionists. Falling short of that—a lot—resulted in us sharing grace, not blame. Others may call the acceptance and support we've always found a way to extend "patience," "leniency," "forgiveness," or "offering the benefit of the doubt." Regardless of the label, we are on the same side, always. So we've made room for each other to take risks, to experiment, and to take action before we know the certainty of the outcome.

Also at the core of our relationship is the humor that from the very start we've leaned on to lighten the burden. When you make as many mistakes as we have, and when you know you're going to make plenty more, sometimes you've just got to laugh, right?

Living a fulfilled life is simple now.

I have my son back. I'm sharing my life with both my boys, connecting in as many ways as we can manage. Turns out, that's all I need to wake up in the morning and know my day will be right.

Some of those days have been packed full of rewards and joy: the births of my seven grandchildren, graduations, heartfelt talks, and watching my sons and grandchildren grow and achieve success. Both of my boys are compassionate men with a deeply rooted desire to help those less fortunate. What could give my life more meaning than to watch them make an enduring impact on the world?

Other days continue to rattle the rafters a bit. There have been deaths, divorces, and sicknesses—enough to keep us grounded in reality, mindful that we won't be on this earth forever. But in those difficult times, no one walks alone. As I write this, we're currently experiencing another one of those challenging times in our family, and yet the unshakable love we feel for each other ensures that no one feels alone.

My goal, always, is to provide comfort and to be there for my sons as we weather each challenge (including how close we are now to losing my mom and dad). It's been a privilege to watch Austin and Alex become supportive caregivers for their grandparents. The generations have switched roles. My loving, compassionate sons are more than up for the challenge. When they see my mom now, they often talk about the oldest of their memories. And she smiles, loving how much her grandsons love the "living" the three of them have shared.

These are sacred moments—both the celebrations and the more difficult times. And despite the potential for unhappiness or even grief in the future, because we've all learned to love so deeply, I find an indescribable beauty in seeing so much of my parents, and even myself, in the strength and character my sons exhibit through all of it.

My boys and my relationships with them truly make me a rich, successful man beyond anything I could have imagined.

WHAT TO DO?

As I mentioned in the opening of this chapter, Austin's and my stories in this last step have already covered much of our "WHAT HAPPENED?" analysis.

We'll wrap any additional insights into the "WHAT TO DO?" section as we help orient you toward the future work you'll be doing with your teen or young adult—and your relationship beyond this seven-step game plan's scope of "getting him back."

Kevin: Take a Deep Breath and Exhale

You've done so much work already.

Both of you.

Your reward is to discover all you will *become* next:

- How will you each grow separately?
- Which parts of life will you seek to share and experience together?
- How will your connection evolve as you both move forward?

The foundational strides you and your son have achieved (and his respective healing) will continue to expand. Each relationship is unique, so we can't offer a definitive roadmap guaranteeing what's in store for you specifically. But know this for certain:

> *It is* absolutely *possible going forward for you to foster an even deeper connection built on everything you've already achieved.*

Likely, you are *not* done helping your son.

The hard work you have already completed now affords you the opportunity to embark on a lifelong journey as teammates.

There will be further, perhaps harder, challenges ahead for both of you. But they will be more "surmountable" now that you're practicing the skills you'll need to successfully navigate them as a unit. And the good times? You'll find them so much more enjoyable because they'll be shared experiences and adventures and memories.

Life is meant to be lived in community. Your son is once more part of *your* community, and you are part of his.

Which also means you're in a better position today than you were before to notice if his life approach slips back into an unhealthy pattern, if his commitment to sustained change seems to veer off track, or if he simply appears to be "off" in a way that triggers your concern that his sense of self and place and confidence has once more begun to lag.

Challenges come in all shapes and sizes and colors.

> *Future conflict won't come calling, looking exactly like the troubles the two of you have faced and dealt with before now.*

Your son is growing, and so are you. Your lives are expanding. And all that exciting growth can also invite you into dynamic new confusion and worries and doubts. Plus, the stakes of how badly things can go wrong will likely increase as your son ages and assumes more responsibility in his personal and professional lives.

Some of the challenges and potential "pitfalls" to come will be of your son's own creation. Other disappointments and trials will simply find him, as they do each of us. And he'll be faced with his next opportunity to prove to himself that he can manage his life confidently and honestly and successfully. And when those sneaky moments grab hold of him when he's least expecting them and he lets you know (either through words or action or reactions), that will be an opportunity for you to prove to him once more that you are there, supporting him and encouraging him and accepting him unconditionally, regardless of the outcome.

You are no longer responsible for directing your son.

Nor is it your job to continually bail him out of his troubles.

You are moving even deeper now into a "reciprocal, supportive role," where your involvement in his choices will be more about discussing with him the situation, potential responses, and the pros and cons of his chosen action. These two-way conversations can be both productive and enjoyable as he takes more ownership of his life and learns, on his own, to turn to you for direction more often. It will also surprise and satisfy him when he discovers you turning to him at times, asking for his input and his advice and his ear as you brainstorm your choices.

In your evolving relationship, you will grow into supporting each other as adults.

Remember, recovery is a lifelong journey.

Setbacks do NOT mean starting from scratch. If and when your son stumbles next, and once he's righted himself (with your support and help), his next journey will most likely pick up from the point at which he stumbled. He will carry forward into his next endeavor all the growth he's achieved despite the interim setback. Your son has now experienced significant success in his journey. He will always have that as a reference from which he can reorient his perspective regardless of the challenges he faces in the future.

For example, Austin and I share the tendency, in times of intense stress or physical exhaustion, to revert to self-doubt and negative thinking about our potential. Hostility toward ourselves and others and our life opportunities can quickly expand from there. But during our time living together, we established a track record of success for implementing healthy habits and intentionally positive behavior patterns to counteract these emotional "rough" patches.

Time and again since then, I've seen my son return to this alternative way of existing, pulling himself back when he's stumbled into a darker place. "Success breeds success," the saying goes. Austin's experience in the past with how well these techniques work gave him confidence that using them would help him the next time he needed them.

Welcome your evolving, changing relationship.

Your son is better able to direct his own life now and contribute to yours.

You will both continue to grow and heal. You'll make more productive choices for your individual lives that don't revolve around how to get him through his darkest period. You will gain confidence in your respective abilities to move forward, continuing to prove yourselves trustworthy and supportive and accepting.

If you're finding it difficult to shift from your role of caregiver to that of peer—I feel ya. Your son no longer requires you to spend countless hours tracking and managing his actions and choices and challenges. He's believing more in his own capability by the day. He's completing more tasks and accomplishing more goals than ever before. You're proud of his success, rooting for him to keep improving. And yet, as a parent, it's natural to feel a bit at loose ends. For so long he's needed you to contribute daily to his recovery.

Now, what he needs most is your support from far enough away that he "gets" how able he is to do this on his own. And perhaps that distance will benefit you as well.

The first time I read one of Austin's papers from the University of Iowa, I was astonished. I could not believe how well a high school dropout who'd never applied himself in school could communicate with the written word. I pointed out his natural ability. English professors had been similarly supportive of his work. The positive reinforcement he received was his alone—for something he'd accomplished totally separate from the "us" that had been his support system for so long. And yet here he is now, confidently coauthoring his first book with me.

Notice and reinforce those successes.

Make certain your son is recognizing and internalizing his achievements.

Remember that shame-prone individuals tend to reduce the chance of failing and facing humiliation, hanging back in their comfort zone until they're unlikely to attempt anything that isn't a guaranteed success. Going forward, you have a continued opportunity to counter this self-protective instinct by celebrating small wins and then progressively larger accomplishments. You will help your son gain confidence in his ability to take risks and tackle larger, more challenging projects despite the increased likelihood of something not working out.

Encourage your son to engage in increasingly complex tasks.

Help him brainstorm approaches and to see potential weaknesses when he invites you to. But also make a point to notice his strengths and successes along the way. Look for opportunities to remind him of past successes that can be connected to the new chance he's taking to expand his horizons.

Sometimes, all that is needed is a recommendation to approach a new challenge in a different way.

He cannot always achieve his desired outcome. That's simply a fact of life.

A great related conversation to have would be a discussion about focusing on the journey or on his overarching goals. In this broadening realm of self-doubt (as he becomes more independent), it is more important than ever that your son know what he's about, why he's making the choices he is, and what he hopes to achieve (long-term) with the effort he's putting into his life.

> *Help him grow more confident in his ability to make decisions with long-reaching effects and to develop areas of expertise that will help him incrementally work toward the future he envisions.*

Perhaps some of his new areas of expertise are those to which you have been less exposed.

Offer him the opportunity to be the expert in your relationship in the areas in which he can instruct or coach you. Admire his skill set and his younger point of view and what he can bring not only to your relationship but to your personal successes. That's a win-win, right?

One caution as you walk down this "partnership" path: avoid arguing. Disagreeing is inevitable and healthy, as it's another opportunity for your son to practice his communication skills. And it's okay to speak your mind and confront issues as they arise. However, constructive confrontation in a relationship is not the same thing as conflict.

Arguing for the sake of winning—to prove who's right and who's wrong—is a no-go dynamic for you and your son. He is gaining momentum and confidence that have taken him light-years away from his downward spiral of not all that long ago. Your job is to fan the flames of his recovery and thriving confidence, not to "put him in his place." Always, always, keep your focus on encouraging and supporting him to *become* even more than he already is—even if you can't possibly agree about everything.

A Note from Austin: Just a Little More about Fathers

I have only two messages left to offer.

They are for you to read and consider as a parent, though one is written to my daughter for the day she's old enough to read this book herself.

The role of a parent, I've learned, is so crucial, so vital. I encourage you to never forget that. Never take for granted what you mean to your child or how much he or she needs you. And never waste a single moment to make an impact with your child, to share his or her life, and to glean as much wisdom and love and joy as you possibly can, relishing your life together.

The letters that follow are in my words, and in places they may be rougher than you'd like to hear. But they come from my heart. Bear with me. Give them a chance to touch your heart too.

To my daughter, Soteria:

Soteria, My Precious Sweetheart,

Know that you're in the forefront of my mind—my favorite person in the world. You have my unwavering commitment to give you my undivided attention as you intentionally will be my only child.

I choose you over having another child because I think you're special, wonderful, and we have so many adventures and journeys on which to embark. There's only enough time for me to give you the life you deserve.

I wish to empower you as a strong woman who reaches happiness through living out your passion. I believe you too were created for something special, my dear child.

My life's work now consists of helping people and being a good father like mine was to me. Sweet Soteria, you deserve that of me.

I love you more than life itself.

Dad

To fathers everywhere:

Whatever else you've got going on is less important than shaping your young man.

Be around as often as you can without being creepy about it. Make sure and pay attention to your child and be active in his life. Please know that even if you've been distant, there's time to repair the brokenness and to build a wonderful relationship.

Don't be condescending. EVER!

You screwed up and made mistakes. Chances are you've butt-fumbled a time or two, so give your son room to fail forward.

Do NOT use shame as a means to gain a superior posture over your boy. He will resent you for it.

Be positive and encouraging because it truly is contagious.

Forgive your son. He will fail you at some point.

Be firm and project strength. He looks up to you.

Create a climate conducive to helping your son discover his passion.

Austin

WHAT'S MOST IMPORTANT?

Once you've reached this transitional point in your relationship, you are no longer trying to "straighten" your son out.

Your focus now shifts toward encouraging him to live his best life.

Your Parent Playbook

Your son will likely continue to struggle in several areas.

Discussing the potential difficulties of these challenges, as well as possible workarounds or solutions, can be a great opportunity for continuing the successful pattern of communication and support you've established.

Opportunity	Consider	Goal
Employment	Participate in his career choices. We spend half of our waking life working, and most emerging adults can feel overwhelmed at the thought of committing to an occupation they're not sure will be fulfilling. Is your son contemplating taking a job as a stopgap, or as a stepping stone to the actual career he desires? Career psychology is an actual field, full of complex theories and assessments.	**Help your son reason through the type of work in which he can actively engage.** What would make him happy to be doing each day? Or if not happy, what tasks would satisfy him, completing them on a daily basis? If his desired field or job is not currently available, help him map out a plan for completing the required steps to make his employment goal more accessible.
Education	A degree can be achieved either by attending a trade school or studying within a more traditional college program. Either choice will benefit your son, and neither is better than the other. And where you start isn't nearly as important as where you finish. Some of the wisest people I know went to trade school, and some of the dumbest people I know have advanced degrees—and vice versa.	**If lack of appropriate education is holding your son back from his goals, encourage him to pursue the needed degree** (despite any doubts he may have that he could complete the program). At first, his focus may be on acquiring what he needs to simply make a living and support himself. That success and experience could then lead him to pursue alternatives to advance him toward his ultimate goals.

Opportunity	Consider	Goal
Taking Action	Few of us ever have life completely figured out. The perfect career or *absolutely right* choices rarely present themselves in a "We're here!" manner. Encourage your son not to allow fear of the unknown to stymie his conviction to make the incremental choices and do the "smaller" work that will place him on a path to tackle the bigger, more complex choices he'll one day make.	**As goals and objectives shift and change, encourage your son not to fall victim to "paralysis by analysis."** At some point, it's essential for him to take that first step, to act, and to experience whatever is needed so he'll grow and gain wisdom and be better able to take the *next* step toward his goals.
NOT Fearing Failure	Failure (and taking risks that put ourselves in the direct path of failure) can be the best thing that ever happens to us. We learn most as we attempt and fall short and then pull ourselves together for the next try.	**Instead of processing setbacks as failures, help your son see "missed" attempts as opportunities for feedback.** Discuss, model, and brainstorm ways to learn from each action and reaction he encounters so that he will feel even more empowered to make the next choice or handle the next opportunity he faces.

Opportunity	Consider	Goal
Saving Money	It may take him awhile to find his passion, but when he does, you will want to act on it. Thankfully, I had saved money throughout my career so that when I was ready to go to graduate school, I had the funds to do so. Impress upon your teen or young adult the importance of planning ahead financially for when he's ready to charge forward in a new, exciting way.	**Help your son prepare to take advantage of opportunity when it presents itself.** To pursue his dreams, he may need to move or go back to school or invest in a start-up business. Help him plan as best he can to be able to financially support his goals once he determines the life direction he wants to pursue.

Purpose

Having a defined purpose can be tremendously beneficial to your son.

Remember Austin's realization that what he truly wanted to do (what would fulfill him) was help people? Having a purpose can make the good times richer and the bad times seem more bearable. We're talking intention and desired outcome rather than job titles and the name of his employer.

> *In her book* The How of Happiness, *Psychologist Sonja Lyubomirsky defines a necessary component of happiness as "a sense that one's life is good, meaningful, and worthwhile."*

For example, my purpose is to help others discover their intrinsic value so they can experience loving connections. It has informed more than how I earn a living as a psychologist (although that is awesome too); it has become integrated with how I live my life. Treating others with dignity and respect is a way of recognizing and validating their value and worth as human beings. Each time I go through a drive-through or check-out line, I try to engage with others in an authentic way. This is how I say that they are worth my time and that I want to interact with them.

In a therapeutic session, my focus is most often centered on improving a patient's self-image, just as many of the technique's shared in this book have targeted improving your son's sense of self-worth and confidence. By living my purpose every day, I experience so much more joy and contentment than I ever did earning money and collecting material things. And the really good news is, I can live my purpose until the day I die. It is not tied to my son's or my career. It is how I have defined my life.

Armed with the same degree of understanding of his intent and desire in life, your son will make increasingly more impactful and ultimately successful choices on his journey to achieve his goals. Knowing his purpose will help immensely with problem-solving, the ability to sustain action through adversity and set-backs, appreciation for accomplishments, and stress reduction while engaging in difficult challenges.

> *Many claim to have the "secret formula" of identifying your life's purpose. I've never found the matter that cut and dried.*

We all have a calling in life. I believe that. And we share many common ideals—for instance, Austin's wishing to help people in a way that he couldn't with his IT job. But finding your purpose is a far more personal pursuit than a high-level ideal.

One recommendation you could make to your son would be to put into motion whatever he feels called to do with his life.

Challenge him to act on it and find out how to execute that ideal in a tangible way that involves interacting with the world around him. For instance, while pursuing my degree in Iowa, I completed six months of volunteer work assisting those who were dying. It wasn't easy work, and it was a hardship to fit it into my schedule, but it was a requirement for my degree, so I was committed. Most importantly, though, I engaged wholeheartedly in my time at that center. It turned out to be one of the most transformative experiences of my life, helping those who had very little time remaining to feel good for the short while I was with them (and somehow in the process making myself feel more alive than ever).

Through that volunteer experience, I finally found my path, my purpose, and the type of work I was uniquely designed to do.

Creating a future with your son.

You and your son, like Austin and I, possess the freedom to create whatever you want from your relationship. You have established a foundation of trust. How many people can say they are fully and unconditionally accepted by someone else? On that foundation, building absolutely anything is possible.

If business isn't how you and your son connect, what hobby would you both like to take up? Where would you like to travel? Is there a volunteer opportunity you could pursue together that might springboard you into a totally new shared reality?

A brand-new world is your playground as a reward for the hard work you've already done. And the more you work and play and grow together, the better you'll become at supporting and loving and inspiring each other. Your relationship will become even stronger and more successful as a result. That is our desire for you and your son.

In fact, take a look at our Life Doctor slogan:

"Better you. Better life. Better world." Dream big dreams with us and then pursue your goals.

So I guess there's only one more question to ask. Perhaps the most important and satisfying query I've made yet.

What would you and your son like to do next?

YOUR NEXT PLAY

The opportunities before you and your son are endless, limited only by your creativity. You are already on your way to creating something magnificent together.

Your Game Plan in Step Seven	Focus beyond recovery toward the future dreams you can now pursue (both individually and together).
As a parent, you will continue to	encourage your son to live his best life.
Your teen is now better able to	direct his own life and contribute meaningfully to yours.
Your relationship dynamic has changed to	a fully connected partnership of mutual respect, support, and acceptance—a rock-solid foundation from which each of you can successfully pursue any goal you set your minds to.
Your Next Step	Take advantage of every opportunity, and encourage your teen or young adult as you both continue to support and love and inspire each other to achieve your dreams.

IN CONCLUSION
Commit to Parenting Change!

Life passes quickly.

We take our first breath, our first steps. We're off to school and out into the world. And, then, before we know it, from way down the road we're looking back, wondering what we've accomplished in the time that's passed.

In this conclusion, let's track our discussion back to the beginning, taking a fresh look at the why and the how of the seven-step game plan this book guides you and your son through. It's important to consider the value of the material presented within these pages, yes. Austin and I have worked hard to relay our message in a personal and impactful way, hoping you will see yourself and your relationship with your troubled teen or young adult in the stories and recommendations we've shared. But our desire for your takeaway from our message goes far beyond "understanding."

We're dreaming big with this book, as we've learned to do for all the projects we pursue.

Our goal with *How to Get Your Son Back* is to offer a transformative, individually customizable approach to better parenting your troubled teen or young adult—the ultimate success of which depends entirely upon your incorporating the techniques and recommendations we offer and absorbing them as an essential part of your everyday life.

So indulge us one last time as we lead you through a final discussion of . . .

WHAT'S MOST IMPORTANT?

In the end, it's our relationships that make life most fulfilling and worthwhile.

And I would argue that it is our relating to our children that outshines the rest in importance.

A parent's journey can be painful and challenging during those times when our kids race off the rails, pursuing a rebellious, destructive path.

We do our best for them using every tool in our arsenal to correct their course. But we learn it's out of our hands: the choices are ultimately our children's to make.

I have witnessed parents' attempts to control, manipulate, coerce, shame, and helicopter their offspring back onto a safer track. Short-term compliance and perceived behavior modification may be somewhat of an immediate reward, but at the expense of their offspring's trust. If this is your method, your actions are likely to lead to your child's loss of confidence and fractured self-image. Worse yet, asserting dominance over your troubled teen's drive for independence (no matter how reckless) can result in his "checking out" relationally—until he breaks away completely, determined to figure things out himself.

> *Relational apathy sends the most devastating signal of all— that your son views his well-being as no longer your concern. "Back off and stay there," his nonresponse demands.*

> *The consequences of this total breakdown can be as devastating to his psychological well-being as they are to your relationship with him.*

But even if you've reached this place of exile, there is hope for you and your son, as Austin and I demonstrate in our stories and recommendations.

Hope, research has shown, is comprised of two elements:

Willpower	Your desire and willingness to get your son back.
"Way" Power	*How* you get your son back.
	Aka the seven-step game plan offered in this book.

Your willingness to reconnect with your teen or young adult, repair your relationship, and help him heal weighs heavily in his battle to achieve his full potential.

> **A warning:** Your current goal may simply be for your son to live as a responsible and independent adult and return to living between the socially acceptable lines in which you do. On the surface, this may seem a good enough result.
>
> **However, consider the potential cost of not pursuing the other objectives laid out in this seven-step game plan.**
>
> Your son's negative self-image, if left unchecked, won't improve on its own. Deeply rooted psychological issues require more extensive intervention. At risk is his ability to pursue healthy and fulfilling relationships as well as other key aspects of his life, such as finding meaning, purpose, or a fulfilling career.

Your son may be able to sustain a life on his own even while framed by a pervasive negative self-image, but it will be all but impossible for him to *thrive*. Consider also any children he may sire himself and the effect of his life view on the generations that follow. Maladaptive family traits rarely "autocorrect," despite our best intentions not to repeat our parents' mistakes.

In committing to the principles and techniques detailed in this seven-step game plan, you have a tremendous opportunity before you.

Influence is the greatest tool you possess for affecting your son's actions.

Austin and I have shared firsthand accounts of the futility of trying to force your son to change. As a parent, making changes in and about yourself is critical. Your "self" work positions you to help your son similarly correct his thought process, behavior, and life direction. Required is your sustained *willpower* to engage in the hard work ahead. And as a parent who's traveled the same road, I assure you that every second of effort and every tear you invest will pay off.

Healing your relationship with your son and helping him grow into the confident, productive, and loving contributor he *absolutely* can become is the opportunity of a lifetime, the long-reaching effects of your efforts likely extending for generations.

> *If this book convinces you of nothing else, if we've opened your eyes to the unparalleled healing opportunities before you, Austin and I have done our job.*

Now, about that "way" power . . .

Parents, the journey of this book is, first and foremost, about you: you and the untapped power you must access if you want to reach your troubled teen.

How to Get Your Son Back's seven-step game plan illustrates how to apply your innate influence as a mother or father. Your parent-child relationship with your teen or young adult has been developing since before your child was born, continuing throughout early adulthood. Even if you are currently geographically separated from your son, he desires a connection with you on some level. He longs to know he is loved and treasured.

For years, I've counseled troubled young adults and grown men who still hunger for this connection. Unfortunately, most of my clients do not believe they will ever achieve a reciprocal relationship with their parents. Consequently, they carry an internal disdain for themselves. They must be unworthy for so much to still be so broken with a person who should love them unconditionally.

Commit today to touch that same hollow place inside your son. Fill it with your love and support and acceptance. In doing so, you will jump-start his flagging self-esteem and trigger a revival of his determination to better care for himself. With that promising start achieved, there's no limit to how successful your relationship can be.

Your son may have greatly damaged his life and yours, but rather than merely seeing him as broken, understand that he is a human being motivated by a desire to belong.

He is afraid that if he is really known by others—the way he *really* is, with all his flaws—he will be rejected. Negate his innate fear that he will never be good enough. Assure him he does not deserve to be rejected. Become once again, as when he was very young, the home and the one person in his world in which he is confident he will always find a safe place to land.

You are not only in a battle to heal your son, you're in the midst of a shared human struggle to find and know and believe in our place and worth in this world. Identify with your son's sharp edges and instinct to withdraw; embrace with empathy and compassion your shared drive to be an individual and yet to be a welcomed part of something greater than you can achieve on your own.

> *Your power as a parent lies not in your "perfection" or authority but in your willingness to recognize and acknowledge your imperfections and to model an effective approach to addressing your own issues.*

To succeed in influencing your troubled teen, you do not have to be "right."

Instead, become willing to expose your own vulnerabilities.

You make mistakes. Own them. Apologize for them. And move forward following a better, more successful path. *This* is what your son needs from you. Rather than "dumping" your problems on your troubled teen, this approach (dealing with the root causes of your own negative self-image) will inspire him to similarly work on himself.

> *Unaware of what to apologize for or change? Ask your son, "What three things could I do to make me better parent?" He'll likely tell you. But be prepared for a shot of truth (likely between the eyes).*

All parents can find something to apologize for.

But remember, apologies are cheap when not followed by action.

Your son will gauge the sincerity of your mea culpa by tracking how well you follow-through on your commitments. Practice what you preach. Consistently improve your parenting approach following the techniques and practices we discuss in our seven-step game plan, in particular the recommendations and notes and progress you've recorded in your personal Parent Playbook.

A Final Note from Austin: My Hope for You

Dad will have the final say in just a little bit, which is more than cool with me.

So much of what you've read has been about his perspective as a parent, and his knowledge and years of experience as a therapist, and about helping other parents achieve with their teens what my dad ultimately was able to achieve with me. But before we've wrapped everything up, at least between the covers of this book, I wanted to share on a personal level a final glimpse of what our journey together means to me.

Building an enduring relationship with my father has enriched my life far beyond what words can express.

He's my best friend, and we are teammates for life. More than that, we're fully committed to using our personal experience to empower other parents and children facing similar challenges.

Your relationship with your child is the most valuable and powerful blessing in your reality.

After reading this book, I hope you come to that same realization. And I hope you decide to act. Engage with your teen or young adult in a healthy, positive, supportive way, better informed and skilled at helping him or her achieve life goals and dreams. Put the seven-step game plan Dad and I have recommended to use. And don't give up.

> *Never, ever give up on your ability to influence your son's life in a positive way.*

Because my father stuck with me, I can now envision a future built upon my passion for helping others. Power is not what I want. Money is not the end goal. I desire to see people achieve their potential. My goal is to help them break the chains preventing them from maximizing their happiness. I hope to help others on a whole new level. That would mean the world to me.

I've embraced the unique vantage point my past has given me.

I've made the same mistakes a lot of troubled kids make. If I can help another teen and family avoid some of the inevitable fallout I faced, I'm in! Which is partially the impetus behind a new book I've begun writing entitled *College Wasteland*.

In *College Wasteland*, I share more about the situations I faced and the dangerous choices I made when I was younger, as well as the acting out with alcohol and the bar scene and associated risky behavior I either participated in or observed as I grew older.

These stories are even more raw and real than those I've contributed in this book: things no kid wants their parent to know about but the very realities parents need to be brave enough to face.

My objective with this new project isn't to shock or offend anyone. Instead, I hope to help parents of college students *better help* their young adults focus on their dreams and future aspirations instead of those same kids limiting or sacrificing their potential to shiny "objects" and short-lived gratification that most often yields pointless destruction.

Recently, I gave a speech about my journey.

When I finished, I gazed out at the audience to discover numerous people wiping tears from their eyes.

I was humbled all over again by the responsibility I feel as a result of the fresh start and opportunities my father's acceptance and support has made possible for me. If I can become that same kind of trusted leader for others, earning their attention as I help guide them, *my* life will be richer for it. I feel an obligation, a calling, to make the most of my experience by sharing what I know to be true. I feel a dedication, beyond what I can convey, to *you* and to others like me, to troubled kids everywhere who aren't a lost cause and to the parents who refuse to give up on them.

A bright future lies ahead for all of us if we'll only stop, look, listen, and care enough to help each other travel this road together.

Your Parent Playbook

The parenting recommendations in our seven-step game plan are primarily about leading by example.

> *How can you get your teen or young adult to listen to and embrace the lessons you're dying to share with him?*

In this last "playbook" opportunity, let's take a deeper look at how to reach your son by "showing" him what you hope he will see rather than telling him.

Opportunity	Consider	Goal
Take Action	Take action yourself. Steadfastly follow the steps needed to become a better person and parent. Fix your own faults and seek help for those issues you cannot successfully address on your own.	**Be ready to change, and then model for your son the exciting results your commitment will produce in both your lives.**

Opportunity	Consider	Goal
Be Patient	For troubled young men, even those trying to change, their next crisis is not usually too far around the next corner. Your son needs help. You both likely do. Going forward, your goal is to be engaged and committed to seeking that help as a team. • Make certain he doesn't ever hear the shaming words "I told you so." • Listen calmly and with empathy. • Make clear your desire to understand and help. • Lead him back to a path of lasting change based on expectations, boundaries, and an enduring commitment to address the issues underling his troubled choices. • Ask for a specific agreement to improve. • Avoid targeting unrealistic results. • Invite him to join you on a self-healing journey to a better future.	**Negotiate a win-win, healing path toward healthy communication.** Once successfully established between the two of you, your connection can be maintained and nurtured and expanded throughout your lives.

Opportunity	Consider	Goal
Make the Investment	If your son needs therapy, rehab, medication, or other things, make it happen. However, getting your son help is not limited to dropping him off at rehab or therapy. Remember, you are an active participant. Forty percent of success in therapy takes place outside therapy and can be accomplished with your help, including providing a safe, supportive environment in which to live and experience healing.	**The money and energy and other resources you spend today will save countless dollars in the future.** This can be difficult work, but your effort will make a game-changing impact. You are no longer a coach but in the game of life with him. As he heals, your opportunity to support him expands as he maintains his gains and continues to improve alongside you.
Fight for Him. Don't Judge.	No matter where you and your son are on the relationship spectrum, whether you are simply having difficulty communicating with him or if he has gotten himself into serious legal and/or addiction problems, he is worth the fight. Rarely, if ever, should a child be written off. Resist judging your son's life, even if it seems he has wasted his potential or ruined it up to this point.	**Resurrect his future and see what miracles can be born from his past.** Help yourself and your son see that his troubled history is the fertile ground from which both his redemption and the healing of others can most definitely grow.

A Final Word from Kevin

Take my word for it.

Getting your son back is the road less traveled, the narrow gate.

The hardest, most costly personal work I have ever done was helping Austin recover his life.

Was it worth it? He was once spiraling toward prison or death. Now we are in the business of helping other parents and children reconnect. And the idea for this book comes from my work with countless desperate parents and hearing them say, "I will do anything to help my son."

Austin's and my seven-step game plan for getting your son back requires commitment, time, effort, and an unshakable iron will. As I've shared, I did most of the relationship work with my son while putting eighty to ninety hours per week into graduate school and holding down two jobs. I wish I'd had a playbook to follow, guiding me and reassuring me and showing me what *not* to do. Instead, I learned everything the hard way, mostly by trial and error, imperfectly feeling my way through the dark as best I could. Now Austin and I feel privileged to pass along this book and the additional website and social media resources listed in appendix C to you.

There are no guarantees with human behavior.

Take the leap anyway. Study and execute your Parent Playbook strategies. Put yourself in the best position possible to reconnect with your son and reboot your relationship and his life. For now, let go of the results. Work the process. Offer yourself the peace you deserve by knowing you've done your absolute best, and then trust that the rest will come.

Rather than quick-fix strategies, How to Get Your Son Back *takes you to the front lines of the battle your son is waging for his identity, his happiness, and his future.*

As you work together, expect wide swings in his behavior. Consistent, daily improvement is unlikely for quite some time.

It took years for you and your son to arrive at the place you find yourself today. It will take time to begin seeing a positive result from your effort to adjust your course going forward.

You have my utmost respect as you embark on this new journey with your teen or young adult. We all share the instinct to improve our lives and help those we love to do the same. Very few of us will commit to the degree required to sustain long-term improvement. But you can do it. You can be the exception, because your son is worth it.

Know that your son possesses limitless, unrealized potential. Use the techniques in this seven-step game plan to unlock the chains binding him to his past. Do all you can to get your son back. He and the generations that follow are worth it.

On your journey, I wish the following for you:

- **Courage**—to deal honestly with your fears, weaknesses, and vulnerabilities so you can get out of your son's way as he heals and so you can set an example for him to follow as he works on his issues.
- **Comfort with the uncomfortable**—to weather any pain you will experience, including your son defensively lashing out at you as he struggles with the path before him.
- **Open-mindedness**—so that you can learn all you need to about yourself and your son to make possible the thriving connection you long for with him.
- **Patience**—to weather the ups and downs with grace and compassion and to remain confident in the long, slow, deeply healing journey on which you've embarked.
- **Faith**—that despite short-term or even longer setbacks, this process can and does work.

You *can* reconcile with your teen or young adult, heal together, and forge a new, sustainable path to a stronger, brighter, healthier future. And you *will*. There is no doubt in my mind that your dreams for your relationship with your son are possible.

May God bless you both on your journey.

APPENDIX A:
HOW TO GET YOUR SON BACK
The Seven-Step Game Plan
at a Glance

To help you better find and chart your and your son's journey through our seven-step game plan, we summarize our recommended approach below. Remember, however, that the recommendations and strategies offered in each new step build on the relationship and individual work that comes before.

> **NOTE:** For more information about how to help you, the parent, find your place in and chart your and your teen's or young adult's course through How to Get Your Son Back's seven-step game plan, refer to "Your Game Plan" and "Your Next Play" at the beginning and end of each step. Shared in these sections is key information about where you and your son should be, emotionally and on your journey toward recovery, before you begin each step.
>
> Also, for a broader, at-a-glance view of the recommendations offered in each How to Get Your Son Back step, see appendix B: "The Parent Playbook at a Glance."

Step		
One	STOP FIGHTING! You are not the opponent.	**Shift first your perspective, and then your son's, so you can reconnect with your teen or young adult, influence his worldview, and begin to work together.** Reestablish a foundation of understanding, empathy, and support.
Two	RECONNECT. Repair your relationship.	**Reboot your parenting approach. Let your son know you're committed to making better parenting choices as you help him make better decisions for his life.** Establish fresh credibility with your teen or young adult.
Three	STEP IN. Be there when your son hits rock bottom.	**When your teen's or young adult's life reaches a crisis point and he turns to you for help, work together to help him act on his newfound commitment to change.** Waiting for your son to make better life choices—allowing him to experience the grave consequences of his behavior—is difficult. Yet your number-one priority remains consistently reflecting your empathy and acceptance of him as a person.
Four	LEAD YOUR TEAM. Give your son an example to follow.	**Model the types of behavior and choices that will help him achieve success while securing for him the professional help he needs to meet his unique challenges.** Continue to encourage your son on the very long journey of change ahead, even when *you* have difficulty grasping what the next milestone should be.

Step		
Five	DEAL WITH DEEPER PROBLEMS. Help your son heal.	**Support your son's work on "deeper" issues—including securing the professional help he'll need to expand his recovery.** Focus on your teen's or young adult's growth rather than expecting immediate, "magical" gains as he deals with the underlying emotional and psychological issues still causing him difficulty.
Six	MAXIMIZE HIS GROWTH. Help your son develop confidence and feel success.	**Prepare your son to become "consciously competent" and adopt the vital "recovery mindset" necessary for his long-term healing and growth.** Encourage your teen or young adult to embrace his growth and healing while at the same time confirming that there are no "quick-fix" solutions to the challenges he faces.
Seven	CREATE YOUR BEST LIFE, both of you.	**Orient your shared perspective of the future toward the next dream you want to achieve (both individually and together) despite the surprises and difficulties and challenges you face along the way.** Shift your son's (and your) focus from targeting recovery alone to striving for broader goals.
In Conclusion	Your commitment to parenting change.	**How can you get your teen or young adult to embrace the lessons you're dying to share with him?** Your relationship with your son is the most valuable and powerful blessing in your life. To succeed in influencing your troubled teen, you do not have to be "right." Instead, become willing to expose your own vulnerabilities. Commit to the principles and techniques detailed in this seven-step game plan and to the tremendous opportunity before you.

APPENDIX B:
THE PARENT PLAYBOOK
AT A GLANCE

How are you doing with your notebook?

We asked you to take your personal Parent Playbook with you everywhere you go, to jot down notes as you read, and to make time to work through exercises and recommendations or think through the questions Austin and I have asked.

We know these aren't quick steps and that every family comes to this material with their own dynamic. And while we hope to motivate and help each and every one of you grow, we know you and your son will progress at your own pace. That's where the idea for your playbook came from—as a way to inspire you, a way for you to hold yourself accountable, and also as a place for you to work and track your progress and to plan your journey ahead with your teen or young adult.

With that in mind, we've included this appendix as a "handy" resource for you to begin building your own playbook or to quickly reference something you remember reading in one of the steps. On the pages that follow, you'll find the goal for each chapter followed by the "WHAT TO DO?" and "WHAT'S MOST IMPORTANT?" elements, strategies, and recommendations we hope you'll work with in your Parent Playbook.

> **NOTE:** Please refer to each step's full materials for more essential details, including vital Parent Playbook practice notes for how to implement the recommended strategies.

STEP ONE
STOP FIGHTING!
YOU ARE NOT THE OPPONENT

Core Behavioral Motivators:

- We all want to belong.
- We all want to avoid rejection.
- If we can't belong and avoid rejection, something has to give.

Your Step-One Parent Playbook

Trust that with every attempt you make to reconnect with your child, you'll become more aware and accepting and successful at having an active presence in your son's life as the loving parent he needs and wants you to be.

Skill	Intent	Practice
Stop pushing him to talk with you. Start listening.	Diffuse the defense mechanism causing him to withdraw and avoid you (because he doesn't want his unhappiness discovered). **NOTE:** If you believe your son is suicidal, get him professional help immediately. His safety is your highest priority.	**Recognize the negative cues that reveal his altered view of himself.** Whenever possible, reflect back an understanding, accepting, and more "realistic" view of his circumstances. Convey your understanding of just how difficult his reality is.
Stop fighting. Start relating.	Diffuse your teen's seeing your concern and attempts to help as personal attacks.	**Proactively understand, and then share your compassion with your teen.**
Stop shaming. Start empathizing.	Shame has been linked to significant risk-taking behaviors.	**Practice a more empathetic approach, modeling healthy interpersonal choices.**

STEP TWO
RECONNECT: REPAIR YOUR RELATIONSHIP

Your Pledge to Change Your Parenting Approach:

- No more yelling, shaming, or physical abuse.
- Talk to your son like a young man deserving of respect.
- Expect your son to make his own decisions with your advice and guidance offered in a noncontrolling, nondomineering way.

Your Step-Two Parent Playbook

As you work to create a fresh start with your son, consider the following tools I utilized in my fight for a better relationship with Austin and Alex.

Tool	Purpose	Goal
Own your mistakes.	Let your child know how much it hurts you that you've hurt him.	**Shine a light on personal issues you know your son is aware of** but which he's likely blaming himself for or thinking you don't see as problems.
Apologize.	Apologizing is not a sign of weakness. True strength lies in one's ability to be comfortable as an imperfect, vulnerable human being.	**Apologizing to your son moves you from a position of power in his life to that of a human being.**
Take the first step.	Be the one to break the stalemate first. Extend an olive branch, even if he doesn't expect one. Especially if he doesn't expect one.	**Leave no doubt in his mind that this new path to put your child first is your choice, your goal, your mission.**
Be authentic.	Our kids are perceptive. They'll spot a superficial, empty apology from a mile away.	**Put to good use the empathy and compassion you developed for your son in Step One.**
Be specific.	Generality (a blanket apology) breeds misunderstanding and distrust. Be specific about the mistakes you've made *and* the changes and goals you're focusing on.	**Focusing on specific behaviors and actions clarifies both your regret and your intent to change. It resets everyone's expectations.**

Tool	Purpose	Goal
Tell your son how important he is to you.	You may think your son knows you want to be close to him, or he may have no idea. Regardless, make it clear beyond a doubt that his well-being and happiness are more important to you than any of the other priorities you've put before him to this point.	**It's a bold gesture, you're really putting yourself out there, but the payoff can be priceless.**
No strings attached.	Reset your relationship by making this about your heart and your wanting to share it unconditionally with your son no matter what he's done or will ever do. No expectations. No need for him to return the gesture or to say he loves you.	**Eliminate any doubt in his mind that what's happened between you two is *your* responsibility.**
Be consistent.	You'll continue to butt heads with your son. He may not trust your intent right away, but be where you say you're going to be, doing what you've promised you'll do, over and over, until he believes you'll never stop.	**When your son realizes your commitment can endure whatever next happens (to him or between the two of you), you've reached a major milestone.**

Tool	Purpose	Goal
Be patient.	Your son must find his own motivation to extricate himself from his problems. And until he does, his actions likely will not improve regardless of what you do. Wait him out. If he rebels, be there when he finds his way back. If he acts out, control *your* reaction and mirror a more constructive, accepting way of communicating.	**Rather than reacting in anger or frustration or disappointment, your pride and love for your son will lead the way.** Your son will pick up on your cues and begin to respond to you in kind, likely sooner than later.

STEP THREE
STEP IN: BE THERE WHEN YOUR SON HITS ROCK BOTTOM

Levels of Change

Precontemplation	Change is not on his radar.
Contemplation	**Change is now a possibility and verbally discussed when prompted**, but internal conflict and barriers remain in play.
Preparation	**Change is now the primary focus**; plans are made. Emotional and behavioral barriers may still exist, but he has taken the steps necessary to take action toward change.
Action	**Action is taken to create sustainable change,** away from destructive behaviors and unsuccessful goals.
Maintenance	**Habits and behavioral practices are created** so that change becomes a routine part of life—the person embraces their new "normal" reality.

Your Step-Three Parent Playbook

How do you teach your son to "fish?"

First, you have some evaluating to do—both on your own and with your teen.

Ask Yourself . . .	Consider . . .	Your Goal
What does my teen really need?	Take the time, before acting, to be confident you are addressing key, underlying behavioral issues rather than merely putting out "immediate" fires.	**Understand the psychological dynamics driving the behaviors that led to your son's crisis.**
Is my son aware of his underlying problems?	Is he still in the precontemplation stage, where his only focus is his immediate crisis rather than sustained change? Is he contemplating change but not at a level that will help him avoid future crisis?	**Understand your son's stage of "change" so** you can plan your approach accordingly.
Are fears and other psychological issues holding him back from making necessary changes?	Is he hiding from the work he needs to do out of a fear of humiliation or failure or loss of acceptance (core motivators that can cause us to behave in ways that seem contrary to our best interest)?	**Encourage your son to consider why he's doing the things he's done and why he's asking for your help.**

Now it's time to act—in partnership with your teen and only with his commitment to the process the two of you agree to follow.

Action	Consider . . .	Your Goal
Set clear expectations for the help he needs and the help you're willing to give.	"I don't know" is not an acceptable answer from your teen when you ask him what he needs if what he really means is "I don't want to talk about it."	**Focus on your son's potential to improve rather than on the end result either you or he thinks he should achieve.** Help him get a quick win so he can begin to build momentum.
Outline a general map that provides direction and gives him attainable goals to pursue. Inspire your son to reach his potential without adding to the pressure he already feels.	Always remember that you are working with a low-self-esteem individual driven by guilt rather than confidence. You are asking a lot of him, and he needs to be committed to asking a lot of himself. **NOTE:** Shame and "fear of failure" should never be used by either of you as a motivator.	**Cast a vision for the future you're confident your teen can achieve.** However, be realistic (and help him understand) how long achieving sustained change can take.
Set expectations for what you need from your son.	Clarify your expectation that he must work hard for the change he wants to make. Support him but let him know that the degree of your support will be set by the level of effort you see him applying toward achieving his goals.	**You are inspiring your son's commitment to relearn how to approach and live his life.**

STEP FOUR
LEAD YOUR TEAM:
GIVE YOUR SON AN EXAMPLE TO FOLLOW

Encourage engagement, not disconnection:

1. Walk the walk.
2. Treat your son as if he's fully capable of achieving his goals.
3. Stop the downward spiral.
4. Get in the game.
5. Model the behavior you expect.

Self-actualizing tools to help reflect all you believe your son is capable of:

- Be genuinely warm, embracing his current situation and him as he is.
- Support his choices (build his trust).
- Share approval of decision outcomes even if there is some degree of failure.

Redirect his fight-or-flight instinct:

- Create a threat-free home environment.
- Interact projecting love, warmth, and acceptance.
- Offer compassion rather than opposition when addressing changes and outcomes.

Be an "experienced warrior" who's been in the trenches too:

- Reveal your weaknesses while modeling confidence with your flaws.
- Reflect that there is no shame in having problems.
- Tolerate and deal calmly with your own issues.
- Model active and proactive problem-solving.
- Talk authentically about your hopes and dreams.
- Share your disappointments and roadblocks.

Your Step-Four Parent Playbook

To support your teen or young adult, you must:

- Reflect your confidence that he can achieve a successful future.
- Help him believe that both his fresh start and his dreams are 100-percent attainable as long as he's willing to fight for his future.

The following table summarizes several key areas on which to focus as you modify *your* behavior and life approach and place yourself on the field, accepted into your son's journey in a position of influence and support.

Model	Consider	Goal
Self-Awareness	Becoming more self-aware of one's feelings helps an individual create a space between behavioral triggers and the resulting reaction.	**Illustrate for your son how to make positive, successful decisions even while experiencing sometimes extreme emotional upset or conflict.**
Flexible Thinking	Your son, like many others, may interact with his world from a very black-and-white perspective.	**Offer examples of how your son can think in more complex ways.**
Dealing with Risk	Your teen or young adult can become risk averse to the extreme, to the extent of refusing to attempt any of the steps needed to achieve their goals.	**Encourage your son to expand his comfort zone.**

Model	Consider	Goal
A Healthy Relationship	Self-disclosure and trust are reciprocal. You get what you give, and it's likely your son has been burned one time too many by people who've betrayed or hurt him when he most needed someone to turn to.	**Prove to your son that while your current relationship is far from perfect and you may still become angry with him, you will always respond from a place of preserving and improving your relationship.**
Help Seeking	The myth that real men (or strong people or people of "true" faith) do not ask for help is ludicrous.	**Emulate for your son your acceptance that you are not afraid or ashamed of seeking help when you need it.**
Empathy for Others	"Troubled" kids tend to be more than a little rough around the edges. Shame-based individuals are overly "self-focused" out of their perceived need to protect themselves from more trouble and hurt. They are likely to think that no one else cares enough to help them, so their top priority is taking care of themselves.	**Reach through your son's emotional walls and help him get back in touch with his heart. Model the rewards of sharing your heart and love with others—and, specifically, that you don't see it as a threat to your well-being.**

STEP FIVE
DEAL WITH DEEPER PROBLEMS:
HELP YOUR SON HEAL

As you wait for your son to commit to lasting change . . .

- Continue to implement our self-actualizing tools.
- Remember that your son does want to change.
- Tap into his drive to heal and to make positive choices (through conversations and reflecting your hope for and confidence in him).
- Positively redirect your son toward removing psychological and behavioral barriers.

Encourage your son in the direction of positive change:

- Encourage him whenever (authentically) possible.
- Reflect your approval of the positive direction he's taking.
- Share your hope and excitement about progress you see.
- Express your confidence in the healthy choices you know he can make and in his ability to commit to change.

Your Step-Five Parent Playbook

Practice these strategies before and after your son asks for the additional help he needs to achieve sustained change in his life.

Strategy	Consider	Goal
Increase your expectations.	Without projecting a "need to improve" on your son while he struggles with all he's facing and the permanent change he's still resisting, find ways to reflect how much more you're certain he can achieve and do better for himself.	**Treat your son as if he's smart and capable, encouraging him to reframe his perception of himself accordingly.**
Help your son find purpose.	Encouraging someone with this emotional deficit to reposition their frame of reference toward a purpose that will help others besides himself create a new value system and a broader emotional connection. His world expands beyond his individual experience, making possible a more realistic view of what's happening to him and others.	**Give your son a more clearly defined sense of the world around him.** Help him consider and refocus on others' lives and if possible on the plight of those truly less fortunate than he is; for example, Austin's insight into the lives of the homeless men I worked with.
Look for and celebrate "quick wins."	You're wanting to keep the focus on incremental achievement while maintaining the open, trusting line of communication that will remain essential going forward.	**Reflect your approval. Celebrate all accomplishments. Be honest and frank but maintain an encouraging role as you wait for future change.**
Approach mental illness as a real and "must-treat" issue to which your son needs to commit.	Research has repeatedly demonstrated that behaviorally troubled individuals who receive therapy and/or mediation benefit more than individuals who receive no treatment at all. However, for sustained progress, the decision to seek treatment must be your son's.	**Offer to pay for professional help once your son knows he's ready, but leave the decision of if and when to start up to him. His responsibility and ownership of his treatment must be your priority.**

Strategy	Consider	Goal
Carefully select the professionals your son will use in his recovery.	Your son's motivation to work on his problems is the primary indicator of whether a therapist, medication, or rehabilitation program will work for him.	Find the resources that will work for your son by observing those in which he engages and works. Encourage and expect him to participate in choosing who he will see.
Expect change to take time.	Sustained change takes time when your son is dealing with multiple underlying psychological problems that impact an array of life areas: occupational, interpersonal, intrapersonal, emotional, etc.	Accept (and make certain your son knows you accept) that you are interested in helping him modify the underlying psychological issues beneath his behavior, for these are the genesis of his problems.
Allow him to do his work.	Therapy and rehab occurs both in session as well as out of session. It is important to let your son continue to live his life and implement therapeutic changes without your interference—even if he continues to make mistakes while in treatment.	Rather than micromanaging, continue to send the signal that you trust him and his doctors.
Participate in therapy when invited.	Expect your son to have unresolved issues with you. It's a guarantee. Forgiveness is a process that takes time to run its course.	Whatever your child needs to feel supported in what he's feeling and the changes he must make to deal more effectively with those feelings—do it.

Strategy	Consider	Goal
Support your son's healing.	If you are disengaged from your son's treatment, how can you support the changes he is trying to make?	**Agreeing on therapeutic goals and collaborating with your son to find solutions (when invited to participate in his at-home therapy work) will produce a more positive outcome.** Your consistent empathy and alliance with your son (particularly in affirming positive feelings and genuinely supporting his work) are more important than ever.

STEP SIX
MAXIMIZE HIS GROWTH:
HELP YOUR SON
DEVELOP CONFIDENCE AND FEEL SUCCESS

Deep, foundational change happens in multiple steps as your son grows in his awareness.

- He must recognize the areas in which change is needed.
- He must understand the process required to make the necessary change and how this will impact his life.
- To sustain results requires a recovery mindset and a continuous recommitment to persevere and practice the changes.

As you gauge his competency in dealing with his issues, observe . . .

- His level of awareness of the need for specific skills (or workarounds).
- His proficiency at executing the techniques he is learning.

There is a clear path to your son's level of competency in dealing with his issues:

Unconscious-Incompetence	Your son is unaware of the need to change and incapable of achieving his goal.
Conscious-Incompetence	Your son is aware of the need to change but unable to achieve his goal.
Conscious-Competence	Your son is aware and able to achieve his goal but only with sustained attention and focus.
Unconscious-Competence	Your son's new approach has become routine, or habit.

Your son craves acceptance above all else—reflect that back to him at all times.

- Offer kind words and compassionate verbal responses and observations.
- Keep your tone and responses respectful regardless of provocation.
- Give as much care and attention to how you speak to your child as you do the actual words you say.
- Work to understand how he's thinking and how he learns. Craft your comments and answers to better support his approach.
- Listen much more than you speak so that he knows you value what he says and thinks.
- Avoid interrupting him as he speaks, which can be perceived as a hostile or aggressive form of verbal rejection.
- Talk with your son as if you expect him to be successful. Your positive expectations will communicate the message that you think he is capable.

Continue to make to make positive changes together, dealing with setbacks as simply part of the healing process.

- Assure him that one incident or mistake does not mean starting over from the very beginning.
- Remind him that shame has no place in his experience of the consequences of his actions. Shame, like depression, can be the result of anger turned inward. Help your son find healthier outlets for the difficult emotions he is experiencing so they do not become weapons used to rip at the positive self-regard he's developed.
- Whenever possible, call attention to the improvement he's made (and continues to make) in other areas of his recovery.
- Help him reposition his disappointment into a determination to learn from the experience and to develop a plan or approach that will reduce the likelihood of further recurrence.
- Reaffirm your nonanxious, positive regard for your son. Extend your hand to help him get back on track, share your continued understanding of how hard his journey has been, and express your pride in the many accomplishments he's achieved so far.

Your Step-Six Parent Playbook

You and your son have accomplished a lot in your journey together. As your son grows, heals, and maintains his emotional and psychological achievements, several important tools will help you support his continued progress.

Tool	Consider	Goal
Focus on authentic conversation with, and interest in, your son.	Proactively express that you are committed to growing and maintaining your relationship long-term. This not a time to smother or force decisions on him. He may make mistakes as he makes more choices on his own, but continue to express your interest, and always make yourself available when he indicates he's ready to talk.	**Make the relationship with your son an ongoing priority. Let him know by your actions that you continue to want to be present in his life. Grow and foster your relationship as a lifelong team. You are his ultimate source of support.**
Recognize your son's strengths as much or more than his challenges.	Highlight his strengths and make certain he recognizes them. Target conversations that discuss how he can utilize his strengths and the same successful techniques he has used in other areas of his recovery.	**Regularly taking inventory of and spotlighting your son's achievements strengthens your relationship.**
Celebrate your successes.	At this point, you and your son have accomplished things together that few could have predicted. Celebrate these milestones.	**Recognizing hard work, success, and key achievements helps set expectations for continued growth in the future.**

Tool	Consider	Goal
Help your son develop a maintenance-/relapse-prevention plan.	A maintenance/relapse plan is not "tempting" relapse or even sending a signal that you anticipate your son falling back into dangerous patterns. Look at it instead as a way to protect the gains your son has made should there be an unexpected future setback.	**Involve your son in not only thinking of ways to maintain his progress (despite momentary setbacks) but also in thinking carefully about all that would be at stake if there were a relapse.**
Empower your son.	Elevate his status from someone who is out of control to someone who's worked hard to regain his ability to make healthy and successful choices for his future. Trust him to make those better choices for himself. Allow him to make mistakes and work through his issues independently. Be there for him every step of the way, but make certain he knows you know he absolutely can succeed in his recovery.	**Treating your son as a competent equal conveys respect.** Let him know you believe in and value his abilities. Treat him as the success you know he can be, and then watch him grow into making even more successful choices.

STEP SEVEN
CREATE YOUR BEST LIFE, BOTH OF YOU

As your roles evolve and he becomes more independent and successful with his new life approach, remember . . .

- Future challenges won't look like those of the past.
- You are no longer responsible for directing your son.
- Grow into supporting each other as adults.
- Welcome your evolving, changing relationship.
- Continue to notice and reinforce successes.
- Encourage your son to engage in increasingly complex tasks.
- Lean on him for support and help.

Your Step-Seven Parent Playbook

Your son will likely continue to struggle in several areas. Discussing the potential difficulties of these challenges, as well as possible workarounds or solutions, can be a great opportunity for continuing the successful pattern of communication and support you've established.

Opportunity	Consider	Goal
Employment	We spend half of our waking life working, and most emerging adults can feel overwhelmed at the thought of committing to an occupation they're not sure will be fulfilling.	**Help your son reason through the type of work in which he can actively engage.** What would make him happy to be doing each day? Or if not happy, what tasks would satisfy him, completing them on a daily basis?

Opportunity	Consider	Goal
Education	A degree can be achieved either by attending a trade school or studying within a more traditional college program. Either choice will benefit you, and neither is better than the other. And where you start isn't nearly as important as where you finish.	**If lack of appropriate education is holding your son back from his goals, encourage him to pursue the needed degree** (despite any doubts he might have that he could complete the program).
Taking Action	Encourage your son not to allow fear of the unknown to stymie his conviction to make the incremental choices and do the "smaller" work that will place him on a path to tackle the bigger, more complex choices he'll one day make.	**As goals and objectives shift and change, encourage your son not to fall victim to "paralysis by analysis."** At some point, it's essential for him to take the first step, to act, and to experience whatever is needed so he'll grow and gain wisdom and be better able to take that next step toward his goals.
NOT Fearing Failure	Failure (and taking risks that put ourselves in the direct path of failure) can be the best thing that ever happens to us. We learn most as we attempt and fall short and then pull ourselves together for the next try.	**Instead of processing setbacks as failures, help your son see the results of "missed" attempts as opportunities for feedback.** Discuss, model, and brainstorm ways to learn from each action and reaction he encounters so that he will feel even more empowered to make the next choice or handle the next opportunity he faces.
Saving Money	It may take him awhile to find his passion, but when he does, you will want to act on it.	**Help your son prepare to take advantage of opportunity when it presents itself.**

IN CONCLUSION:
YOUR COMMITMENT
TO PARENTING CHANGE

Hope, research has shown, is comprised of two key elements:

Willpower	Your desire and willingness to get your son back.
"Way" Power	How you get your son back.
	NOTE: These are the seven steps contained within this book.

On your journey, I wish the following for you:

- **Courage**—to deal honestly with your fears, weaknesses, and vulnerabilities so you can get out of your son's way as he heals and so you can set an example for him to follow as he works on his issues.

- **Comfort with the uncomfortable**—to weather any pain you will experience, including your son defensively lashing out at you as he struggles with the path before him.

- **Open-mindedness**—so that you can learn all you need to about yourself and your son to make possible the thriving connection you long for with him.

- **Patience**—to weather the ups and downs with grace and compassion and to remain confident in the long, slow, deeply healing journey on which you've embarked.

- **Faith**—that despite short-term or even longer setbacks, this process can and does work.

Your Concluding Parent Playbook

The parenting recommendations in this book are primarily about leading by example.

How can you get your son to listen to and embrace the lessons you're dying to share with him?

In this last "playbook" opportunity, let's take a deeper look at how to reach your son by "showing" him what you hope he will see rather than telling him.

Opportunity	Consider	Goal
Take action.	Take action yourself. Steadfastly follow the steps needed to become a better person and parent. Fix your own faults and seek help for those issues you cannot successfully address on your own.	**Be ready to change, and then model for your son the exciting results your commitment will produce in both your lives.**

Opportunity	Consider	Goal
Be patient.	For troubled young men, even those trying to change, their next crisis is not usually too far around the next corner. Your son needs help. You both likely do. Going forward, your goal is to be engaged and committed to seeking that help as a team. • Make certain he doesn't hear the shaming words "I told you so." • Listen calmly and with empathy. • Make clear your desire to understand and help. • Lead him back to a path of lasting change based on expectations, boundaries, and an enduring commitment to addressing the issues underling his troubled choices. • Ask for a specific agreement to improve. • Avoid targeting unrealistic results. • Invite him to join you on a self-healing journey to a better future.	**Negotiate a win-win, healing path toward healthy communication.** Once successfully established between the two of you, your connection can be maintained and nurtured and expanded throughout your lives.

Opportunity	Consider	Goal
Make the investment.	If your son needs therapy, rehab, medication, or other things, make it happen. However, getting your son help is not limited to dropping him off at rehab or therapy. Remember, you are an active participant. Forty percent of success in therapy takes place outside therapy and can be accomplished with your help, including a safe, supportive environment in which to live and experience healing.	**The money and energy and other resources you spend today will save countless dollars in the future.** This can be difficult work, but your effort will make a game-changing impact. You are no longer a coach but in the game of life with him. As he heals, your opportunity to support him expands as he maintains his gains and continues to improve alongside with you.
Fight for him. Don't judge.	No matter where your son is on the relationship spectrum, whether you are simply having difficulty communicating with him or if he has gotten himself into serious legal and/or addiction problems, he is worth the fight. Rarely, if ever, should a child be written off. Resist judging your son's life, even if it seems he has wasted his potential or ruined it up to this point.	**Resurrect his future and see what miracles can be born from his past.** Help yourself and your son see that his troubled history is the fertile ground from which both his and the redemption and healing of others can most definitely grow.

APPENDIX C:
ADDITIONAL RESOURCES

The recovery experience you've read about in *How to Get Your Son Back* is merely one father and son's story.

This seven-step game plan was designed to be adapted to different family dynamics. However, there wasn't room for us to exhaustively address all the issues families, parents, teens, and young adults face on their healing journey.

Addressing Your Unique Family Situation

We encourage you to embrace your Parent Playbook and our recommended strategies, but we realize that your family faces its own combination of obstacles and challenges.

Your efforts as a parent to reconnect with your teen or young adult and to repair your relationship are vital to your son's recovery and future success. We would be honored to coach you through your own seven-step game plan, dealing more in-depth with your family's unique concerns.

The areas in which Dr. Fall and Austin offer individualized parental coaching and consulting services working in-depth and one on one with clients, include:

- Divorce
- Mental illness
- Physical abuse
- Incarceration
- Substance abuse
- Nonresponsive teen/young adult
- Estranged teen/young adult
- Family dysfunction
- *I've tried everything!*

To find out more about these services, please visit their website:
www.LifeDoctor.com/Consulting

Events, Speaking Engagements, and Workshops

Dr. Fall, an award-winning speaker, and Austin have spoken nationwide.

Through their engaging programs, they provide attendees a thoughtful and emotion-provoking growth experience. Targeting audiences that look to make an impact on their organization or community, Dr. Fall and Austin will work with you to develop a presentation that best fits your needs.

To learn more about how their services can propel your impactful message to the next level, visit their website:
www.LifeDoctor.com/Engagements

Stay in Touch

Dr. Fall and Austin would love to hear from you.
Please stay connected!

Email: info@LifeDoctor.com
Facebook: www.facebook.com/RealLifeDoctors
Blog: www.LifeDoctor.com/blog

ABOUT THE AUTHORS

Dr. Kevin Fall is an award-winning speaker, author, psychologist, and leading expert in human connectedness. He received his PhD from the University of Iowa in psychology and spent years working with some of the most hardened and dangerous individuals with histories of violence and severe mental illness. Today Dr. Fall specializes in helping parents and their young-adult sons overcome the barriers that prevent them from truly connecting and discovering a deeper, more meaningful relationship.

Prior to becoming a psychologist, Dr. Fall was an information technology consultant specializing in managing outsourcing engagements and large-scale projects with various Fortune-500 companies. He was also licensed as a certified public accountant in the state of Texas. Despite a successful career, he found his work unfulfilling. As he progressed in his own introspective journey of personal growth, he began helping others and consequently discovered his purpose in life. As his discontentment with his career grew, it soon became too much to ignore, and Dr. Fall walked away from it to pursue his calling as a psychologist dedicated to helping others live happier, healthier, more fulfilling lives.

At a young age, **Austin Fall** was left internally broken and without direction as a result of his parents' painful divorce. By the time he reached his teen years, he'd disconnected from his parents and turned to a destructive lifestyle of violence and heavy drinking to mask his pain and compensate for low self-esteem. As Austin's behavior continued to deteriorate, he dropped out of high school, was convicted of several felonies, and found himself at a dead end. At the point where he considered suicide his only alternative, he decided to ask for help.

For the next six years, Austin lived and worked with his dad to reengineer his life. Today he is a college graduate with a clean legal record, a loving father, and a thriving professional whose purpose is to help parents reconnect with and inspire their troubled teens to reach their full potential. Austin brings a unique and valuable perspective as he consults with parents trying desperately to reach their teens and repair their relationships.

Made in the USA
Las Vegas, NV
30 December 2020